TREASURES OF
Ontario

Canadian Parliament Building and the Rideau Canal

by Damon Neal

a part of the Morgan & Chase Treasure Series
www.treasuresof.com

MORGAN & CHASE PUBLISHING INC.

Morgan & Chase Publishing, Inc.
531 Parsons Drive, Medford, Oregon 97501
(888) 557-9328
www.treasuresof.com

Printed and bound by Taylor Specialty Books–Dallas TX
First edition 2008
ISBN: 978-1-933989-31-0

THE
TREASURE
SERIES

I gratefully acknowledge the contributions of the many people
involved in the writing and production of this book. Their
tireless dedication to this endeavour has been inspirational.
–*William Faubion, Publisher*

The Morgan & Chase Publishing Home Team

Operations Department:
V.P. of Operations–Cindy Tilley Faubion
Travel Writer Liaison–Anne Boydston
Shipping & Receiving–Virginia Arias
Customer Service–Elizabeth Taylor
IT Engineer–Ray Ackerman
Reception–Samara Sharp

Production Department:
Office Manager–Sue Buda
Editor/Writer–Robyn Sutherland
Photo Coordinator–Wendy L. Gay
Graphic Design Team–Jesse Gifford, Jacob Kristof

Administrative Department:
CFO–Emily Wilkie
Accounting Assistants–David Grundvig, Tiffany Myers
Website Designer–Molly Bermea
Website Software Developer–Ben Ford

Contributing Writers:
Mary Beth Lee, Harry Fawcett, Clara Nunes, John Alex Mosley, Karen Paton, April Higginbotham,
Jeanie Erwin, Jennifer Buckner, Kate Zdrojewski, Laura Young, Marek Alday, Patricia Smith, Paul Hadella,
Prairie Smallwood, Tamara Cornett, Todd Wels

Special Recognition to:
Casey Faubion, Pam Schalow, Betty Holland, Gordon Haas, Linda Klee, Megan Glomb, Eric Molinsky,
Heather Allen, Mary Murdock, Clarice Rodriguez, C.S. Rowan, Vikki West, Gene Mitts

We dedicate this book to Clevelands House, a resort in northern Ontario that has served vacationing families for generations. This traditional, upscale, family-oriented resort was managed and run by the dedicated Cornell family including mother and father Fran and Robert along with their children. Robert started there as an employee in 1949 and met Fran in 1955 while she worked there as a waitress. Eventually they were married. At the end of 2007 this resort changed hands and an era came to an end. We wish the Cornell family well.

~ Harry Fawcett
Ontario Travel Writer

Foreword

Welcome to the *Treasures of Ontario*. This book is a thoughtful resource that can guide you to some of the best places in Ontario, a province of astounding natural beauty. Ontario is located within the east-central part of Canada and is a leader in hydroelectric energy due to the massive power generated daily at Niagara Falls. Ontario is one of four original provinces created July 1, 1867 by the British North American Act, and today it has the largest population in Canada.

During our visit we found Ontario is home to very friendly, imaginative and hard working people. They make Ontario a special place to live or to visit. This province is filled with chances to experience the rich traditional and cultural diversity that's as vast and as endearing as the Ontario landscape. Whether you choose to hike the Canadian Shield or sunbathe at Sandbanks Provincial Park, you will have an unforgettable experience.

From the beginning of this project we were blessed to see incredible works of art and explore communities that were so much more than just a place to visit. Whether you are a world traveller or you have spent your entire life in Ontario, you will find people and places in this book that will both inspire and interest you. The idea for the Treasures Series of books was created over 20 years ago by entrepreneurs who were both raised in family-owned and operated businesses. Today they continue to oversee overall book quality and to maintain the high selection standards for the Treasures who are featured within the Treasures Series books.

In preparing the *Treasures of Ontario* we talked to literally thousands of business people about their products, their services and their vision. We spent time photographing the Wanapitei Reserves and the Niagara Escarpment. We were amazed by the view from atop the CN Tower and we visited art galleries with eye-catching glimpses of creativity. You are holding the result of our efforts in your hands. *Treasures of Ontario* is a 217-page compilation of the best places in Ontario to eat, shop, play, explore, learn and relax. We had the privilege of seeing all the people and places this book is about. All you have to do now is enjoy the result of our efforts.

~ Cindy Tilley Faubion

Toronto skyline at sunset

How to use this book

Treasures of Ontario is divided by region and category. Categories range from accommodations to wines, with headings such as attractions, fashion, galleries, restaurants and shopping in between. In the index, all of the Treasures are listed alphabetically by name. We have provided contact information for every Treasure in the book. They are the places and businesses we encourage you to visit during your future travels through Ontario.

We sincerely hope you find this book to be both beautiful and useful

The CN Tower in downtown Toronto

Ambassador Bridge
Photo by Norris Wong

Southwest and Toronto

Niagara Falls

Briar Hill

Briar Hill is an adult lifestyle community offering award-winning home and apartment suites. The Nottawasaga River meanders through the property, and you can savour the lovely views of lush forested valleys and ravines. Homes are available with brick or stone exteriors and a choice of 13 floor plans. All provide luxurious amenities and are peaceful, affordable and virtually maintenance free. The Renaissance apartment complex features one and two bedroom suites. Briar Hill and the Renaissance are meticulously constructed with the professionalism that has consistently earned the developer the coveted Excellent rating from Tarion, the regulator of Ontario home building. Home and apartment suite owners also enjoy the world-class resort facilities offered at the Nottawasaga Inn Resort, just next to Briar Hill. Resort facilities include the fabulous indoor Sports and Leisure Dome, which offers tennis, squash and racquetball. Swimmers delight in the 25-metre pool with a sauna and whirlpool bath. The dome houses a health and fitness centre, along with a full-service salon and spa. The Centre Ice Sportsplex provides an NHL-sized ice arena for ice skating and hockey. The resort offers 45 regulation holes of golf and is rated among the top 25 Canadian golf resorts. Depending on the season, you can enjoy tobogganing, hiking, bocce, baseball or soccer. Lou Biffs, president of Briar Hill and the Nottawasaga Inn Resort, invites you to Briar Hill, an irresistible choice that suits your active lifestyle.

6015 Highway 89, Alliston ON (705) 435-5503 *www.briarhill.on.ca*

Nottawasaga Inn Resort

Just 45 minutes north of Toronto, the Nottawasaga Inn Resort has been a favoured resort destination for business and recreational travellers since 1968. The Nottawasaga River winds gracefully through the resort's 575 acres. It's no surprise that the inn has received the *Reader's Choice Gold Award—Favourite Ontario Resort*. With 269 guest rooms, including 34 suites with Jacuzzi tubs and fireplaces, you are assured a comfortable stay. The inn provides unrivaled convention, meeting and banquet facilities—36 newly renovated meeting rooms with wireless Internet access and audio-visual systems, plus copying and fax services. The 70,000 square foot Sports & LeisureDome offers exceptional indoor recreational facilities, including a 25-metre pool with a water slide, whirlpool baths and sauna. You can play squash, racquetball or work out at the Fitness Centre. Check out the NHL-sized professional ice arena or the three indoor tennis courts. A spa with massage services and a full-service hair salon are just some of the other amenities. Three restaurants, ranging from casual fare to elegant dining, complete your experience. Outdoors, golfers enjoy 45 regulation holes, which place Nottawasaga among Canada's top 25 golf resorts. The inn arranges exciting and diverse events on request, including mini-Olympics, murder mysteries and medieval feasts. Those who would like to make these amenities a permanent part of their lives can settle at Briar Hill, the next-door adult lifestyle community. Visit the Nottawasaga Inn Resort soon. You'll be glad you did.

6015 Highway 89, Alliston ON (705) 435-5501 or (800) 669-5501
www.nottawasagaresort.com

Unto the Hills Bed & Breakfast

Unto the Hills Bed & Breakfast was voted the Best Accommodation for 2007 by the Hills of Headwaters Tourism Association. At Unto the Hills Bed & Breakfast, you will experience some of the most beautiful scenery in all of creation. The bed-and-breakfast is located in the green hills of Mono, and the view extends more than 50 kilometres over the lush woods and hills of the Hockley Valley. Owners Don and Lynne Laverty designed this modern French farm house, which was built by Mennonites in 2004. Each room is equipped with an electric fireplace and is designed for guest comfort. Whether you're staying in the Relessey Room, with its king-size bed, air tub and beautiful attached deck, or the Dorthea Room with its ensuite, you will delight in the view and amenities. Unto the Hills was designed with the environment in mind and sports a geothermal heating and cooling system that keeps it comfortable in all seasons. The famous Bruce Trail abuts the property and connects to the Mono Cliffs Park to the north and the 4,500 acre Hockley Valley Reserve to the south of the bed-and-breakfast. Enjoy the beauty of all seasons at Unto the Hills Bed & Breakfast, one of the best bed-and-breakfasts in Ontario, according to travel writer Janette Higgins.

15th Sideroad off 3rd Line, Orangeville ON
(519) 941-2826
www.untothehills.ca

The Irvine House Bed & Breakfast

Lovingly restored by owner Helen Kellow, the Irvine House Bed & Breakfast recalls Victorian life in the late 1800s. Built in 1885 by Robert Irvine, a local painter and founding father of Orangeville, the house and surrounding gardens provide the perfect hideaway for business meetings or a couples' weekend. The home, furnished with period antiques, provides both comfort and enjoyment. Bedrooms are roomy and sun-filled. Select one of four rooms with private bath or shared bath with soaker tub. Architecture buffs will marvel at the two sets of pocket doors, the splendid staircase and original hardwood floors. Mornings in the cozy dining room include a full breakfast and rousing chit-chat with other guests. Enjoy a second cup of coffee on the front porch while you relax and take in the beauty of tree-lined Alexandra Park, directly across the street. When you're ready for a little exercise, Irvine House is only steps away from Theatre Orangeville, fine cafes and restaurants, art galleries and shopping. The entire house can be reserved for special events such as weddings, showers or family reunions. The downstairs area is available for meetings and conferences. For old-fashioned, homey ambience, a stay at the Irvine Bed & Breakfast simply can't be beat.

25 1st Avenue, Orangeville ON
(519) 940-0260
www.irvinehousebb.ca

Village Inn

In setting the tone for the rest of the Village Inn, the lobby at this establishment is like the living room of a friend with really good taste. Its leather chairs, fireplace and pretty lamps extend an invitation to guests to linger and get comfortable. This atmosphere of casual elegance extends to the guest rooms where luxurious duvets and an abundance of fluffy pillows await to soothe you. Choose from a variety of room sizes and arrangements, including Jacuzzi suites. Couples seeking a getaway should consider the romance package. It comes with dinner and breakfast-for-two at Monet's, the on-site restaurant. Other packages combine overnight accommodations with a round of golf or motorcoach tour. The Village Inn is Sarnia's only full-service boutique hotel, featuring not only the restaurant but a fitness facility and banquet area. Whether you come to town to try your luck at the casinos, attend the theater or frolic in one of the waterfront parks, you will be no more than five minutes away when you stay at the Village Inn—all the more reason to make this charming boutique hotel your choice for casual elegance.

751 Christina Street N, Point Edward ON
(519) 344-1157
www.villageinnsarnia.com

By The Park Bed & Breakfast

By The Park Bed & Breakfast is located in the west end of Toronto in a serene neighborhood off Bloor Street West, near High Park. Owned and operated by artists Margo and Ziggy Rygier, the inn consists of two century-old homes, beautifully restored to their original character with all of the modern conveniences and surrounded by lush garden landscape. The house at 92 Indian Grove, with its leaded glass windows and hardwood floors, is a traditional bed-and-breakfast with full vegetarian breakfast. A small dog and friendly cat will greet you. The accommodations include bedrooms and suites with private and shared bathrooms. The elegant Loft Suite has 1,200 square feet of space, a conservatory with sitting area and two fireplaces. The accommodations at 89 Indian Grove include a one-bedroom efficiency suite, with a private bathroom and kitchen, plus second, third and basement-level renovated bedrooms with en suite bathrooms and shared kitchens. Each is beautifully decorated, warm and inviting. By The Park Bed & Breakfast is not far from the centre of town and is just a two-minute walk to the Keele subway station. All of the city's attractions are easily accessible. Visit By The Park Bed & Breakfast, where hospitality abounds.

92 and 89 Indian Grove, Toronto ON
(416) 520-6102
www.bythepark.ca

Posh Digs

While vacationing, Marge and Cliff Lopes got the idea of opening their own vacation suites. They saw the need for beautiful accommodations with the comfort, privacy and independence of home. Soon, they opened an impressive red-brick Victorian property. Nestled in a tree-lined street in an upscale Toronto annex district, Posh Digs provides three beautifully appointed, self-contained suites surrounded by planted grounds. Choose from the charming, bright and spacious Pied-a-Terre, an open-concept three-piece bathroom and a cute walk-out balcony. The sky-lit Loft Hideaway has a separate bedroom with a queen bed, a four-piece bathroom with a Jacuzzi tub and a walk-out balcony. The newly renovated Luxury Garden Suite features a stunning open-concept huge living room, gourmet kitchen, two bedrooms, two bathrooms, a cedar deck and gardens. Plan a getaway and visit the beautiful Posh Digs.

414 Markham Street, Apartment 2, Toronto ON
(416) 964-6390
www.poshdigs.ca

Norfolk Guest House

Walk into Norfolk Guest House and you are welcomed into a world of elegance and comfort. Located in the heart of the city and short stroll from shopping, dining and entertainment, Norfolk Guest House is a restored 1865 mansion and a haven to appreciative visitors. Owners Janet Perry and Ken Friedmann love old houses with character and charm and share that feeling with others. This boutique-style hotel offers five themed guest rooms and two exquisite suites, all luxuriously appointed marrying Old World charm with modern amenities. Guests enjoy a complementary full breakfast, room service, central air conditioning, and convenient on-site parking. You can count on being pampered during your stay with custom fireplaces, hydro massage whirlpool tubs, heated floors, jetted showers, imported fine linens and private terraces. Bath amenities include hair dryers, toiletries and salon shampoo and conditioners. A landscaped garden waits for guests to enjoy its beauty. Janet and Ken's establishment has been featured in *Decorating Ideas* and is the winner of a Guelph tourism award of excellence. Whether you plan a long or short stay, you will enjoy the spectacular and stylish Norfolk Guest House. It is truly a more personal accommodation option.

102 Eramosa Road, Guelph ON
(519) 767-1095
www.norfolkguesthouse.ca

Jordan House Bed & Breakfast

Jordan House Bed & Breakfast has a history like no other. It is the only designated provincial heritage bed-and-breakfast in Chatham-Kent. Built in 1900, the Edwardian estate is located on a 50-acre farm where a succession of Jordans have been stewards since 1838 when it was granted to Richard Jordan by the Canada Company. Start your day with a full, hot breakfast, prepared just the way you like it. Graceful wicker furniture beckons you to the verandah where you enjoy a cup of coffee or tea while overlooking the glorious gardens. Relax in the Edwardian atmosphere of the tastefully decorated sitting room. The ornate fireplace hosts a cracking fire on chilly winter nights, flooding the dining room with a feeling of warmth and well-being. Ensuite baths enhance each of the four guest rooms. Lavender scented sheets topped with down duvets embrace your bed, creating a safe haven for pleasant dreams. Many of the original fixtures remain in this charming home, while modern amenities have been unobtrusively added to make your stay more memorable. Unwind from the stresses of the day with a stroll on the two-acre manicured grounds. End your day with a drink or a cup of tea on the upper balcony. John and Barbara Jordan are seasoned re-enactors. As a special seasonal package, they can bring the past alive to enchant and delight you. Jordan House Bed & Breakfast provides a first-class experience in comfortable elegance you won't want to miss.

7725 8th Line, Chatham-Kent ON (519) 436-0839
www.jordan-house.com

Ripley's Great Wolf Lodge

Right on the Niagara River, close to the famed falls, Ripley's Great Wolf Lodge redefines the year-round family resort. This resort offers quality accommodations and dining, outstanding customer service and safe, but always exciting, family recreation. Climate never interferes with the fun. No matter if it's sub-zero or raining cats and dogs outside, the 103,000-square-foot indoor waterpark is always a balmy 84°. The huge log resort features a 30-foot high fireplace, glass-sided elevator with a viewing balcony of the waterpark and the largest waterslide in Canada. Its Bear Track Landing has 13 water slides, from gentle kiddie slides to adventurous plunges, as well as four pools. Get soaked in Rainbow Lake, an indoor wave pool. Loon Lagoon offers water basketball and plenty of fun kiddie activities. Fort Mackenzie, the interactive four-storey water fort, is a child's delight. Adults bask in the family flume, spa and hot tubs. Browse the lodge's well-stocked souvenir and gift shop or take a helicopter ride next door. General Manager Keith Simmonds keeps operations running as smooth as glass. Come and soak up the fun at Ripley's Great Wolf Lodge.

3950 Victoria Avenue, Niagara Falls ON (905) 354-4888 or (888) 878-1818
www.greatwolf.com

Domes on the Grand

On the West Banks of the Grand River, one of the most beautiful heritage rivers in southern Ontario, you'll find Domes on the Grand, an intriguing and romantic retreat. Owners Debbie and Ted Whitelaw got the idea to rent out one of their twin geodesic dome homes after

tourists and passersby kept asking if they could see inside. They now offer one dome as a guesthouse and rent rooms out of the other, where they live. You can enjoy one of two guest rooms, a shared bathroom and a wonderful home-cooked breakfast at the bed-and-breakfast, or, for the full dome experience, rent the guesthouse. The guesthouse offers two bedrooms and two complete bathrooms, a fully equipped kitchen and dining area. The living room is complete with satellite television, a CD player and Internet access. Situated on 14 acres, the domes offer great views of the Paris countryside. Horses run in the fields, and migrating birds visit the river, just a five-minute stroll from your door. You can fish, kayak or canoe on the Grand or take on the nearby trans-Canada trail. Historic downtown Paris offers quaint specialty shops and beautiful architecture. Discover the charms of Paris from the storybook dome homes, the Domes on the Grand.

272 West River Road, Paris ON 519-442-5641
www.bbcanada.com/9362.html

Winston's Fine Dining & Guest Rooms

Bill and Maggie Foley bring European hospitality to Winston's Fine Dining & Guest Rooms. As owners of a small hotel in England, they learned the fine art of elegant, yet relaxed, customer service. As proprietors of this charming bed-and-breakfast, their professionalism shines through. Table settings, menu selections and presentation, and room service all reflect attention to detail. Winston's mission is to protect your privacy while catering to your needs. Meals are prepared by chef Tony Rennolds, the Foley's son-in-law. Dinners include homemade delicacies such as butternut squash soup and medallions of beef tenderloin, garnished with garlic fried rice in spinach cream sauce. Dinners are served Tuesday through Saturday. After your meal, enjoy a glass of sherry out on the patio overlooking the countryside. If you need a place to stay, you can choose among three guest rooms. Awaken to a lavish, full-course breakfast in the morning. Since 2005, the Foley family has been welcoming diners and travelers into their 100-year-old home. They'll help you with wedding, group and corporate events. Stop by for dinner or stay a night or two. Either way, you'll meet the wonderful folks at Winston's Fine Dining and Guest Rooms.

475 Lindsay Road, Peterborough ON (705) 743-0968
www.winstonsinn.com

Admiral Inn—Mississauga

The recent Mississauga addition to the Admiral Inns chain makes it a trio, or maybe it should be referred to as the trifecta, because all three inns are superb. The newest inn has an in-house saltwater swimming pool and spa, a sauna and a fitness facility. A free home-style, continental breakfast is laid out daily. Besides the standard amenities, the inn provides free local fax services, cable television and a daily newspaper at the front desk. There is a 24-hour convenience store on the premises for those last minute items so often left behind. Jacuzzi suites are available for romantic getaways and kitchenette suites for the traveler who requires apartment-style accommodations. Like all the Admiral Inns, the inn at Mississauga boasts an inviting décor of solid colors and clean, modern lines, decidedly unlike your standard chain hotel décor. The inn offers a total of five rooms for meetings and banquets—more than 4,300 square feet in all. The largest room can seat up to 100 people. Ambient lighting, catering services, Internet connectivity and a library of high-tech audio/visual equipment are available for your event. Let the cheerful staff help you plan and set up. Travel in style when you stay at the Admiral Inn in Mississauga.

2161 N Sheridan Way, Mississauga ON (905) 403-9777
www.admiralinn.com

Crossroads Television System–CTS TV

In an age where, according to a Canadian Heritage study, children have come to assume that the violence shown on mainstream television is an accurate depiction of reality, David Mainse wanted to produce Television You Can Believe In. That was the inspiration behind Crossroads Television System, a station dedicated to promoting traditional morals and family values. Mainse launched the network in 1998 after witnessing the inspiring success of its flagship program, 100 Huntley Street, which first aired in 1977. The popularity of the show proved an untapped appetite for uplifting programming. CTS programs depict strong families who confront modern problems with moral values. You'll find family favourite Full House, which details the travails of a single father forced to balance work and the needs of three young daughters. The high-rated 7th Heaven is a family drama about a minister, his wife and their seven children. Happy Days takes an affectionate look back at the 1950s. In addition to fictional programming, you'll find many inspirational nonfiction shows, including The Michael Coren Show, On the Line with Christine Williams, Faith Journal and Behind the Story. Tune in to CTS to help your family get with the program.

1295 N Service Road, Burlington ON
(905) 331-7333
www.ctstv.com

Crossroads Centre

A major landmark attraction in Burlington, the Crossroads Centre is the home of Crossroads Christian Communications Inc. (CCCI), producers of a variety of popular Christian television programs, such as *100 Huntley Street*. Crossroads is also home to Crossroads Television System (CTS), a commercial television station serving the Golden Horseshoe region, as well as London, Ottawa, Calgary and Edmonton. It also houses a National Ministry Centre, chapel, café and bookstore. When Crossroads outgrew its original Toronto facility at 100 Huntley Street, due to the overwhelming success of its programs, the company held an open competition to elect the architect of the new broadcast centre. The winner was Australian Rob Adsett, who modeled the Crossroads Centre after a Toronto streetscape that joins Victorian row housing to more modern buildings. The marriage of old and new influences reflects the spirit of Crossroads, which hopes to uphold time-tested moral values through modern media. One of the major attractions to the Crossroads Centre is the opportunity to be a part of the live audience in the *100 Huntley Street* studio. Most weekdays you can also tour the state-of-the-art facilities. The Promise Theatre hosts special presentations for children and adults. The Towne Square Café is an elegant place to lunch or to host a special event, with its soaring, three-story glass ceilings. Stroll the quaint Olde Towne Square, stop in the chapel for a moment of reflection, then browse the Blessings Christian Marketplace bookstore for inspiration. Visit the Crossroads Centre for a rewarding stop on the road to faith and fellowship.

1295 N Service Road, Burlington ON
(905) 335-7100
www.crossroads.ca

Willowbroke Stables

The land surrounding Willowbroke Stables makes a strikingly beautiful backdrop to the horses, nature's most handsome animal. Owner Jane Longmuir came to this 90-year-old farm ten years ago. She has added barns and outbuildings to Willowbroke's expansive acreage, and today, neat fencing surrounds the fields, ponds and trees. Jane's father, Rod McAuley, in his nineties, and her son, Ryan, both help out on the farm. Willowbroke Stables specializes in breeding services. It sells seed from its top stallions to horsefolk who seek quality for their mares. Ashanti, the son of King Conch-Miss Trillium-Balanced Image, is the star of the program, with a service fee of $2,000. Willowbroke Stables also offers many of the other services you might expect, though usually on a small scale. It boards a number of horses, including some magnificent Clydesdales that grace the fields. Riding lessons are offered on a limited basis. Students from local high schools can perform their mandatory community service here, sometimes feeding and grooming the horses. Pay a visit to Willowbroke Stables if you're looking to breed some magnificent horses of your own—or just to watch them run.

1622 Highway 6 N, Hamilton ON (905) 659-6060

Southwind

Southwind is definitely the lamb farm—it is owned by the Lamb family who raise sheep! Stop by and a bevy of creatures will be on hand to greet you. Along with owners Mary and Jim Lamb, son James and daughter Shannon, watch for dogs Bear, Chinook, Whipple, Pepper and three-legged Scooter. You might even see Smitty, the miniature donkey who dips in and out of sight, working with a llama named Quito to keep the coyotes away. The grazing sheep are sheared and the wool is sold annually. Southwind also raises high-quality breeding sheep for sale. Mary Lamb grew up on a farm in Nova Scotia and is an old hand at the farming game. Milking a cow and priming a water pump come as natural as churning cream to make butter. The picturesque property features rolling hills, sprawling trees and bountiful gardens. Mary has been voted Woman of the Year for her local volunteer efforts, which include pet therapy with senior citizens, group homes and hospitals. She has also organized the Flamborough Santa Claus Parade and served as president of Animal Adoptions of Flamborough for 13 years. For an unusual glimpse of farm life, stop by Southwind and visit with the Lambs and their lovable brood.

1602 #6 Highway, Hamilton ON (905) 659-1592

Ripley's Believe It or Not!

Located on Clifton Hill since 1963, Ripley's Believe it or Not! Museum still holds on to the reputation as Niagara's best museum. Authentic shrunken heads, the world's rarest egg and two-headed animals are only the beginning. Housing an impressive collection of the odd, strange and unbelievable from around the world, the museum showcases over 700 mind-boggling exhibits, oddities, curiosities and illusions. Several videos and interactive displays allow for a first-hand experiences. Take a stroll through what is perhaps the most humorous of cemeteries. The Niagara Theater offers guests the opportunity to witness ultimate risk first-hand in a film showcasing daredevils brave enough to face the wrath of Niagara Falls, and those who accidentally took a trip over the falls. Plenty of photo-ops are scattered around the museum, from an 18th Century Spanish Public Humiliation Stock to the world's tallest man's Chippendale Chair. Ripley's Wacky Explorative Room challenges kids with various curiosities and interactive displays, such as the shadow wall. After you exit, stop by the Wax Zone where you are invited to dip your hands in wax to create a personalized souvenir of your visit to Ripley's Believe It or Not! Niagara Falls.

4960 Clifton Hill, Niagara Falls ON (905) 356-2238
www.ripleysniagara.com

Liuna Station

Events at the extraordinary Liuna Station Banquet & Convention Centre are reminiscent of the grace and elegance of another time. The 80,000-square-foot train station, built in 1930, was in desperate need of restoration when it was purchased by the Labourers' International Union of North America (LIUNA) Local 837 in 1999. A designated National Historic Site, the majestic Station with its soaring ceilings, terrazzo floors and Italian marble columns was once a major gateway for immigrants seeking a better life in a new land. The impeccably restored Grand Central Ballroom was once the central entrance of the rail station, while the Continental Express Ballroom was a restaurant. Today, these two ballrooms offer conferencing space for 1,000 people. In addition, an executive boardroom, furnished with a handcrafted cherry table, bar and marble fireplace, accommodates a gamut of smaller events, from business meetings to intimate gatherings. The state-of-the-art facility offers high-speed Internet access, video conferencing and audiovisual equipment. The building has a distinctive look and regal presence, which accounts for its use in the filming of many productions, including the movie *X-Men*. At Liuna Station, your event will take on the lavishness and opulence of a golden era. Come and experience the idyllic and timeless luxury of Liuna Recation and experience first hand the many reasons why Liuna Station has been a consecutive winner of *The Hamilton Spectator*'s Reader's Choice Awards for Best Banquet Hall and Best Executive Chef.

360 James Street N, Hamilton ON
(905) 525-2410 or (866) 525-2410
www.liunaevents.com

Liuna Gardens

Elegant reception halls and a spectacular garden setting on the shores of Lake Ontario make Liuna Gardens worthy of extraordinary events. The Labourers' International Union of North America (LIUNA) Local 837 purchased the 12-acre Stoney Creek property in 1982, turning the popular Club El Morocco into an events centre that would generate income and continue to enhance its well-known reputation. Today, this breathtaking and picturesque location in the heart of Niagara's wine growing region welcomes conventions, weddings, balls and private celebrations. Liuna Gardens boasts 1,000 feet of lake frontage and handsome architecture reminiscent of 18th-century Europe. Romance abounds on the property, with a classic gazebo in the gardens and a marquis tent for alfresco events in fair weather. The professional staff at the Gardens can coordinate every aspect of your event in three separately styled rooms, each with its own outdoor patio and fireplace. For large gatherings, the Grand Ballroom offers classic style, with vaulted ceilings, plaster mouldings and magnificent chandeliers above a hardwood dance floor. The Renaissance Ballroom features a modern design that combines crisp lines and exquisite décor with Italian crystal chandeliers that glimmer under the skylights natural sunlight. The Botticelli Room with its cozy fireplace brings a touch of elegance to all small functions. Prepare for enchantment at Liuna Gardens, winner of *The Hamilton Spectator*'s Reader's Choice Award for Best Area Banquet Hall.

526 Winona Road N, Stoney Creek ON (905) 643-3117 or (866) 331-3875
www.liunaevents.com

Always Fun

Burlington Bowl

Always Fun! Renowned as Ontario's premier bowling centre, Burlington Bowl is a favourite gathering place and party destination. Decked out Las Vegas-style with vibrantly coloured carpets and special effect sound and lighting, Burlington Bowl hosts glow-in-the-dark bowling, birthday parties, corporate outings, group events, fundraisers, bowling leagues and lots of family fun. Burlington Bowl showcases Brooklyns Fun, Food & Bar. The restaurant, featured on Food TV's hit show, *Restaurant Makeover*, offers casual dining with 1950s fun and today's flair (see its story in the Restaurants & Cafés section on page 65). Touring this large bowling and entertainment venue, you will also discover pool tables, arcade games, a fully-stocked pro shop and much more. This community landmark is a must-do experience for those visiting or living in the area. Open 365 days a year. Expect outstanding service and a great time. Reservations welcomed. Visit Burlington Bowl today.

4065 Harvester Road, Burlington ON
(905) 681-2727
www.BurlingtonBowl.com

Toronto Conservatories and Greenhouses

Enjoy plants indoors all year round at Toronto's conservatories. Allan Gardens and Centennial Park Conservatory host important plant collections and educational programs and are stunning backdrops for wedding photos. Floral displays change seasonally at both conservatories—bulbs in the spring, hydrangea and lilies at Easter, chrysanthemums in the fall and a poinsettia festival at Christmas. Allan Gardens Park, located downtown and dating to 1858, is a true urban retreat. The conservatory located in the park features a global collection in six connecting greenhouses, the oldest being the Palm House, which opened in 1910. Others are the Arid House, Tropical House and a Temperate House. The 12,000-square-foot Centennial Park Conservatory, located in Etobicoke, offers three glasshouses, including a tropical display with fruit trees, ferns and palms and also an arid house. The Riverlea Allotment Greenhouse provides a unique program of indoor allotments. Permit holders range from hobby gardeners to keen horticulturists. The 12,000-square-foot greenhouse operates from October to June every year.

Allan Gardens Conservatory:
19 Horticultural Avenue, Toronto ON
(416) 392-7288
Centennial Park Conservatory:
151 Elmcrest Road, Etobicoke ON
(416) 394-8543
Riverlea Allotment Greenhouse:
919 Scarlett Road, Toronto ON
(416) 394-8543

Eagle's Nest Apiaries

Located on 50 acres filled with breathtaking views, Eagle's Nest Apiaries features a variety of bee products, from hand-dipped beeswax candles to the famed royal jelly. In addition, the store stocks propolis, bee pollen and offers seven flavors of unpasteurized honey, which you can sample before you buy. Bee products are well-known for their healing properties, with applications ranging from skin blemishes to Alzheimer's disease. Ask for brochures detailing the remarkable uses of these bee products. The store also carries pure Canadian maple syrup. Eagle's Nest Apiaries is a favorite year-round family outing spot. Come enjoy the grounds, have a picnic or tour the lovely flower gardens. Students from local schools come here to learn about the bees and their hives. In summer, see the display of radio-controlled planes. In winter, you can snowmobile or snowshoe around the land and refresh yourself with apple cider. Owner Henry Vilčinskis has a passion for tropical fish and invites you to take a look at the aquarium when you visit. View his collection of model cars, from antique to present day models. Eagle's Nest Apiaries is certainly a must-see destination.

308020 Hockley Road, Orangeville ON
(519) 941-5920 or (866) 759-9969

Remember When

The hectic world never intrudes upon Remember When, a charming tea house located inside a Heritage home in downtown Brooklin. The menu doesn't say it, but a sense of refinement and calm is what owner Daniela Harflett provides every day, along with her freshly made foods. High tea is an extravagant affair featuring a fresh scone with clotted cream and jam, plus assorted sandwiches, a cookie and a baked tart. The fine china adds to the pleasure. Remember When is a perfect place to meet friends for an unhurried lunch. Take your time, chat and finish your tea while soaking in the atmosphere of this beautiful old house. Built in 1847, it is decorated with antiques to capture the feel of grandmother's place in the country. Remember When proudly takes part in the Eat Smart Program, so you know your meal will be a healthful one. The staff makes everything on the premises, including the delicious soups and scrumptious desserts. Take time out from a busy day to enjoy the calming mood of yesteryear at Remember When.

61 Baldwin Street N, Brooklin ON
(905) 425-0505
www.rememberwhenteahouse.com

ScoopOn Ice Cream House

First Susie Schilling attended school in Munich, Germany to become a pastry chef, then she put her skills to work in Hamilton, opening an ice cream and pastry shop in 2007. The cute standalone farmhouse with awnings and white clapboard siding is a lovely addition to the city's West End shopping district. Susie's life has a European rhythm to it. She lives above the escarpment and walks down the mountain to her store each day. Her son Kyle helps out at the shop. Susie uses the weather and the tastes of Hamilton residents as product guides, which means she emphasizes ice cream in summer and pastry in winter. Fudge and chocolate are always in season as are truffles and peanut brittle. Susie does a big business in birthday cakes and saves such pastry specialities as tarts and strudel for weekends. You can taste the quality in Susie's European-style products, which feature fine, rich ingredients. Whether you are seeking cool refreshment on a summer day or a rich treat for winter entertaining, you will want to explore the delights at ScoopOn Ice Cream House.

139 Locke Street S, Hamilton ON
(905) 527-0707

Walker's Chocolates

A family-owned and operated business, Walker's Chocolates has been handcrafting high-quality confections at its flagship store on Fairview Street since 1983. Year after year, Walker's has scored as the area's top chocolatier in Readers Choice and Consumers Choice awards. There's always something tasty being concocted in the candy kitchen, where centres are made in small batches and hand-stirred in copper kettles to let the full flavour of fresh butter, fruit and nuts develop slowly in the traditional way. Walker's makes more than 60 kinds of centres for its chocolates and truffles, plus fudges, brittles, delicious chocolate chunk cookies and one of the largest selections of novelty chocolates around, in shapes ranging from airplanes to zodiac signs. Walker's Escargot, a swirl of caramel and marshmallow dipped in chocolate, has long been a fast mover. In 2005, it won the Retail Confectioners International Awards for Best New Piece and Best Presentation. The mint meltaways, if not yet world-famous, are certainly famous locally. Discover the unforgettable taste of Walker's Chocolates at a shop near you. Check the website for locations.

4391 Harvester Road, Burlington ON (905) 333-4463
www.walkerschocolates.ca

Capistrano Caffé Bar

Consistency is the key to Capistrano Caffé Bar, a long-running coffeehouse and bistro in Guelph. That's the philosophy of owners Nicole Shortreed and Peter Marchment, both employees before they purchased the business in 1999. Customers have come to expect fast, friendly and efficient service, and that's what they get every time. A friendly server is always on hand to whip up even the most complicated coffee concoctions. Order a cappuccino or espresso and watch the coffee masters work their magic. A reverse osmosis system that purifies the water, along with 100-percent Arabica beans, makes for a most satisfying java experience. All beans are freshly ground before brewing and coffee is then poured into pre-heated cups, which also adds to the perfection. Bistro luncheons, served every day but Sunday, include tasty treats such as pizza, salads, European sandwiches and a variety of wraps. In 2001, the partners were awarded the Young Entrepreneur Award from the city of Guelph. Great staff and an inviting atmosphere make Capistrano Caffé Bar a great place for discovery.

42 Wyndham Street N, Suite 102, Guelph ON (519) 763-8905

McGinty's Café/Antiques, Gifts & Collectables

Owners Kevin and Linda MacInnes opened McGinty's Café in 2002, and two years later they added antiques, gifts and collectables. The marriage of good food and eclectic inventory proves to be a winning combination. While the 1887 building and the antiques are certainly

old, McGinty's Café menu is definitely nouveau. A grilled chicken breast sandwich comes with caramelized onions, goat cheese and roasted red pepper pesto. Try a tortilla wrap with chicken, tuna, egg or grilled veggies and a glass of wine or a cool beer. The beverage list includes lattes, cappuccinos, hot chocolate and fruit smoothies. On a cool fall day, caramel apple cider hits the spot. Top off your meal with a dessert and specialty coffee or tea. You can sit inside or outside on the lower or upper deck. A visit to the antique and gift shop across the building is a must. Linda MacInnes selects only the most unusual items to add to her inventory. With shelves of cards, pottery, furniture, lamps, jewelry and dainty china teacups galore, you won't know where to look first. Their inventory changes regularly, so plan to visit McGinty's Café/Antiques, Gifts & Collectables often. They'll be waiting for you.

45 and 47 Sykes Street N, Meaford ON
(519) 538-0092 or (866) 413-4453
www.mcgintys.ca

Heirlooms Bridal Shoppe

Step into Fran White's Heirlooms Bridal Shoppe and the fairy tale begins. Brides forget time and enjoy the unequaled shopping experience. Service is paramount in the bridal business. Fran's trained consultants know that your wedding day is your dream come true and perfection is in the details. They will help you select your gown and can ensure a perfect fit thanks to the excellent alterations department. An exquisite selection of gowns by major suppliers is on display. Heirlooms Bridal Shoppe offers full-service shopping for all members of the bridal party. Dresses for flower girls, bridesmaids, and mothers, ranging in size from 4 to 30, make shopping easy and fun for everyone. Located in the historic Hugh Walker Hardware Store, Heirlooms is proud to be a walk down memory lane. Before the grand opening of the bridal salon in 1987, Fran oversaw restoration of the interior with its original hardwood floors, sweeping counters, winding staircase and stunning 14-foot ceilings. Artifacts, including the original ceiling lamps, wall sconces and ceiling décor, were also preserved. When the time comes to select that special gown for that special day, choose Heirlooms Bridal Shoppe, where the staff takes the time to cherish quality.

19 King Street W, Dundas ON (905) 628-4555

Cadence Clothing

Since 1997, owners Chris Reid and Candi Clements have been bringing the latest in hip hop clothing to Kitchener. The only store of its kind within hundreds of miles, Cadence Clothing stocks urban/denim wear difficult to find in any other store. Cadence has its finger on the rhythm of the culture and truly caters to its customers. Cadence Clothing sells fashion, not just clothes. Not only is this the store where you can find current, legit gear for hip hop heads, it has also been the first to introduce new upscale lines to Canada. You'll find Diesel, DKNY and now Firetrap and Jack & Jones. The clothing is stocked in limited quantities—you will not see everyone wearing your vibe. Consistency, style, knowledge, integrity and value are all reasons this shop is a hit. Every season, staff research the markets to know what is going to be hot next and order that, not what was hot before. Tastes from Atlanta, New York, Los Angeles, Miami and Vegas go into the Cadence style. To find clothing for every rhythm, come to Cadence Clothing—never fake, phoney, or fraudulent and always fresh.

87 King Street W, Kitchener ON
(519) 742-5550
www.myspace.com/cadenceinc

Inception

Inception is a sleek, sophisticated shop that provides women and men with fashions that match their life style. Young professionals appreciate the functional and stylish selection that ranges from career wear to casual attire. You'll find the best lines from Europe, Canada and America. Inception's independence allows it to offer unique collections—the shop maintains its own style and creativity. Take advantage of the wardrobing service and let Inception's talented staff help you build a collection from names such as Michael Kors, Buffalo and Kenneth Cole. A wonderful selection of accessories brings the outfits together for that polished look. Wherever you wear these outfits, you'll always feel classy. Men will find a fusion of style and ease with pieces that blend quality and longevity. They will love the lines from Kenneth Cole, Matinique, Buffalo and others. Inception goes beyond the traditional mall experience. Desiring to help create a diverse downtown, owners Erin Young and Andre Atkins combined their talents to create this inspired store. Visit Inceptions for a dynamic and stylish collection of clothes and accessories, presented by employees who have a passion for fashion.

26 Kings Street E, Kitchener ON
(519) 342-0714
www.inceptionstyle.com

Baroque Pearl Lingerie Boutique

The philosophy behind the Baroque Pearl name makes it one of the finest boutiques in Ontario. Each Baroque Pearl is unique from the others—no two baroque pearls are alike and each has its own shape and size, yet each is exquisitely beautiful. Baroque Pearl is known for its fitting services and the bra sizes range from 30A to 52J. Each bra is well-designed for the purpose of giving the best shape and comfort possible to a variety of needs, including women who have had breast surgery. All personnel are trained in fitting prosthetics for women who have had breast surgery. Baroque Pearl's sleepwear and loungewear lines are made of fine silks, cotton, modal and wicking properties. The yoga wear and swimwear lines are of superior quality and beautifully fashioned to fit women of all ages and sizes. Ki Ki Chic is the name Baroque Pearl has given to its accessories boutique. You will feel *tres chic* wearing handmade jewellery, beautifully made purses, hats, scarves and gloves. The boutique also carries high-quality bedding, travel accessories and a variety of spa products. Let the caring staff at Baroque Pearl Lingerie Boutique help you show off your own individual beauty.

5 Victoria Street E, Alliston ON (705) 435-0617 *www.BaroquePearl.ca*

The Scented Drawer
Fine Lingerie Boutique

This lovely boutique was founded in January 2005 by proprietor Nicole Bechthold-Coon. The Scented Drawer's philosophy is to provide the community and surrounding areas with a non-aggressive, comfortable, relaxed atmosphere where trained bra specialists are there to help fit the most unusual size. It offers clients an extensive variety of brand name ladies and men's sleepwear and loungewear, from classic to romantic and sizes petite to voluptuous. The lingerie is elegant, alluring and truly feminine, combining flattering styles with exciting colours and fabrics. There is also a menagerie of specialty items for prom, bridal and maternity with all the accessories, from clear straps to scented drawer liners. The Scented Drawer also believes in supporting local artisans that provide exquisite handmade Chinese silk brocade corsets by Noah Brown Collection, jewellery designs with Swarovski crystals by Y-Knot Jewellery and organic handcrafted bath and body products by West Wind Farm. Whether shopping for yourself or someone special, The Scented Drawer Fine Lingerie Boutique offers a truly special shopping experience, and a world of gift-giving ideas.

143 Broadway, Orangeville ON
(519)941-9941
www.thescenteddrawer.com

Habit

With elegant clothing and excellent customer service, Habit is indeed habit-forming for fashion lovers. Though owner Angie Jorge works hard to make shopping here addictive, she actually named the store after the French word that means clothing or an outfit. Habit has everything it takes to build a complete lady's wardrobe for any occasion. The store specializes in business casual wear. It stocks beautiful shoes and clothing from Nine West, upscale urban fashion by InWear and casual outfits from Esprit. Angie's specialty is in finding items that will go just as well in the boardroom as they will on a night on the town. In addition to beautiful clothing, you'll also find gorgeous gold and silver jewellery to add sparkle and colour to your ensemble. Habit carries a large variety of accessories, including striking beaded handbags. If you're looking for some help in putting together the ideal wardrobe, you've come to the right place. The friendly staff at Habit will work one-on-one with you to create ensembles that will have you looking and feeling great. Experience fabulous clothing and sterling service at Habit.

195 Broadway, Orangeville ON
(519) 941-3451
www.habitapparel.com

Nostro Moda

"There is nothing better than a hand-made garment," says Mauro Reda, owner of Nostro Moda. A purveyor of fine men's clothing, Nostro Moda offers custom tailoring, one-of-a-kind hand-made garments made to your measurements. Originally from Calabria, Italy, Mauro found his passion for tailored and tasteful clothing while working in men's retail at age 15. In Toronto, he built his reputation on workmanship and elegant fabrics. Nostro Moda Design House carries high-quality, luxurious fabrics by Dormeuil, Zegna, Lessona and Vitale Barberis Canonico, with cottons by Thomas Mason. Mauro has secured the trust of CEOs, bankers and assorted professionals with his impeccable fashion sense and world-class style. Stop by the Nostro Moda Design House showroom and enjoy an espresso and Old World charm. Nostro Moda carries silk ties, handmade shoes and the finest in leather accessories. You can choose suits and leisure wear from Mauro's own custom label, Su Misura. If you prefer, Mauro or his staff will come right to your home or hotel suite and update your image with the latest fashions and fabrics. Services include a first-class personal shopper, car service if you are from out of town, an elegant lunch, grooming and exclusive boutique shopping. A wardrobe consultation relieves the stress of what to wear to that important meeting. With a closet assessment or help with event dressing, fashion becomes a way of life. Update your image with a visit to Nostro Moda, where clothing is tailor-made for a gentleman's style.

186 Davenport Road, Toronto ON (416) 922-1624 *www.nostromoda.com*

New Day

New Day features fine-crafted handbags and shoes from Vietnam, along with specialty boutique items from around the world. Its Gracie collection of handbags, shoes, scarves and jewelry captures expressions of beauty in yesterday's styles. Handbags are skillfully designed in traditional motifs. High-quality pieces are beaded or embroidered very finely on beautiful silk-textured fabrics and are both durable and stylish. Classic patterns, both vibrant and exciting, appeal to the fashionable woman of today. New Day relies on jewelry designers who have mastered the use of patterns to create exquisite sterling silver pieces. Necklaces, bracelets and earrings compliment the handbags, shoes and scarves. Owners Viet and Sean Harrington started in the wholesale business in 2003 as the Vieta Trading Company. As their clientele grew, they decided to open a boutique in 2006. Viet and Sean continue to welcome wholesalers and retailers as well as the general public. Competitive pricing rounds out top-notch customer service. New Day invites you to step inside and see their wide selection of beautifully crafted products.

3409 Yonge Street, Toronto ON (416) 483-7878
www.vietatrading.net

Boa

Twin sisters Ofra and Daphne Nissani offer two stores to serve you that offer the utmost in contemporary couture. Boa in Yonge Lawrence Village was their first foray into business. In 2005, their success led to a second Boa opening, at The Beaches. Boa caters to the fashion-forward, price-conscious, urban-chic female. Funky, original accessories such as earrings, necklaces, handbags and belts polish the look that make you shine. The socially-conscious sisters take a hands-on approach to solving world problems. Purchase one of their custom-made Canadian Flag T-shirts, and every penny of profit goes to the AZT Prophylaxis program in Zimbabwe, dedicated to stopping the spread of AIDS/HIV. In an effort to reduce the amount of carbon dioxide in the atmosphere, Boa uses paper bags instead of plastic. Boa was rated one of the Best Places to Shop in Toronto by *Toronto Life* magazine. If you visit on your birthday, you'll receive a 10-percent off coupon for any item in the store. Let the Nissani sisters at Boa put together the perfect outfit just for you.

3217 Yonge Street, Toronto ON (416) 485-9372
2116B Queen Street E, Toronto ON (416) 694-6867
www.theboaroom.com

Diane Kroe

After nine years of traveling throughout Canada displaying her designs, Diane Kroe decided to settle down in one spot. Her boutique on Avenue Road displays the distinct style and panache Kroe's clients have grown to expect and enjoy. Known for her sleek, elegant and easy-to-care-for fashions, her current collection comes in a variety of colors, seasonal add-ons and accessories. The Jersey Collection, inspired by vintage Hollywood but made in Canada, is an asset to any woman's wardrobe. A luxurious, wrinkle-free jersey blend makes each piece a favorite for traveling. The Ten-In-One Dress can be worn ten different ways, as back and necklines effortlessly adjust to flatter all body types and create the ten styles. You even have a choice of hemline: straight or kerchief. Her Current Collection, which consists of three tops and three bottoms, combines into eighteen exquisite outfits. Comfortable, lightweight and of course, wrinkle-free, the entire collection fits into a small 13-foot by 12-foot overnight bag—perfect for the woman on the go. If you're looking for high standards in design, fabric and workmanship, a visit to Diane Kroe's is a must.

1693 Avenue Road, Toronto ON (416) 256-4221
www.dianekroe.com

Melmira Bra & Swimsuits

Melanie Heenan opened Melmira Bra Boutique in 1992. Within five years, her business grew to include swimsuits—and her daughter Amie. Together, they own and operate Melmira Bra & Swimsuits, a three-floor boutique that fulfills every woman's fondest wish to find the perfect fit. A visit to Melmira means taking the time to be enlightened and educated about the advantages and pleasures of proper fitting undergarments, no matter what your age, shape or size. The professional, friendly fitting consultants minimize your insecurities and maximize your confidence. Once they assess your size, consultants bring a range of attractive, stylish choices to you in the privacy of your fitting room. Staff take a European-inspired approach to teaching each woman the proper way to select undergarments and swimsuits that flatter the figure and heighten comfort and confidence. Seamstresses on-site make appropriate alterations. You can invite a group of friends and hold a private showing of lingerie, swimsuit and cruise wear. Wine and cheese are served at such events, along with personal fittings and style suggestions. A wide range of sizes are always available. If you have specialized needs, such as a first bra or a fitting following a mastectomy, the highly-trained staff are there to help. With 25 staff members who speak six different languages, you can count on the best of service at Melmira Bra & Swimsuits.

3319 Yonge Street, Toronto ON (416) 485-0576 *www.melmira.com*

Mirella's Ladies Boutique

Mirella's Ladies Boutique is at the forefront of formal and contemporary fashion with garments from well-known Canadian and European designers. If you're seeking a smart modern look and distinctive pieces to complement your existing wardrobe, Mirella's is your one-stop

fashion destination. Clothing and accessories by JS Collections, Powerline and Avanti grace the shop's racks in sizes 2 petite to 22 plus. Put the finishing touches on your outfit with the perfect pair of shoes imported from Italy, including lines such as Anne Klein, Enzo Angiolini and Nine West in sizes 5 to 11. Mirella's offers alterations, home showings and complimentary wardrobe consultations at the customer's convenience. Mirella knows her clients value personal attention and makes it her top priority to provide optimal customer service. At Mirella's Ladies Boutique, you'll find seasonal fashions well before anyplace else, assuring that you stay on top of current fashion trends. This charming boutique has been honored with many community awards since it opened in 1992. Whether you have a formal event on your calendar or not, you'll find something you can't live without at Mirella's Ladies Boutique.

374 Brant Street, Burlington ON (905) 592-9292
www.mirellas.on.ca

Foot Tools

When you think about it, shoes are the tools you use to help your feet move you from place to place. Foot Tools has the shoes that will have you getting there quickly and in both comfort and style. Owners Paula Desjardins and John Lawson have operated this Burlington store for more than 10 years. Their focus is on high-performance footwear. Whether you're looking for shoes for racing or for a leisurely walk on a mountain trail, you'll find them here. You'll also find comfy sandals to relax in when you're done with the fancy footwork. Looking for spiked sports shoes? There are plenty here, including models made for cross-country running and the high jump and long jump. Foot Tools has options for both men and women, including renowned brands such as Adidas, Nike, Puma and Montrail. The store also stocks a variety of technical apparel and performance accessories. Runners can check in at the store for information on local events. Foot Tools also hosts walk and run clubs—and even its very own racing team. Run on into Foot Tools for the finest in performance footwear.

2013 James Street, Burlington ON (905) 637-1888
www.foottools.ca

J.J. Orr Designer Collection

A vibrant yellow awning seems to point the way to the second-floor showroom on Brant Street that is the home of the J.J. Orr Designer Collection. Jackie Orr still possesses that genius for fashion design that made her such a favorite a few years ago on the Shopping Channel. However, her focus has shifted from covering the full range of clothing, accessories and jewellery to concentrating just on jewellery. In fact, J.J. Orr is one of the leading jewellery designers in Canada. Prepare to be dazzled, because her pieces use the highest quality metal and only Swarovski crystals. Ms. Orr designs and manufacturers her own collection, which includes sterling and semi-precious pieces as well as freshwater and faux pearls. Necklaces, earrings and pendants as beautiful as those in a Fifth Avenue boutique in New York are always on display at the showroom, enticing the beholder with their shimmer and glamour. Ms. Orr designs for many high-end stores in Canada and Europe, proving that her sense for setting trends is as sharp today as it was when she captivated her television audience with advice and opinions. Select something to enhance your beauty from the J.J. Orr Designer Collection.

421 Brant Street, Burlton ON (905) 333-1205

Danya Fashion Shoppe

Women's clothing to complement a sophisticated lifestyle has been the signature of Danya Fashion Shoppe since 1985. Women of discriminating fashion taste count on this store for stylish professional wear and elegant dresses for a night out. The store carries lines from many Canadian, European and American designers of distinction. Due to its longstanding commitment to fashion quality and outstanding personal service, this business has won many local awards, including being named the top women's clothing store in the West End of Toronto and Etobicoke for many years. Owner Danya Chuma learned the fashion business from her father, Dmytro Nahirnyj, a New York City tailor to such fashion legends as Bill Blass and Arnold Scassi. Mr. Nahirnyj also counted many celebrities among his clientele, including Judy Garland and Leonard Bernstein. Danya, with a degree in economics from St. John's University in New York, brought her vast knowledge of fabrics and style from New York to Toronto in 1979, when she and a partner opened a small boutique called the Room Upstairs. Danya Fashion Shoppe, her next venture, has been at its present location since its first day. Several members of Danya's staff have been with her nearly as long. Viewers have seen Danya on television, giving advice on style and opinions on trends, and she has contributed fashion articles to many publications. Look your sophisticated best by dressing at Danya Fashion Shoppe.

2378 Bloor Street W, Toronto ON
(416) 766-4511

Gems Custom Jewellery

If you have ever gazed spellbound at a dazzling gem stone, then you will understand what makes Ralph Schroetter, GG., FGA, tick. A lover of rare beauty, he is the owner of Gems Custom Jewellery, a high-end custom jeweller specializing in fine, rare and unusual gem stones. Since 1983, Ralph has fashioned hundreds of quality jewels for customers; everything from shimmering diamond earrings to brilliant blue sapphire rings and alexandrite pendants. His gift is to feel the personality of a gem stone and then design the right setting to bring out its special character. Ralph designs jewellery that become heirlooms that will last a lifetime and then some. Gems offers a very large selection of fine custom-made silver and pure silver jewellery at very affordable prices. Looking for something special for that young person in your life? Gems has it. Are you curious to know what a piece of your jewellery is worth? Ralph is a Graduate Gemologist with degrees from both GIA in American (GG) and The Gemmological Association and Gem Testing Laboratory of Great Britain (FGA), he offers appraisals while you wait, by appointment.

211 Brock Street S, Whitby ON (905) 666-4612
www.yourpersonaljeweller.ca

Ted Hendry's No Mean Feat

Ted Hendry was practically born with a silver shoehorn in his hand. His father founded Hendry's Family Shoe Store in Hamilton in 1928. Ted opened the first of his many shoe stores at the age of 22. Ted Hendry's No Mean Feat is the culmination of 50 years' experience. This charming boutique tucked into Westdale Village's popular shopping centre appeals to McMaster University students and fashion-minded professionals. Ted's feat with the shop has been to strike a magical balance between the fashion requirements and budget constraints of youth. The shop offers name-brand shoes for every consideration, whether it be walking, working or dating. Ted stocks the largest selection of high-comfort Naot shoes in the city and the complete collection of Blundstone Australian boots. You'll find classic Birkenstocks, trendy Emus and sensuous heels by Steve Madden and Chinese Laundry. Under Ted's half-money-down plan, you can pay the second half of your bill two months later with no interest. The highly trained staff will consult with you to help you find the perfect shoes for you. Ted is first and foremost a people person, and he understands the difference that the right pair of shoes can make. Let him help fix up your feet at Ted Hendry's No Mean Feat.

1028 King Street W, Hamilton ON (905) 525-9977
www.westdalevillage.ca/merchants/hendry

Nu-2-U Consignment Store

The Nu-2-U Consignment Store offers clothes for every size, shape and mood. Owner Cindy Fox wants to save you money on gently used clothing. The shop has clothing for women, men and children—it can outfit the entire family. Lady's apparel ranges from business to sportswear, in sizes that include plus and pettite. Dresses, jeans, coats and jackets come in an array of colours, styles and eras. Formal wear features sequins, bows and bangles that you won't find at department stores. Accessories include designer-inspired purses, shoes, belts and jewellery to enhance that special outfit. Maternity wear serves a special purpose, according to Fox: "Maternity wear is an example of something that is needed temporarily, but must be functional and look good at the same time." Children's clothing fits babies through teenagers, and includes some fine formal garments a child can wear to a wedding or other special occasion. Baby equipment, toys, books and videos are also on display. The shoes, boots and dresses turn over quickly with the ebb and flow of fashion. What was old can suddenly become new again as retro styles come full circle. You'll always find something to please your personal sense of style at Nu-2-U Consignment Store.

23 Main Street, Dundas ON (905) 628-1055

Simmons & Co.

The pursuit of fashion has been bringing women to Simmons & Co. since 1867. Jeans would not have been in the inventory back then, but today you'll find the hottest couture jeans from Italian designer Cappopera. Simmons specializes in all the latest fashions from Europe. You'll find skirts and dresses from the runways of Berlin, courtesy of the German line Blacky Dress, and femininity without frills from the label Nougat London. Do you possess the self-confidence and sophistication to slip into something from Mondi, whose motto is Fashion is Art? Find out by allowing the Simmons staff to dress you in the latest from this designer. Other featured brands include Tuzzi, Capponi and Perani. Whether you are seeking a complete wardrobe or just that one terrific outfit, someone on staff will spend the time with you to make sure you find something that expresses your personality and style. Daughter-mother team Angela Ingoglia and Paola Ingoglia purchased the business in March of 2007. They are proud to carry on its tradition of excellence. Shop the world of fashion at Simmons & Co.

39 Dunlop Street E, Barrie ON
(705) 728-4023

The Boutique

Anita Peng opened a gallery called The Boutique more than 20 years ago and realized a dream. Since then, she has been presenting art at its best. Peng travels Canada coast to coast in search of artists and artisans who display versatility, creativity and a flair for combining yesterday's techniques with today's materials. Specializing in sterling silver jewelry and art glass, Peng highlights designers and artists who create one-of-a-kind pieces. A specialty is Venetian masks that are traditionally embellished with gold and silver leaf, feathers and precious lace. The masks are imported and handmade. Masks have never been worn with such panache as in Venice. They eliminated social class—faceless, everyone was the same. Eventually, masks were reserved for carnevale (also called mardi gras). Stunning glass art work by Robert Held is featured throughout the store. A pioneer in hand-blown art glass, Held oversees the largest hot glass gallery and studio in Canada. Inspired by artists such as Monet, Klimt and Tiffany, his color-infused pieces dazzle the eye. Held's goblets grace the tables of royalty. A visit to The Boutique is like a course in art history. Peng welcomes you to experience artistry that stirs your senses.

944 King Street West, Hamilton ON
(905) 527-6966

Cardinal Glass Studio

Cardinal Glass Studio has been serving Brantford and the area since 1981. With over 25 years experience, Gordon Hill creates brilliant glass art pieces using the traditional lead came method and modern copper foil. Gordon mainly uses high-quality hand-blown glass from France and Germany. He enjoys the challenge of fusing glass at high temperatures, creating one-of-a-kind glass art and functional glass accents, such as slumped glass vases or kiln-formed glass mirror's bejewelled with crushed glass. Churches come to Gordon for advice, restorative work and stained glass windows, as Gordon still practices the traditional paint-and-kiln-fired method. Gordon offers four and six week beginner and intermediate lead or copper foil classes, and a full day workshop in glass fusing. Cardinal Glass Studio also has the assistance of Vanessa Fraser, a local fine artist and professional graphic designer. Vanessa has an outstanding ability to visualize what Gordon's clients want and can produce a full colour preview of a finished product before Gordon cuts a single piece of glass. Take a tour of Cardinal Glass Studio's intriguing showroom, located three doors down from the Sanderson Centre, and directly across the street from downtown Brantford's new Civic Square.

82 Dalhousie Street, Brantford ON
(519) 754-4307
www.cardinalglass.ca

Coldwater Gallery

Luba Huzan has a poet's way of explaining how she chooses work for Coldwater Gallery. "Visual beauty infused with good energy, produced with a high level of technical skill, that elicits an immediate gentle 'wow' is what I seek," she says. If the works also inspire us to a higher level of consciousness, or help us understand and relate better to each other and our planet, they are even more likely to get her attention. One look at the gallery's busy exhibition schedule indicates that she has no trouble finding local, out-of-town, even international artists who share her passion for art that lifts the spirit. Large paintings by local artists sell particularly well for the owner, and once you've experienced the feast of dazzling colors that often characterizes these canvases, you will understand why. Describing the village of Coldwater as a gem waiting to be polished, Luba uses the gallery to bring more culture to the area and, thereby, to assist in the polishing process. The gallery breathes new life into a building that has served its community well since its construction in 1903. Overlooking the Coldwater River, it was a bank for 20 years and a post office for 30 more. Enjoy its current existence as the home of Coldwater Gallery and of art created with a pure and positive attitude.

14 Coldwater Road, Coldwater ON
(705) 686-3035
www.coldwatergallery.com

BeMused
Fine Art Supplies & Studio

Lora Gibson, owner of BeMused Fine Art Supplies & Studio, wants to bring out the artist in you. The studio offers a place to relax, learn and most important, create things of beauty. According to Gibson, putting brush to canvas may be the best way to soothe your soul. Trained as a social worker, Gibson has spent many years as an amateur artist. As a way of sharing her passion, she opened BeMused to offer a large and reasonably priced selection of art supplies. Oils, acrylics, watercolours, pastels, brushes and canvases fill the supply store end of the building. You'll find oil bars, gouache and the associated media and tools. From easels to palette knives, sketch books to charcoal, matt boards to drawing inks, BeMused has it all. The shop can prepare gift certificates and gift baskets. The studio end of the shop offers a relaxing, calming atmosphere to feed and bolster your creativity. If you need a little coaxing, both group and one-on-one classes are available. Gibson promises a life-changing experience if you decide to spend just an hour or two at BeMused Fine Art Supplies & Studio. It's certainly worth a try.

185 Marsh Street, Clarksburg ON (519) 599-2993

Lou Hanson Pottery

Pottery for everyday and special occasions, that's what you'll find at Lou Hanson Pottery. The sun-filled showroom highlights ever-changing displays of her award-winning work, from pottery for mixing, baking and serving to her signature pedestal cake plates for weddings and anniversaries. Lou also makes raku-fired wall tiles, ornaments, mirror frames and welcome signs in a riot of colours and themes. Every piece starts with a lump of clay and is hand-built or wheel thrown, glazed and fired right in her Dundas studio with the help of her beloved Newfoundland dogs and Manx kitties. Since 1977, Lou has been using clay as a medium to find expression for her humour and love of life. Lou also creates limited-edition pottery featuring the Newfoundland dog and marketed under the name Prairie Dog Pottery. She has made fundraising easy for churches, schools and organizations with her custom ornaments and tiles. Special studio events include a spring and fall open house and a location on the wildly successful Dundas Studio Tour, always held the weekend before Thanksgiving. Collectors world-wide already appreciate the quality and diversity of Lou Hanson's work. Discover it for yourself. Visit Lou Hanson Pottery in the historic town of Dundas.

62 Sydenham Street, Dundas ON (905) 627-8632

King Framing

Creating a frame for artwork, mementos or mirrors is a delicate process, involving precision and artistic sensibility. You can count on those attributes from Nick Sokolovic, the owner of King Framing. Nick discovered his affinity for the trade when he went to work for his brother-in-law after moving to Canada, and he followed up by taking classes in framing. In 20 years of business ownership, Nick has seen several frame shops come and go from downtown Kitchener. He has outlived them all with a mix of affordable pricing, fine product lines and the kind of dedication to customers that has earned him corporate accounts and the loyalty of countless customers. Once Nick handles a frame job for a customer, chances are that person will keep coming back for frames, even if they have moved away from Kitchener. All framing takes place on the premises, where Nick stocks about 300 frames, including a wide selection of ornate frames, suitable for paintings, mirrors and needlework. When you need your treasures framed, come to King Framing, where you can count on extraordinary attention to detail.

42 Ontario Street, Kitchener ON (519) 578-5290

Textures

In July 1983, local bookbinder Sharon Beasley, silk painter Janne Hackl and textile artist Margo Griffith had an idea. Realizing there wasn't a year-round outlet for Hamilton-area craftspeople to sell their work, other than government-supported galleries or small owner-operated shops, these artisans dreamed of something better. After discovering an ideal location in a converted Victorian house in Hess Village, their idea began to take shape, and Sharon, Janne and Margo set to work building a business that would be totally self-sustaining in an environment where most artisans relied on government grants. One month later, six craftspeople were on board to invest in opening and operating the shop, becoming the core members of Textures, and an additional 11 artisans eagerly paid a small yearly membership to join the fledgling enterprise. Thus, Textures, a combined effort of area artisans, was born. In the 25 years since its inception, Textures has changed locations twice, but the original philosophy of a not-for-profit shop that is managed, stocked and staffed by member artisans remains the same. Loyal customers support its efforts and have helped Textures grow. From an initial group of 17 to more than 50 talented craftspeople between 18 and 80-plus, members continue to work together to guarantee a broad range of fine-quality original craft pieces in a welcoming environment. Custom orders are encouraged and its Happy Endings service can complete that expensive craft project you began so long ago, but never quite seem to finish. Come see some old friends today and meet some new ones at Textures.

236 Locke Street S, Hamilton ON
(905) 523-0636

Sue Jagt Custom Stained Glass

For artisan Sue Jagt, stained glass work started out as a hobby—she first took a class in it when she lived in Guelph. In 1986, she moved to Meaford and opened her own studio. Her passion for stained glass led her to offer custom pieces as well as ready-to-sell items such as lamps, night lights, vases, jewelry boxes and panels for kitchen cupboards. As her customer base grew, she began to receive orders from around the world. Eventually, she didn't have time to run her store and decided to work solely from home. Jagt often uses apple and maple leaf motifs, but if you show her a picture of a design, she will recreate it in the stained glass item of your choice. Garden sculptures, suncatchers and church windows have featured her designs. Jagt also carries a very popular variety of all-vegetable and ecological friendly silks (soaps) and lotions in many colors and scents. Naturally, they are good for your skin and the environment. If you're looking for a way to beautify your home or garden, contact Sue Jagt Custom Stained Glass for a one-of-a-kind treasure. Sue has also participated in artists' studio tours.

82 St. Vincent Street, Meaford ON
(519) 538-4184

Laura Berry Gallery

From a snow-covered cabin in the woods to a row of teddy bears dressed in their pajamas, Laura Berry's images are precise in their details and heartwarming in their effect. Local to the area, this self-taught artist has been painting her delightfully vibrant impressions of animals, rustic settings and young children since 1987. The Laura Berry Gallery, located in the Hockley Village, is home to a varied display of her original watercolours and limited edition prints, as well as calendars, cards and collectibles featuring her images. Laura is present at the gallery a few days every month to meet with clients and to personalize purchases. Working from photographs, she has created beautiful paintings and pencil drawings of homes, retreat properties and children for clients. She welcomes corporate commissions and has completed projects for Labatt and the Starlight Foundation. Her paintings, more than just photographic depictions of everyday moments, take the viewer beyond the everyday and into the realm of the imagination. Find art to warm the heart at the Laura Berry Gallery.

Hockley Road at Airport Road, Township ON
(519) 943-0053 or (866) 310-7739
www.lauraberry.com

Leonardo Gallery

Leonardo Gallery presents and promotes contemporary art by Canadian and international artists. It also offers the finest quality custom framing and expert art restoration. The gallery has two very attractive show-spaces in Yorkville and Forest Hill Village that may be rented for exhibitions, lectures and private events. While exhibitions change every six weeks, the collection includes fine works in oil, acrylics,

drawings, water colours and photography from both emerging and established artists. The premium-quality framing service that uses archival materials exclusively, offers its services at reasonable prices. The gallery provides expert restoration of old frames as well as for works on canvas, paper, wood, textile, stone and ceramics, and can transform your valuable art works of any media, including family photographs, to their original splendour. The gallery's staff always takes genuine interest in your art, and strives to facilitate and improve your method of collecting, preserving and displaying art. If you are looking to build your collection, frame or restore a piece of art, be sure to pay a visit to Leonardo Gallery in one of the two locations.

Yorkville: 133 Avenue Road, Toronto ON
(416) 924-7296
Forest Hill Village: 417 Spadina Road, Suite 210, Toronto ON
(416) 488-4057
www.leonardogalleries.com

La Couture Studio & Day

Burlington's finest & most prestigious Salon & Spa
receive the "Ultimate experience". Whether you in
one of our Ultimate Spa Days, a bridal experience,
a "New You" makeover including hair and makeup
romantic retreat in our Arizona Oasis suite with st
chocolate & Champagne, followed by a steam room
will be taken away with a magical vision that is sur.
Couture Studio & Day Spa "There are no limitation
Couture owner & operator of 19 years experience. "
tranquil holistic haven located in north Burlington o
as Beautiful Millcroft, one of the finest and most est
of Burlington where you will find this astounding re
Couture originally developed the miraculous studio
of a spa to follow in the future. In only one year, the
studio had grown to 4000 sq feet over night with five
treatment rooms and a one stop shop oasis for anyor
pampered including a medical spa. "The expansion i
states Tracy as she has mentioned a patio pedicure ar
cabaña is on the way next with lots of greenery and a
getaway feeling….without the expense of a getaway..
your pleasure or relaxation experience may be, at La
& Day Spa we will realign and define the beautiful yc
yourself in our Barbados Oasis room with any luxuri
of your choice, under a palm tree with the sounds of t
hitting the sandy beaches. Be whisked away in our me
rock water room, with waterfall sounds flowing, and
of fresh mountain air as you breathe deeply in a sanct
aromatherapy. Indulge in a lavish gentle touch sensa
our Orchid suite and cleanse yourself all over with the
of our Italian skincare line, "Bioline" or anti age your
with "Seductage" and feel the youthful sexy you. Rela
fireplace and enjoy a luxury manicure & pedicure wit
tea. Indulge in our medical spa, Rose Room where we
you with the ultimate in professionally trained medica
for both Restyalane and Botox treatment injections to
yourself back to the youthful you. No matter what you
to do, La Couture Studio & Day Spa will provide you
ultimate makeover & experience that you have wanted

2180 Itabashi Way, Burlington ON
(905) 319-0025
http://www.lacouturestudio.blogspot.com

eyes on brant

All eyes will be on you when you wear stylish specs from eyes on brant. Owned by optician James McLean and his wife, Stephanie, the store is managed by Jen Cook. "We always tell people that glasses are the most important fashion accessory," Stephanie says. More important than style is function—and that's where James excels. James' expertise is known across North America, and he is a former chairman of the Ontario Board of Ophthalmic Dispensers. James and his staff specialize in providing thin, lightweight lenses with crystal-clear optics. Jen and her team of eyewear stylists specialize in making sure you get the perfect frames for your face. "We get excited about making people look good," Stephanie says, noting that the staff will offer honest appraisals on how each design will look on a customer. You'll find plenty of gorgeous designer frames to choose from. Eyes on brant carries frames from high-end companies including Bellinger, ic berlin! and Traxion. Whether your style is conservative or far-out, you'll find something to make you look great. The store also offers maintenance and repair services. You'll also find an array of gifts at the shop, including steel Storm watches and Carrol Boyes' functional art from South Africa. Cast your eyes toward eyes on brant for all your eyewear needs.

433 Brant Street, Burlington ON
(905) 525-0788
www.eyesonbrant.com

Westdale Optical Boutique

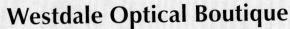

Westdale Optical Boutique is the talk of the town among its many satisfied customers. "I get really excited when I put something fantastic on someone," says owner Stephanie McLean, who has operated the business with her optician husband, James, for the past 14 years of the business' 38-year existence. James' reputation for excellence is such that even owners of other eyewear companies come to him for special orders. Jim specializes in beautiful lab work, providing thin, light lenses with flawless coating. Once your vision needs have been taken care of, it's time to mind your looks, with the help of Westdale Optical's eyewear stylists. "There is no way I would tell someone a frame looked good if it didn't," Stephanie says. With a selection of elegant frames from brands including Alain Mikli, Face a Face, Theo and BeauSoleil, you're certain to find something for every taste, be it funky or traditional. Westdale Optical also has gifts—surround yourself with beauty with items such as kettles and tableware from Alessi of Italy, functional art from Carol Boyes of South Africa and funky jewellery to keep your glasses handy. Let the expert staff at Westdale Optical Boutique help give you better vision and looks.

1050 King Street W, Hamilton ON
(905) 525-0788
www.westdaleoptical.com

The Spa on Main

Owned and operated by Joan Scott and Greta Markus, The Spa on Main provides a serene and relaxing environment into which you can escape. Its focus is on enhancing your natural beauty and wellness. The Spa on Main offers treatments that soothe away tensions while helping you look and feel your best. Try a luxurious facial designed just for you. It will leave you cleansed, toned and rejuvenated. The Spa on Main uses Bioline products from Italy for its advanced scientific breakthroughs, purity and remarkable results. Whether you need sun defense or anti-aging, Bioline products will give you what you are looking for. You'll love the Jato Wellness Experience, which promotes a feeling of wellbeing through invigorating aromas, body scrubs and a full body massage. Enjoy one of the many other luxurious body treatments or massage treatments that the spa offers. Spa packages can be tailored to your needs. The Spa on Main also offers professional makeup services using Jane Iredale Mineral Skin Care makeup. In addition to professional makeup application, the spa offers lessons and consultations. The Spa on Main will host your party or special event, such as a bridal, birthday or girls-night-out. The staff at The Spa on Main will do their best to ensure that your visit will be relaxing and rejuvenating.

40 Main Street S, Georgetown ON
(905) 877-1500 or (866) 477-SPAA (7722)
www.thespaonmain.ca

Sinkin' Ink Tattoos

Express your individuality with the custom body art creations from the gifted artists at Sinkin' Ink Tattoos. With seven talented designers and a piercing studio, Sinkin' Ink can do virtually any design or idea you've got in mind. Owners Jeff Beckman and Greg Schwab are accomplished tattoo artists themselves, and are proud to run a business that embodies their skills and passions as well as providing a gathering place for body art aficionados. Each tattooist has a distinctive style and specialty, and you're encouraged to browse the pictures on display to choose the right artist for you. Greg's tattoos include colourfully detailed scenes with a Japanese influence. He's not afraid of any job. "The bigger the tat the better," he says. While Jeff can do any custom tattoo you can dream up, he finds his style often leans towards Gothic and portraits. Almost every customer that gets work done at Sinkin' Ink can't resist coming back for more. In fact, Sinkin' Ink has been so popular since opening in 1994 that it recently expanded into another location. Whether you're looking for a full body tattoo or a simple flower on your ankle, you'll leave Sinkin' Ink Tattoos with a new, colourful piece to show off.

102 Parkdale Avenue N, Hamilton ON
(905) 548-6667
32 Hess Street S, Hamilton ON
(905) 777-9335
www.sinkin-ink.com

Albert Snow Hair Design Group

For more than 35 years, an understated salon on King Street called Albert Snow Hair Design Group has been offering clients everything they want and need in personal hair care. Master stylist Albert Snow and his team of licensed professionals offer top-notch service, the latest in beauty products and years of award-winning experience. Their mission is to give you a good haircut that makes you feel great and you can care for easily. Whether looking for a new cut, colour or something stylish and fashionable, the friendly staff is here to help. All stylists have been trained under Albert's watchful eye. Services include perms, straightening, colouring, foil highlights and deep conditioning treatments. Men, women and children are all welcome. The salon, a destination shop for chic clientele from throughout the region, has a reputation among celebrities and stars. In 2006, it reached the semi-finals in the Canadian Team Championships, and it has been voted the Best Hair Salon in Hamilton. Albert Snow Hair Design Group continues to lead the way in presenting the most innovative, creative ideas in beauty. For styling tips and the perfect cut, pay a visit to Albert Snow Hair Design Group and leave feeling great.

1036 King Street W, Hamilton ON
(905) 525-0831
www.albertsnow.com

The Glass & Pillar Spa

With services specially tailored to both men and women, the Glass & Pillar Spa offers clients a chance to relax in the lap of luxury and emerge looking and feeling their very best. Linda Vandenbroek and her daughter, Marnie, had owned the Sarnia Merle Norman Cosmetic franchise since 2000. When their initial location proved too small, Linda and Marnie, with the help of friend and client Gayle Tidball, decided to realize their dream of owning a full-scale spa. The designing, planning and building of the new location was a two-year process, in which the three owners researched what would be the perfect spa for both men and women. The result is a facility that will relax you from the moment you enter, with its soft lighting, warm colours and tranquil music. Services range from anti-aging facial treatments to aromatherapy salt glow scrubs for your entire body. Let the cleansing waters of a Vichy body treatment wash away the tension or enjoy a massage from the highly trained therapists. Gentlemen are invited to enjoy the amenities of the Pillar Spa, a completely private and exclusive section of the spa, which offers treatments geared toward men as they enjoy news and sporting events on the high-definition flat screen satellite television. The spa also offers a couples room, parties, retreats and bridal packages, featuring Merle Norman cosmetics. Come place yourself in the capable hands of the professionals at the Glass & Pillar Spa for a relaxing, rejuvenating experience.

563 Front Street N, Sarnia ON (519) 337-9998
www.glassandpillarspa.com

Perceptions Hair Design

The crew at Perceptions Hair Design knows its customers so well that they can probably tell just by the footsteps who is coming to the door. Entering this pretty stand-alone house with the cute blue sign and awning, you'll feel more like a neighbor coming for a visit than a customer. Newcomers feel right at home in this small salon, which scores of regulars have come to love for the friendly and caring attention of its staff—the kind of service that supposedly can't be found anymore. Because they are made to feel special, these folks would never think of going anywhere else to get their hair cut, coloured or permed. Each hairdresser brings to the job the pride of an independent business person working under the same roof with other individuals in the same position. Catherine Suter owns the salon. Tired of the daily commute to Toronto, she decided to plunge into the world of business ownership, and is glad that she did. When her customers come back time and again, she can't help but feel that she is doing something good for the community. Get your hair done at Perceptions Hair Design, specialists in making everyone feel welcome.

514 Guelph Lane, Burlington ON
(905) 634-2241

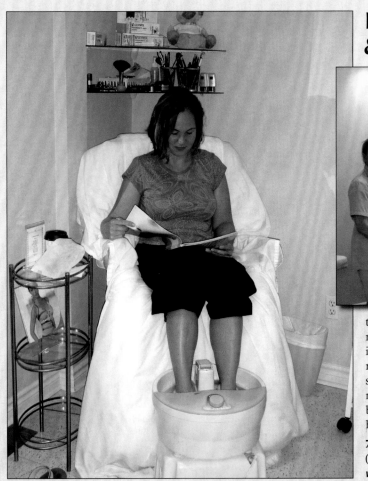

Eva Skin & Beauty Centre Limited

Since 1977, Eva Skin & Beauty Centre Limited has been helping people achieve a sense of balance, beauty and well being in their lives. Silke Lester, owner of this holistic day spa in the heart of Dundas Valley, recommends a monthly facial to ward off what pollution, stress and hormonal changes can do to your skin. Each facial on the extensive menu is designed to accomplish a specific goal, whether you are a teenager battling adolescent breakouts or a mother of a teenager committed to maintaining a youthful glow. The spa also offers algae seaweed treatments, sea salt body glows and other body care services, including massage. Nail care and esthetic services complete the menu. Ms. Lester is proud to carry on the tradition that her aunt Eva started of using only natural elements, combined with the soothing power of touch, in her spa treatments. With four separate rooms, the spa can accommodate multiple guests in privacy. Spa packages allow folks to leave their cares behind and experience hours of relaxation and pampering. Spend an hour or a day getting revitalized at Eva Skin & Beauty Centre Limited.

75 King Street W, Dundas ON
(905) 628-3866
www.evaskinandbeauty.com

Adora Day Spa

Kathy Cullis, owner of Adora Day Spa, believes that pampering oneself and taking good care of oneself are inter-related and equally important. To help you achieve both, she and her team of professionals offer a wide variety of services, including body treatments, facials and nail care. With its five rooms, Adora Day Spa promises an intimate, boutique-style experience for individuals or couples, while being flexible enough to accommodate groups of up to six people. The pedicure room boasts a gorgeous view of the St. Clair River. Light lunches and fruit smoothies, as well as a variety of specialty coffees and teas, are available to make your experience completely relaxing and delightful. Maintain your healthful sheen after you leave Adora by stocking up on skin care products from Ginot of France and the pure mineral makeup line from Jane Iredale. Kathy has nurtured her passion for customer service while being in business for 30 years. She purchased the spa in 2007 as an opportunity to concentrate everything she has learned about hospitality and exceeding customer expectations into this one venture. Come to Adora Day Spa when your body needs a tune-up to enhance its vitality and a little polish to bring out its beauty.

234 Front Street N, Sarnia ON
(519) 337-9212

Country Manor Antiques & Spa

Located on 15 lovely country acres, Country Manor Antiques & Spa offers antique furniture and exceptional spa treatments in one stop. Owners Barry Brand and Cheryl Spalding-Brand gave up conventional careers to follow their hearts. Barry is the antiques expert and Cheryl is an aesthetician and certified reflexologist. The spa provides a retreat-style environment that immerses you in serenity, emphasizing your personal well-being from head to toe. Naturally, spa furnishings include lovely antique pieces, fireside chairs and vintage décor amidst soothing scents. The spa uses only the finest quality products, such as the Allpresan foot care line, Gernetic customized facials and green tea therapy. Choose from a full lineup of individual treatments or one of the spa packages. Now refreshed, you may want to browse for antiques. You'll find two showrooms, one in an elegantly restored 1880s carriage house. Barry is a well-known antique restoration and refinishing specialist with a wealth of knowledge dating back to his teens. He can answer all your questions on period furniture from primitive through 1930s vintage pieces. All restoration work is done by hand. Country Manor Antiques & Spa offers a delightful way to spend a day.

207535 Highway 9, Orangeville ON (519) 942-4977
www.countrymanorantiquesandspa.com

The Body Bar

The Body Bar is an upscale salon that offers a comprehensive menu of beauty treatments, with affordable prices and exceptional service. The Body Bar is renowned for consistently excellent service and product quality; it has also been voted Best Hair Salon and Best Esthetics in Differin County by the Reader's Choice. Its Heads Up Hair Design services run the gamut, from a simple wash and wash to multi-dimensional foiling. Choose from an extensive list of manicures and pedicures, facials and body treatments. The Body Bar also offers eyelash and eyebrow

tinting. Inquire about a free consultation on electrolysis or hair extensions by Great Lengths. Waxing, massage and ear piercing services are offered, along with make-up applications and lessons. The salon's staff is happy to come on-site for your wedding day. Spa packages feature dozens of relaxing and rejuvenating combinations. All of the staff are highly certified and participate in seminars all over the world to keep on the cutting-edge of beauty treatments and products. Co-owner Gillian Rouse is a certified Colour Master with both Davines from Italy and Goldwell colours. Co-owner Maggy Moriarty has a background that covers all facets of the beauty industry, from a simple brow shaping, make-up for special occasions to Dr. Schrammek's Herbal Green Peel. For a blissful experience, visit The Body Bar.

279 Broadway Avenue, Orangeville ON (519) 942-BARR (2277)
www.thebodybar.ca

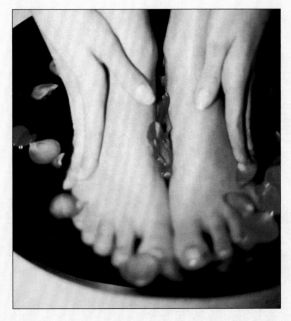

Sue's Magnolias

Sue's Magnolias is a full-service spa-style salon offering dozens of ways to indulge yourself. Sue's beauty treatments pick you up and make you feel brand-new. If you're preparing for a special occasion, this salon ensures your appearance is a premier event. The salon offers manicures and pedicures, all types of waxing and brow and lash tinting. Relieve stress with an exceptional massage. Facials are available for both teens and adults. Hand and foot treatments range from a polish-only manicure to the ultimate pedicure. Ear-candling services are also offered. Makeup application is another option when you want to look your best. If you're getting ready for a special day, such as a wedding, anniversary or prom, indulge yourself in one of the salon's relaxing and rejuvenating spa treatments. Discounts are offered for seniors, students and birthday celebrations, and there are group and wedding packages. Sue's Magnolias caters to both female and male clients. Owner Sue Bell graduated as an aesthetician in 1999. In 2006, she decided to strike out on her own, opening the fabulous Sue's Magnolias. Come and spoil yourself at Sue's Magnolias.

280 Broadway Avenue, Orangeville ON (519) 938-8600
www.suesmagnolias.com

The Soap Opera

Nikki MacKenzie has opened an eclectic shop to bring you the latest and most whimsical bath and body soaps imaginable. The Soap Opera, located in Alliston, is run by MacKenzie, with the help of her sister Virginia Nothrop. Soaps of every shape, size and scent line the aisles of store. The heavenly smells of fresh banana, cherry, pineapple and peach saturate the air as you ponder your choice. All soaps, gels, bath bombs, bubble baths and body lotions are handmade with natural ingredients that offer the utmost in health benefits. Organic products soften and rejuvenate your skin. Fresh scents relax and restore even the most overworked, weary customers. Feeling a little jittery? Try the green tea aromatherapy soap, guaranteed to soothe your nerves. Soaps are created for every occasion from baby showers to weddings. Novelty items such as soap in the shape of a martini glass or a guitar offer gift ideas for those hard-to-please folks. Kids love the dolphin and dragon soaps. MacKenzie also designs the popular citrus-strawberry shampoo bar, perfect for travelling. For natural bath and body products with a little fun and whimsy, visit the two sisters at the Soap Opera.

49 Victoria Street W, Alliston ON
(705) 434-2328
www.thesoapopera.ca

Self Spa & Wellness Centre

A contemporary spa with an Asian tone, Self Spa & Wellness Centre has carved a niche for itself by offering treatments not commonly available in and around Barrie. Chinese acupressure, Shin Tai and Mehta facial massage are a few of these. Owner Tammy Martin has seen her business grow since 1997 from a hairstyling salon to a wellness centre that empowers clients from the inside out. Responding to her clients' demands for a wide range of services, she has incorporated skin care and microdermabrasion into her business in downtown Barrie, as well as body treatments and stress therapy. Other specialties include hair removal, threading and makeup. Bridal party packages are popular, and customers are also welcome to create their own packages. Though Tammy's business has grown over the years, it has not lost its personal touch. A small professional team of three estheticians and two other hair designers join her in serving clients. Hair services include cutting, styling and colouring. Tammy trained at the College of Hair Design. Schedule some time for yourself at Self Spa & Wellness Centre.

123 Dunlop Street E, Barrie ON (705) 734-0031
www.selfspa.ca

R.H.Studio Cosmetics

Makeup artist Richard Halliday began his career as a hairstylist and model in Toronto. His winning smile and joie de vivre led to television, film, theatre and fashion appearances that thrust him into the international spotlight. At R.H.Studio Cosmetics, his brushes become magic wands that spread beauty to whatever they touch. Richard Halliday offers fashion for your face. His studio also purveys its own line of cosmetics, which are sheer, soothing and long-lasting. Halliday has a growing celebrity client roster and a Hollywood presence—he understands noveau beauty and what it entails. Richard Blackwell, composer of the infamous worst-dressed list, has labeled Halliday the Image Ambassador. With a degree in broadcast journalism, Halliday is a popular on-air personality, a passionate lecturer and teacher, and an event and fashion producer for television and stage. He also has a strong commitment to major charities. If you're looking for a world-class makeup personality who believes "If I can make you laugh, I can make you beautiful," make an appointment for a private consultation with R.H.Studio Cosmetics.

421 Brant Street Suite 201, Burlington ON (908) 633-1280
www.richardhallidayinternational.com

e-spa

If you value quality service, then e-spa is for you. Nestled in Stratford's beautiful downtown, e-spa is an enjoyable retreat from the busyness of your day. Located one block south of the City Hall, one block west of the Avon Theatre and right beside the Olde English Parlour Historic Inn & Suites, e-spa offers everything from a quick visit to a relaxing day long experience. The extensive menu revolves around pampering and high-quality service in a beautiful new barrier-free building. Private treatment suites cater to your every whim, or you can book with a friend and share the fun. Custom packages are available and only the Dermalogica skincare line is used. The skincare professionals at e-spa are carefully chosen, not only for their proficiency in aesthetics, but for their love of what they do. They have decorated and arranged with your comfort and pleasure in mind. Come see the rich, deep chocolate and sun-dried tomato hues on the walls, breathe in the subtle aromatic candles and essential oils, listen to the soothing sounds of the wall of water and enjoy all that e-spa has to offer. Erin Strathdee and the staff at e-spa invite you to select a service and place your soul in their capable hands, whether you have an hour or a day.

20 Cooper Street, Stratford ON (519) 272-1293
www.e-spa.ca

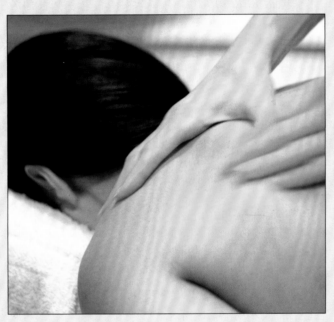

Skindeep Day Spa

For Rikki Vangoethen, being an aesthetician is not like a real job—it's more like hanging out with the girls all day. Rikki started working at Skindeep Day Spa in 2001. She loved it so much that in 2006, she bought the business from her employer. Skindeep is notable for being the greenest day spa around. The spa uses only certified organic skincare products and nail care products that are formaldehyde, toluene and dibutylphthalate-free. Eminence Organic Skin Care products from Hungary use Old World botanical knowledge to address such skin concerns such as premature aging, sun damage and acne. Eminence also uses wind and solar power in manufacturing and 100 percent recyclable packaging. Skindeep Day Spa's consideration for the earth extends to people, naturally. Whether you come for a massage, manicure, facial or body treatment, Rikki will welcome you like family and use the riches of the earth to pamper you body and soul. All body treatments take place under a rainforest canopy complete with steam and a massaging rain bar. A complimentary scalp massage and hydrating body massage finish the job. Treat yourself to the best that nature has to offer at Skindeep Day Spa.

90 Dundas Street E, Paris ON (519) 442-7232
www.skindeepdayspa.ca

Beauty Reflections Skin Care Institute

Beauty Reflections Skin Care Institute offers treatments that deliver dramatic improvements to the condition of your skin and your spirit. Owner Irene Batruch graduated from Marvel Beauty School in 1993. Batruch is a fully licensed aesthetician who worked diligently to gather the experience necessary to open her own exceptional treatment center in Bloor West Village. Her path took her to aesthetics shows throughout the world, including Paris, where she was trained on the ultrasound skin care unit now used as part of the facial treatment at Beauty Reflections. Other services include treatments by an aromatherapist, massage therapist or licensed reflexologist. Eva Gold uses essential oils and massage techniques, including a lymphatic massage, to balance the body, mind and spirit in aromatherapy treatments. An oxygenating mask is used in the specialized facial treatment to refresh skin. There are a variety of treatments to address hands, feet, face and body, including waxing and lash tinting. In addition to the skin treatments, Irene offers a line of body care products including lotion, scrubs and cuticle oils. Beauty Reflections offers the highly respected Nelly De Vuyst products from Belgium and Sothys from Paris. You'll be treated like family in this friendly, charming environment, and you'll leave looking better than ever.

2397 A Bloor Street W, Toronto ON (416) 766-3000

Kasha

Tim Corbett had already been a key hair stylist in Hamilton for 10 years when he had the inspiration to open a new, different kind of salon. His vision was to create a salon that is healthy, homey and comfortable to spend time in, without all the chemical fumes and sprays of other salons. In 1995, he opened Kasha, an Aveda Concept Salon. Aveda produces only natural, botanical products that are gentle on the environment and on the body, and smell nice too. Kasha is unique in Hamilton for using a single product line for all its services, including hair styling, facials, makeup and massage. The product line is popular with retail sales too, so clients can maintain their skin and hair at home. Kasha's mission is to provide beauty and wellness together. Aesthetic consultations at the salon are free. Kasha is a cozy salon with five chairs for hairstyling and professional lighting fixtures for makeup application. It's known for friendly faces and a great hair cut, with Tim leading the hair styling team. Let him treat you to a classy makeover with a gentle touch at Kasha.

258 Locke Street S, Hamilton ON
(905) 522-5468
www.kasha.ca

Hair It Is...

Lori Houtzager's gift for cutting and styling hair seemed to come naturally. She couldn't help but wonder during the three years that she worked for someone else if she also had what it takes to run her own business. Now that Hair It Is has been going strong since 1999, she can confidently say that she was a born entrepreneur as well as an artiste. Not one to take herself too seriously, however, she keeps the mood upbeat and fun at her shop, where having a good laugh while having your hair done is to be expected. Lori, who treats her customers as her extended family, enjoys doing everything there is to do with hair, from cutting and styling to perms and colouring. Not exclusively for women, Hair It Is welcomes men and children as well. The owner is also an esthetician and offers eyebrow and eyelash tinting, facial and body waxing, spa manicures and pedicures, plus ear piercing and tanning. Lori first felt the desire to be a hairdresser when she was a little girl, and the urge only got stronger in her teen years. Come get your hair done from a natural at Hair It Is.

216 William Street, Stayner ON
(705) 428-5757

Wild Birds Unlimited

Wild Birds Unlimited is the place to come for bird supplies and to learn more about the satisfying hobby of backyard bird feeding. The shop's Certified Birdfeeding Specialists provide expert advice—they can show you how to make your garden come alive with the songs and colors of wild birds. Wild Birds Unlimited designs bird feeders and bird feeding equipment of the finest quality. Dave and Eleanor Wood, the owners of the Burlington Wild Birds Unlimited, are backed up by a franchise system consisting of more than 300 stores across North America. The Burlington shop stocks birdhouses, pigeon guards and both tube and wooden feeders. It also builds custom cages. Featured binoculars include the Eagle Optics line and the Swarovoski 8 x 42 EL binoculars. Look for lovely natural gift items and gardening ornaments such as the Wind Deva and Music of the Spheres chimes. You'll also find specialty items, such as the Bird Identiflyer and song cards. The shop carries educational software, useful to both the novice and expert birder. The popular Thayer software includes the *Birding* and *Birds of Ontario* CDs. Excellent book selections cover the bases on birding. Beginners find books that increase their knowledge and enjoyment of birds, while the expert becomes a better birder with more advanced texts. Brighten up your life and your garden with a visit to Wild Birds Unlimited.

3350 Fairview Street, Burlington ON
(905) 634-7700
www.wbu.com

The Plumbing Mart

Does your bathroom need a makeover? Opened in 1959, the Plumbing Mart is Canada's oldest and most experienced kitchen and bathroom renovation company. For 38 years, the Plumbing Mart has held true to its philosophy of providing complete service to its customers, and it has earned a solid reputation for comprehensive service and skillful execution. The professionals at the Plumbing Mart understand the challenges customers commonly face during home renovations. To ease the process, the experienced staff can manage all aspects of your renovation and customize every detail based on your tastes and budget. With a complete selection of faucets, fixtures, and a full range of kitchen and bathroom remodeling packages, you're guaranteed to find the look that suits you. The shop also offers a complete selection of fixtures for the do-it-yourselfer. Not only will you find the products you want, but you can buy confidently knowing that your products are backed by a five-year warranty. With almost 20,000 renovations under its belt, the Plumbing Mart is a sure bet to getting that beautiful new bathroom done right. In addition to the Burlington store, the Plumbing Mart has locations in Mississauga and Richmond Hill.

3235 Fairview Street, Burlington ON
(905) 639-7106
www.plumbingmart.ca

Freem's Home & Garden Accents

Gord Munroe has been a treasure hunter all his life. You can enjoy the fruits of his labour at Freem's Home & Garden Accents, his showcase for distinctive finds that are just too good not to share with the public. Freem's is a one-man show, with a little extra help from Gord's wife, Sylvia, and other family members. Sylvia makes wonderful botanical arrangements for the shop. Gord ferrets out the rest of the goods, an ever-changing assortment of home and garden accents that include cast iron sculpture, reclaimed and rustic furniture, pictures, mirrors and antiques. It's a search he knows and loves well. Gord has spent his life as a buyer in the retail industry. He used to shop for footwear all over the world. Antiques and woodwork were always his personal passion, though, and he made a hobby of scouring markets, fairs and trade shows for beautiful and unusual finds. You'll find something for every budget at Freem's, and Gord will be on-hand to tell you the story behind each piece. Barrie is a growing city, but still relatively close-knit, and Gord understands the value its people place on personalized service. He'll make sure you're as much in love with your purchase as he is when you shop at Freem's Home & Garden Accents.

580 Bayfield Street, Barrie ON
(705) 727-0932

The Home Shop

The Home Shop offers furnishings, home décor and gift items for every taste and budget. The store itself is reminiscent of a metropolitan boutique. It provides a relaxed and enjoyable shopping experience, and has become a place where people gather, chat and exchange ideas. Owner Shaye Robertson is dedicated to exceptional customer service and a sense of community. The staff are knowledgeable, friendly, ready to offer advice on choosing the perfect gift and are always on the lookout for unique items. Bring in a picture or colour chart and the staff will help you put together your overall concept. The store stocks a variety of furnishings with many multi-purpose pieces. If you don't find what you're looking for on the showroom floor, the store will place custom orders. The Home Shop also focuses on environmentally friendly items, from bamboo products to an organic kitchen line. Among the home décor items are bedding, linens and fine prints. Other items include a wide range of kitchenware, specialty candles and jewellery. The store values its clients above all else and prides itself on being part of the Orangeville community. The Home Shop welcomes your visit and hopes to make your shopping experience a simple pleasure.

520 Riddell Road, Suite B, Orangeville ON (519) 941-2873

From the Kitchen to the Table

Sigrid Wolm has cooked up a dream destination for those who love to feed and entertain guests. From the Kitchen to the Table has everything you need to prepare and present delicious meals for your friends and loved ones. Sigrid had worked in the corporate world for much of her career, and was on the verge of securing a big job with a pharmaceutical company when the chance to open her own business presented itself. With the encouragement of her husband, Sigrid opened this cooking store, a kind of business that has never been seen in Orangeville before. Sigrid is dedicated to providing the best in cookware and cutlery. Among the store's lines of knives are Wüsthof-Trident, Global and Mac Knife Canada. You'll find high-quality cookware such as the renowned Le Creuset pans. The ceramic cookware includes the Emily Henry line from France as well as Denby from England. Sigrid also stocks a variety of small appliances. You'll also find gourmet food for sale. The atmosphere is bright and friendly. Sigrid and her knowledgeable staff are ready to answer any questions you have. Come in and see what's cooking at From the Kitchen to the Table.

125 Broadway, Orangeville ON (519) 942-5908
www.kitchentotable.com

Pear Home

Featured in *Style at Home* magazine, Pear Home is a stylish, avant-garde home décor shop. A look at its creative window display invites you to come in and browse. The shop's distinctive collections range from furniture to nursery items. Each product in the shop is handpicked for

quality. You'll find something to love in the living section, which features Canadian art work, furniture and cushions, as well as a variety of home accessories. For your dining needs, the shop offers lovely French glassware, Trattoria dinnerware and a beautiful selection of table linens. The bath and bedding section includes lush down micro-cotton towels from Portugal, Canadian bedding from such designers as Rieva and Reine, and many bathroom accessories. The shop proudly features baby gift items, including the Bunnykins line from Royal Doulton. For personal luxuries, check the shop's array of lotions and body fragrances, including the Fruit & Passion and Archipelago Botanical product lines. You'll also want to take a look at its sterling silver jewellery collection. Pear Home is known for its warm, personal service and affordable pricing. Come visit Pear Home, where customers are greeted as friends.

185 Broadway Avenue, Orangeville ON (519) 941-1101
www.pearhome.ca

Let's Landscape (together)

Do you want to redesign or upgrade your landscaping, but just don't know how to get started? The professionals at Let's Landscape (together) are at your beck and call to help you achieve the yard of your dreams. As their name implies, they carry out all of your projects in harmony with your own landscaping goals. You can do-it-yourself with their guidance or let them complete the entire job from start to finish. Their fully landscaped showroom and design centre helps you put together a plan that is professional, affordable and artistic. The enterprise delivers all the ingredients required to transform your vision into reality. Full-service assistance includes creating custom plans, swimming pools, outdoor kitchens, ponds and other water features, decks, patios and choice of plantings to accent your special garden. A simple hand-drawn sketch of a particular area is included in the price of a consultation. The computer-assisted design (CAD) option gives you the highest degree of detail Gand quality. The staff takes budget, style, personal taste and the surrounding environment into account on every project. Add to the enjoyment of your home while enhancing its value. Call in the experts from Let's Landscape (together) and create your own paradise.

3235 Fairview Street, Unit 5, Burlington ON
(905) 639-7292 or (888) 727-3411
www.letslandscapetogether.net

Photo by Angela Sevin

Quipus Crafts

Quipus Crafts celebrates new handicrafts from the heart of South and Central America, South Asia and Europe. The owners of this unusual home decór source display a panorama of silver and semi-precious stones, outerwear imported from Ecuador and Peru, and wool sweaters. Find delicately hand-carved items fashioned from wood, vibrant pottery made by Mexican artisans and groupings of wrought iron furniture. Wooden sculptures and furniture from Indonesia and Mexico create a warm ambience, and an array of wooden masks provide fascinating wall ornaments. In their travels, they search for the captivating gifts that find their way to Quipus Crafts, including the much sought-after Mexican chimenea. The store has such a wonderful representation of handcrafts throughout the world that it has been the destination of field trips for schoolchildren learning about cultural arts. Walk into a delightful, colourful blend of art when you arrive at Quipus Crafts and embark on your own journey of discovery.

2414 Bloor Street W, Toronto ON (416) 760-7133

Inner Luxe

The current and evolving design trends that Tara Dalla-Nora and Erica Dalla-Nora espouse are in plain view at Inner Luxe. With their degrees in interior design from Ryerson University, they have arranged the store to display living scenarios, each putting forth a concept that seamlessly combines furniture, soft goods, accessories and artwork. You will notice that they favor contemporary designs that are warm and inviting, with architecturally clean lines reminiscent of the Bauhaus period. For bedroom, living room and dining room alike, these are comfortable designs for the everyday home. Many of the furniture pieces and accessories have been designed and manufactured in Canada. Some customers fall so completely in love with one of the vignettes in the store that they buy the complete concept, though Inner Luxe also customizes designs for the individual client. The owners are ready to consult with you on anything from paint colour for a single room to a grand remodeling project. They collaborate with a team of trade workers capable of handling renovations of every size. Find design concepts to enhance your home at Inner Luxe, located in the Bloor West Village.

2358 Bloor Street W, Toronto ON (416) 915-3982
www.innerluxe.ca

Anything Grows

Gardeners delight in Anything Grows. Owned and operated by Allan Watts since 1994, this store has everything the garden artist will need and more. Twice voted one of the top ten garden stores in Canada by *Gardening Life* magazine, Anything Grows has a wonderful selection of plants, supplies and ornaments. Everything you need to get you started is available, including gloves, hats and shoes. Customers find unusual flower bulbs and organic seeds as well as some rare species of annuals and perennials. The store has a wide selection of decorative pieces, many from Canadian artisans, that you will not find in any of the big stores. It stocks containers to suit any style or need. After creating your perfect garden, you will want to highlight it with outdoor lighting, which is also available here. Kick back and enjoy relaxing in your paradise with furniture and some well-placed garden benches from Anything Grows. Don't forget to invite in some animal life with bird feeders and birdhouses. For smaller spaces, you can get creative and enjoy window boxes or hanging baskets. If you love to garden or are a budding garden artist, visit Anything Grows to be inspired.

235 St. Patrick Street, Stratford ON (519) 272-1100
www.anythinggrows.com

Back in Thyme

Back in Thyme opened in the year 2000, though it looks and feels as if it has been around a lot longer than that. Rich in quaint charm, this shop featuring antiques, reproduction furniture and primitive wares is located inside the late-1800s building that once housed the Coldwater General Store. Inside, the original tin ceiling and wooden slat floors add to the sense of time standing still. The mood is enhanced by the merchandise itself, which hearkens back to an age before mass production. Handmade dolls, artistic hand-hooked rugs and beautiful crafted birdhouses complement the antiques and rustic furniture. Satisfy your appetite while you're at Back in Thyme by tasting a variety of home-baked goodies. Handmade Italian pasta and meat pies are also available. Dealing in antiques runs in the family of owner Loree Lennox, who began her business career by holding Homespun Harvest and Old Fashioned Christmas shows in her log home in Horseshoe Valley. With the inspiration of her mother, Betty, and the help and love of her husband, family and friends, Loree took the big step of starting Back in Thyme. Find ideas at this shop for transforming your home, cottage or garden into a beautiful rustic setting.

12 Coldwater Road, Coldwater ON   (705) 686-3493   *www.backinthyme.on.ca*

The Door Centre

When you call on the Door Centre, they'll respond with more than 25 years of professional service and expertise. Owners Rick and Mary Block and their son Derrick believe success is more than supplying doors and windows. It's about personal service and partnerships with clients to fulfill their home design dreams. Doors and windows can add charm and value to your home. The Door Centre custom-builds its own French doors, mirrors and closet doors. It also features Tru-Tech steel doors, fiberglass doors by Fibercraft and Ostaco windows. Interior doors brighten and update rooms and hallways. You can select from the Calabria, Catalina, Portabella or Cordoba collections, exciting lines of iron art glass inserts. For an Italian flair, choose from the Rome, Venice, Tuscany or Milan designs by Arteferro. Voted the Best Door and Window Centre by the *Burlington Post* Reader's Choice awards for the past seven years, the centre has been recognized for its first-class service and its quality craftsmanship and carpentry. The newly expanded showroom displays a wide choice of styles and designs. Add the beauty of fine windows and doors to your home with a visit to the Door Centre.

4280 Harvester Road, Units #3 and #4, Burlington ON (905) 333-4044
www.burlingtondoorcentre.on.ca

Space Age Shelving

Space is more than just the final frontier—it's something we could all use a little more of right at home. You'll have a whole lot more when you visit Space Age Shelving. Owner Fedor Rip opened the Burlington store after years of travel as a metallurgist. In his travels, he often found himself purchasing a variety of organizational tools, including shelving and basket systems from Space Age Shelving. He liked them so much that he decided to open a branch of his own. Space Age Shelving has something for every room in your house. Get your closets organized with shelves, wire baskets, tie and belt racks. For the bathroom, Space Age Shelving offers such useful solutions as over-the-tank magazine holders and heated towel racks. You'll find all kinds of space-saving devices for the bedroom too, including Murphy beds that fold into the wall when not in use. Those looking to save space in the garage will find free-standing shelves and bike racks. "People can come into the store and we can have something designed for them in minutes," Fedor says of the fast, friendly service you'll find here. Come to Space Age Shelving for everything you'll need for a clutter-free future.

3350 Fairview Street, Burlington ON (905) 333-1322
www.spaceageshelvingburlington.com

Chatelet

Shabby-chic and French Country-inspired décor fill Chatelet with a trove of uncommon items befitting a simple but charming dwelling. *Chatelet* means *small chateau* in French—a size that is accessible to nearly everyone. Creativity and style reign supreme at Chatelet. One-of-a-kind dressers are painted, distressed and fitted with decorative pulls. A three-light chandelier is adorned with crystal swags, and a birdcage lantern bursts with colorful embellishments. Teresa Samad, owner, is a trained interior designer who studied at Toronto's International Academy of Design & Technology. She also has a music degree from the University of Western Ontario, which perhaps explains the fluid symphony of style she exhibits in everything she does. Her design experience spurred the decision to launch Chatelet into the design arena; customers can now work one-on-one with Teresa in the design of a single room or an entire home. An accomplished seamstress, she can translate your vision into reality. Visit Chatelet in Hamilton or Toronto and step into a world whimsy and practicality that will reinspire you with the possibilities of simple home décor.

170 Locke Street S, Hamilton ON (905) 527-2278
717 Queen Street W, Toronto ON (416) 603-2278
www.chatelethome.com

Booth Furniture & Interiors

Nestled in the heart of downtown Dundas, this designated historical building has been in the Booth family for 50 years. Step inside the large double doors where you are welcomed by a charming showcase of furniture, art and design. Two floors and a glass-enclosed atrium feature living room, dining and bedroom settings from traditional to contemporary chic. Canadian-made Gibbard, Bermex, Barcalounger and Booth's own private label, Furniture Craftsmen, reflect the top quality you can expect. With in-house interior decorators, Booth and his staff can help you transform a room into a showpiece. Custom upholstery and draperies in luxurious fabrics, as well as home accents from curio cabinets to framed mirrors and vintage-style lamps, represent a lifestyle as individual as you are. Everything your home deserves awaits you at Booth Furniture & Interiors, a family business since 1958.

49 King Street W, Dundas ON
(905) 628-2821

Flamborough Patio Furniture

Winter comes early and sticks around late in Ontario, making folks all the more appreciative of those summer days when they can relax in the backyard. Flamborough Patio Furniture has been making those precious July afternoons more enjoyable since 1979. Its selection of gazebos, garden swings and benches just could be the largest in the region. The showroom features playhouses, hot tub enclosures and garden swings, too. If you are looking for chairs, this complete patio furniture outlet carries everything from beautiful cedar loungers and loveseats to gliders and rockers. Flamborough went international a few years ago, and now ships its high-quality product to Europe and Asia. It all started when Gilles Fortin bought three swings for his family that he assembled on his front lawn. People kept stopping to see what he was doing, and a few were so interested that Gilles wound up selling the swings to them. Soon after, he began taking orders for furniture, which he made after work in his shop at home. Each and every piece at the store in Hamilton is superbly designed and crafted in the Flamborough Patio Furniture tradition. The store, by the way, is easy to spot. It's the one with the life-size replica of a Tyrannosaurus Rex in front. There's a dinosaur out back, too, standing watch over the stock in the yard. If only those critters could scare winter and stop it from lingering. Spend summer days sipping lemonade in your chair from Flamborough Patio Furniture.

823 Highway 6 N, Hamilton ON (905) 689-7676 or (800) 769-4645
www.flamboroughpatio.com

Visions from the Heart

A floral shop specializing in weddings, Visions from the Heart has set the tone for every style of ceremony. From chic and exotic to traditional-romantic, its beautiful floral designs have added elegance to corporate events, parties and many other special occasions as well. Drop by this cute store inside a 1900s building not only when you need flowers, but when you are shopping for someone special on your list. You will find a fine selection of candles, cards and collectibles. Visions from the Heart is a family-owned business and whole family is involved in its day-to-day operations. Designer Grace Graham enjoys helping customers put together gift baskets that combine these items with her remarkable flower arrangements. Grace enrolled in the School of Floral Design at Guelph University, where she developed a flair for floral work and wedding arrangements and has never looked back. Now, more than 10 years into her second career, she is a master at what she does. She has created beautiful floral and décor designs for such events as the Hamilton Gallery of Distinction awards ceremony and the Accacia Lodge anniversary. The official florist for Staybridge Suites in Hamilton, she has also done work for McMaster University, Women for Women of India and Petro Canada. Let Grace at Visions from the Heart create floral masterpieces for your next special occasion.

222 King Street W, Hamilton ON (905) 529-5577
www.visionsflowersandgifts.com

Westdale Florists

Westdale Florists is known for personal service, magnificent designs and the freshest flowers you'll find anywhere. Westdale Florists has been at the same location for more than 50 years, making it the oldest flower shop in the Hamilton area. This shop goes the extra mile to provide sweet memories. Weddings are a big part of its business, with 80-plus clients each year. Of these, 60 percent are referrals. In addition to arrangements, the store offers gourmet and baby baskets, stuffed toys and balloons. Westdale Florists even sends customers reminders of important dates—men love this service. Each bouquet comes with instructions for the care and long life of your arrangement. The shop's talented designers regularly attend courses which keep them on the cutting edge of the latest trends. You'll find a host of fun and romantic items to nestle amongst the flowers, including berries, feathers and beaded butterflies, pearls and rhinestones. The shop offers reliable same-day delivery service to all metro and suburban locations. Worldwide delivery is available. Expect the same personalized service and quality when purchasing through the website. Westdale Florists provides the very best in floral services.

1041 King Street W, Hamilton ON (905) 527-4127 or (800) 463-4127
www.westdaleflorists.ca

La Jardinère Flower Market

Located in a historic brick building in the quaint shopping district of Hamilton, La Jardinère Flower Market is reminiscent of a corner flower shop in Europe. The striped fabric awning and sidewalk lined with vibrantly blooming buds transport visitors to another country while the friendly staff and relaxed atmosphere invite the passerby to drop in to pick up a bouquet or just chat. The owners enjoy providing an alternative to modern-day flower shops where the bustle of sales dominates the atmosphere. At La Jardinère, customers come for the calming ambiance and personal service as much as they do for the fresh blooms and original designs. Specializing in European hand-tied bouquets, La Jardinère can adorn any special occasion with fragrant accents that add the perfect touch of class and style. Be sure to browse the stunning displays for weddings, which can be customized to suit individual preferences and themes. If you're looking for something truly different, La Jardinère offers a wide selection of tropical and imported flowers, as fresh as the day they were cut. Stop by La Jardinère Flower Market on your way home tonight and enjoy the sweet-smelling air of this old-fashioned flower shop.

246 Locke Street S, Hamilton ON (905) 529-5909 or (800) 879-6615
www.lajardinere.com

Insight to Interiors

A professional interior decorator, Cheryl Ashby has been giving in-home consultations since 2000. In 2006, she decided it was time to open her own home décor store. Insight to Interiors is located in a lovely 1835 brick house in downtown Brantford. Its four rooms are filled with stylish and distinctive home furnishings that you can use to accent your designs. Look for such labels as Steven & Chris, the well-known duo of the hit television show *Designer Guys*. You'll see fabulous tables, unusual lamps, artisan mirrors, vases and framed art. Insight to Interiors has a wide variety of tableware, including crystal. Cheryl is a wiz with window treatments and colour schemes, and her staff is all well-experienced and knowledgeable. Bring your questions and design problems into this friendly, inviting store and let the staff help you work out a solution. Bring Cheryl home with you to take full advantage of her insight. Make Insight to Interiors your first stop for interior design ideas.

108 West Street, Brantford ON (519) 720-0606

Once-A-Tree Country Furniture & Gifts

Once-A-Tree Country Furniture & Gifts is the place if you're looking for a cast aluminum lion lavabo fountain or an Arctic reindeer hide for your home or cabin. The shop specializes in solid wood furniture with a rustic flair, but its wide assortment of items, from furniture to knick-knacks, makes shopping an adventure. Owners Jeff Cole and Tara Smith offer solid oak, pine and teak tables, chairs, benches, rocking chairs and blanket boxes. Contemporary to classic in design, pieces feature quality craftsmanship. Cast aluminum reproductions add a slice of whimsy to your entry, patio or garden. Outdoor street lamps, hitching posts, mail boxes and weather vanes are available in color-coordinated themes. Bunk beds, dressers, garden arbors, swing sets, log or twig furniture, picnic tables, muskoka chairs and end tables, all Canadian-made from natural cedar make the perfect accessories for your mountain cabin or lakeside retreat. Home décor items include pottery, candle holders, Mexican and Indian artifacts, sheepskins, wall rugs and much more. Jeff and Tara enjoy welcoming locals and visitors who have heard about their unusual emporium. Once-A-Tree can be easily recognized by the moose, gazebo, sheds and antique buggies visible on the east side of Airport Road. For some really neat stuff, pay a visit to Once-A-Tree Country Furniture & Gifts in Mansfield, one hour north of the Toronto Pearson International Airport.

936577 Airport Road, Mansfield ON
(705) 434-0200 or (800) 893-0830
www.once-a-tree.ca

Gray's Florist

A Dundas institution since 1912, Gray's Florist is worth visiting just for the landmark building. With its beautiful architecture and hardwood floors, the store evokes a former era when pride of craftsmanship went into the very structure of a business. Long and deep, the shop seems to go on forever in space as well as time, swallowing shoppers into a floral paradise. Brother and sister Brandon and Dana Thurley grew up here, helping their mother, who ran the store for 20 years. The elder Mrs. Thurley took the shop over from the namesake Mrs. Gray. Brandon and Dana continue to run a first-class floral business. They design for weddings and bar mitzvahs and are a community standby for Mother's Day bouquets and prom corsages. They import fresh-cut flowers from the tropics to offer their customers the most exotic and fragrant flowers available. Come in to browse and you may find yourself inspired to create your own arrangement out of the flowers the shop has to offer. The staff will help you find the right basket, vase and ribbon to pull it all together. Uplift your senses and your spirit with a visit to Gray's Florist.

22 King Street W, Dundas ON
(905) 628-6315

Photo by Kevin Tostado

Collins Brewhouse

Since its days in the 19th century as Dundas' grand hotel, the building that now houses the Collins Brewhouse has been a busy gathering place, drawing people from all walks of life through its doors. The current restaurant embodies the perfect combination of class and casual, its plank flooring, large booths for six and garage doors that open out to the patio lending to an atmosphere rich in character. If you come to sample the beer, you will find two brewed on the premises, Brewhouse Red and Brewhouse Lager. The bar boasts ten other beers on draft in addition to a voluminous wine list and a variety of tantalizing martinis and cocktails. As for the food, an entire section of the menu is devoted just to burgers. The award for heartiness goes to the Beefeater Onion Ring Burger, an eight-ounce patty of Canadian beef topped with gigantic onion rings and smothered with provolone cheese. The menu also features ribs and pasta, while exhibiting a New Orleans influence with such dishes as jambalaya, gumbo and Creole shrimp salad. With indoor seating for 100 and a patio that can hold 60, Collins Brewhouse is a lively place where a perpetually festive mood reigns. The building, which dates to 1841 as the Collins Hotel, was granted designation as an historical landmark in 1994. Enjoy libations and good eating at Collins Brewhouse, a fixture of downtown Dundas.

33 King Street W, Dundas ON
(905) 628-9995
www.collinsbrewhouse.ca

Sizzle Steakhouse

Located in the heart of Hamilton's historic Hess Village, the newly refurbished Sizzle Steakhouse serves five-star cuisine in a stylish atmosphere. Sizzle Steakhouse is renowned for perfectly prepared food, artful presentation and impeccable service. This hip yet elegant restaurant is a converted vintage house, with peaked roofs and original picture windows. Earth tones, two large fireplaces and candlelight lend a warm, romantic note. The spacious wooden wraparound terrace has a delightful European feel with seating under large red umbrellas. There is also a nightclub, with an innovative design joining the 2nd and 3rd stories. Sizzle Steakhouse uses only the best-quality ingredients to deliver an exquisite meal served with fresh artisan breads. The menu includes delicious appetizers, such as the Cognac shrimp, served with raisins and butter-roasted shallots. Signature dishes include the cappuccino-crusted Cumbrae Farms filet mignon and the three-inch thick miso-roasted black cod. The lobster bisque is divine. Vegetables are always fresh and crisp. A private dining room is available, with seating for 12. The large bar stocks premium brands to make the best martinis and cocktails, as well as a wall of fine wines. After 10 pm, the cocktail lounge is a popular gathering spot, especially in the summer. This is an ideal destination for a romantic dinner for two, a family lunch gathering or a corporate event. Whatever the occasion, you're assured a wonderful experience at Sizzle Steakhouse.

25 Hess Street S, Hamilton ON (905) 522-3500
www.sizzlesteakhouse.com

Koi Restaurant and Cocktail Boutique

Catering to the tastes of professionals aged 25-50, Koi Restaurant and Cocktail Boutique is a trendy, cosmopolitan dining establishment. Owner Dean Collett set out to provide a complete dining and entertainment experience to rival the best of Toronto. The cuisine is an inspired version of Japanese-American fusion. Not a Japanese restaurant in the traditional sense, Koi Restaurant and Cocktail Boutique offers a menu anchored on the fresh, colorful and striking presentations of Japanese dishes. The menu is the result of the collaborative efforts of Dean with Executive Chef Robert To and Sous Chef Michael Lyons. Along with fabulous sushi, you'll find incomparable filet mignon, grilled salmon and a simply remarkable stuffed chicken breast. Dean remarks that the healthful qualities are just an added bonus. The restaurant's magnificent décor is anchored by sleek, modern lines and colored lighting. You'll find an abundance of plasma-screen televisions in the bar and a terrific dance floor. The bar offers a choice of 25 exotic drinks and no less than 15 varieties of vodka. A shared outdoor terrace joins Koi with its sister restaurant next door, Sizzle Steakhouse, also owned by Dean. For exciting and unusual dining, check out Koi Restaurant and Cocktail Boutique.

27 Hess Street S, Hamilton ON
(905) 308-7507
www.koirestaurant.ca
www.koilounge.ca

Olive's Casual Cuisine

Since 2003, Olive's Casual Cuisine has been taking guests back to the way that restaurants used to be. The Polynesian salad, a signature dish, is a case in point. All of the fruit is fresh, and the coconut dressing scores points not only for being homemade but for being inventive. Everything at Olive's, including the desserts and bread, is made from scratch by someone who takes pride in creating food that is a joy to behold and a pleasure to taste. Whether you come for lunch or dinner, you will find nothing deep-fried on the menu, only foods that have been prepared so that their flavours ring out. Olive Archibald ran a popular tea house in Sarnia for 15 years before opening Olive's Casual Cuisine, and the lunch menu of salads and quiches is reminiscent of the lighter fare of such an establishment. Dinner is more elegant. Feel free to visit the wine table in the middle of the dining room to taste different wines and to pick something to go with the Ontario rack of lamb, served with a maple brandy sauce. Salmon and steaks are also popular. Olive is a hands-on type who enjoys mixing with her guests. Join her for a meal that will satisfy your appetite for fresh, creative cuisine.

1591 London Line, Sarnia ON
(519) 541-1333

Bean Bar

Owners Robert Wilton and Debbie Molot call the Bean Bar a lifestyle restaurant. Located in the beautiful Westdale area, the contemporary and stylish restaurant attracts all kinds of customers. Enjoy an apple martini and a plate of warmed Brie with cranberries before the theater. The ambience is intimate. Spend the evening dining on grilled salmon or seared tilapia, or go Mexican with sweet potato quesadillas. Rich chicken curry made with sweet and savory chicken slowly cooked in coconut curry sauce. Some like it hot, and if that's you, order the Blow Your Top Burger with hot peppers, chipotle mayo and avocado. Remember to leave some room for dessert—the Bean Bar features 40 selections at any one time. Cheesecake, mousse, meringues, tarts, biscotti, brownies, and the Best Ever Butter Tarts are freshly made to satisfy the most discriminating sweet tooth. Staff picks include the baklava cheesecake, white chocolate raspberry bombe and the Wacky Apple, a winning combination of apple caramel custard with pecans in a shortbread crust. Coffee delights such as espresso or cappuccino complement the dessert. Specialty drinks, both alcoholic and non-alcoholic, are mixed, stirred and shaken to your liking. The catering department is happy to plan and staff your wedding, corporate event or special family celebration. For a exhilarating trip into the world of high cuisine, come to the Bean Bar.

1012 King Street W, Hamilton ON
(905) 524-BEAN (2326)

Ray's Place—The Boat House

Sports fans get as attached to their sports bar as they do to their favorite teams, which accounts for the affection folks around Hamilton have for Ray's Place—The Boat House. It was fish and chips that launched Ray Paquette into the restaurant business 30 years ago. He was working as a disc jockey in a nightclub when a customer told him where he could purchase a fryer for making fish and chips. He opened his fish and chips restaurant in 1976, and by 1981, he had expanded into a full-fledged sports bar with autographed shirts and photos lining the walls. Not only do the televisions stay tuned to all the games, but you'll find posters and memorabilia from the NHL, NFL, NBA, MLB and NASCAR. The venerable old building with its peaked roofs, verandah and glassed-in extension looks as inviting and established as it is, and Ray gives his customers plenty of reasons to visit besides sports events. Customers belt out their favorite tunes at karaoke every Friday and Saturday throughout the summer, and specials change each night, so you can come for rib night and return for specials on pasta, wings or steak. Pizza is a perennial favorite, along with salads, burgers and wraps. As in the beginning, fish and chips is the house specialty. Ray's Place is a big player in local social calendars. The town shows up for weekend breakfasts and signs up for a monthly email newsletter that describes products, specials and upcoming events. For games, food and good cheer, visit Ray's Place—The Boat House.

303 Dundurn Street S, Hamilton ON (905) 522-4800
www.raysplacetheboathouse.com

50/50 Restaurant

50/50 Restaurant just steps from Burlington's waterfront gives diners a stunning destination for celebrating the fine things in life—art, wine and food. Chef Harnek apprenticed in classical French and Italian cuisine while in Frankfurt, Germany. He incorporates European elements into his menu while embracing the local ingredients in a fusion fashion to carefully blending tropical and citrus fruits for pairing wines around the world. Harnek changes the menu seasonally offering dishes such as cured Salmon Carpaccio, beef tenderloin, his signature Agnolotti and daily fresh fish. He is an expert at blending spices from all over the world for his sauces and recipes, such as roasted cumin, garlic-crusted Ontario lamb and preserved ginger veal chops in red wine reduction. You will find four dining rooms on the main floor centered around a glass room enclosure for your corporate meetings and events as well as a balcony under the city's biggest skylight that seats 120 and a lower level wine bar with a fireplace and live entertainment. The architecture, punctuated with a glass ceiling and imported marble floors, elegant interior décor and unique settings invite you to celebrate the finer things in life with a visit to 50/50 Restaurant.

1445 Elgin Street, Burlington ON (905) 333-5050
www.5050restaurant.com

Sonzi Restaurant & Rooftop Patio

Mediterranean cuisine in a warm and relaxed atmosphere make dinner at Sonzi Restaurant & Rooftop Patio memorable. Chef Jay Trefethen uses only the freshest and finest ingredients to whip up entrées and desserts. Start with crispy calamari or pan-steamed East Coast mussels. Move on to an entrée such as rigatoni with basil sauce, grilled lamb sausage and kalamata olives. Heartier appetites can choose between a New York strip steak or Marble Farms pork tenderloin. Follow up with Sonzi's signature dessert, warm upside-down chocolate pecan tart with espresso sour cream ice cream. If you still have room for more, order a Sonzi coffee infused with Frangelico and dark crème de cacao or a Monte Cristo coffee laced with Grand Marnier and Kahlúa. The well-trained staff is happy to help you with wine selection. Teas, cognacs, ports and dessert wines are also available. A moonlit night beckons you to relax and enjoy your dinner on the new rooftop patio. Hear classical guitar Tuesday and Wednesday nights and jazz on Friday and Saturday evenings. Sonzi Restaurant and Rooftop Patio have been serving satisfied customers for 10 years. Let owner Jeff Mason welcome you to one of downtown Burlington's treasured restaurants.

370 Brant Street, Burlington ON (905) 632-6682
www.sonzi.ca

Saigon on Brant Restaurant

With its location on the main street of downtown Burlington, Saigon on Brant fills up every day with workers from the nearby shops, offices and City Hall. The restaurant's reputation for authentic Vietnamese cuisine at a good price makes it a popular place for students as well. The pungent fare is especially welcome on a frigid day. For a filling and delicious meal that will cut through the chill, try a bowl of beef and noodles. Elizabeth Way, food critic for *View*, the area's alternative magazine, called this dish "the perfect respite from a cold and blustery fall night." The beef is cut very thin and comes layered on top of the noodles. An aromatic broth fills the bowl to the top. Pork rolls and deep-fried wontons are just two of the many crowd pleasers from the list of appetizers. The main menu features noodle soups, vermicelli dishes and steamed rice entrées galore. Helpful pictures guide you in choosing from all the exotic choices. The two large rooms in this pleasant, family-owned establishment are nicely appointed with Vietnamese artwork. Make like a local and head to Saigon on Brant for generous portions of tasty Vietnamese cuisine.

474 Brant Street, Burlington ON (905) 633-9262

La Scala Ristorante

The tastes of Italy come alive at the intimate La Scala Ristorante in the heart of the St. Catharine's business district. Owners Lori and Joe Marchese restored the 1800s era building in 2003 to resemble a rustic Italian eatery, complete with painted walls that reproduce ancient Italian artistry. In summer, enjoy the Tuscan patio with its water fountain and exotic plants. Diners can sample traditional dishes from all regions on the Mediterranean and choose private label wine from around the globe to accompany their meals. Head Chef Lyra Alexander takes special pride in offering bona fide Northern Italian Florentine dishes. Specialties include homemade gnocchi, cannelloni and ravioli, each dashed with light cream or wine-based sauces. For lunch or dinner, look for an assorted menu of seafood, soups, salads, antipasta, panini and La Scala's signature dish, veal scallopini. The Ristorante is open to special menu requests, offers catering and hosts wine tasting events. You can wear your jeans or your best jacket to this classy restaurant, where high standards extend to taste, service and presentation. Visit La Scala Ristorante, where the staff promises nobody leaves hungry.

26 Church Street, St Catharines ON
(905) 684-5448
www.goldbook.ca/goldbook/niagarafalls/Restaurants/lascala.html

Angel's Diner

Would you like to have breakfast with Elvis? Eating at Angel's Diner promises the next best thing. Pictures of many 1950s idols, including the man with the blue suede shoes, hang on the walls of this popular establishment, which faithfully recreates the look of a diner from that era with its checkered black-and-white floors, chrome trimmings and lots of reds and greens. With the beat of "Hound Dog" or some other sock hop hit in the background, feel free to order breakfast all day. If you're in the mood for something other than pancakes or an omelette, you'll find more than enough choices on the menu. From soups and salads to burgers, pasta and seafood, Angel's has something for everyone. A deli within the diner offers even more possibilities. The smoked meat sandwiches, in particular, are crowd pleasers, and the ribs have won first prize at Ribfest Guelph. Part of a small chain of Canadian restaurants founded by John Kokoris, Angel's Diner has been written up in the Guelph Mercury and other local publications for its delicious low-cost meals and nostalgic atmosphere. Gaze at Elvis, Marilyn and James Dean while enjoying breakfast, lunch or dinner at Angel's Diner.

18–64 Hamilton Street N, Waterdown ON
(905) 690-4109
www.angelsdiner.ca

Il Fiasco Café & Wine Bar

Italian chiantis are traditionally sold in a straw-wrapped bottle known as il fiasco, and this served as at least one inspiration for the name of Il Fiasco Café & Wine Bar. Il Fiasco is also the name of a delicious red wine featured here. Ian Glenday and Judith Birchall have produced a merry atmosphere to match their outstanding culinary approach and smart service. The professional expertise is no accident—Judith has impressive credentials. She is a former sous-chef at a leading hotel and chef at the prestigious LoPresti's. Il Fiasco's global cuisine is affordable gourmet, and has attracted a dedicated following as the word spreads. Tempting entrées include pasta dishes such as a penne with smoked salmon, vodka cream and capers. Tasty meat dishes include medallions of venison with a wild blueberry red wine glaze. Pizzas are fantastic creations with descriptive titles. The volcano is topped with spicy sausage, hot peppers, pineapple and tomato sauce. The Mediterranean décor contributes to the overall celebratory spirit. Il Fiasco will even come to you. Eat This is Il Fiasco's catering division for groups ranging from 4 to 200. Visit Il Fiasco Café & Wine Bar for a festive meal in an intimate setting.

182 Locke Street S, Hamilton ON (905) 522-8549
www.ilfiasco.ca

The Village Green Bistro

A recent graduate in culinary management from George Brown University, Allison Gordon has joined her mother Gwen in running the Village Green Bistro. Featuring vegetarian and fish dishes, this year-old bistro boasts a high-quality, healthy cuisine made with love. Spicy and tantalizing, the menu includes regional dishes ranging from India to China to the Mediterranean. Breakfast, served all day, includes choices such as crème brûlée French toast and eggs Panini. The green side of things features poached apple with candied almonds, Greek goddess or Israeli salads. For the adventurous gourmand, the restaurant offers creative fusions such as orange-glazed tofu stir fry and salmon fried rice with spicy duck sauce. Slightly more traditional choices are gourmet pizza, lasagna, the falafel and hummus platter, quesadillas or beer-battered fish and chips. The pink and green décor urges you to stay a while and enjoy the atmosphere. If you're in a hurry, you can get your order to go. Surprise your colleagues and have the Village Green Bistro cater your next business luncheon. The Village Green Bistro is located in the heart of the charming Westdale village. Drop by and enjoy home cooking with an edge.

925 King Street W, Hamilton ON (905) 296-6300
www.villagegreenbistro.ca

Flying Saucer Restaurant

There's more to Niagara Falls than earthly wonders. Just a short way down Lundy's Lane, you may be surprised to discover that a large-as-life flying saucer has landed by the side of the road. Curiosity is rewarded at the Flying Saucer Restaurant. Step inside and you'll find a classic old-time diner in the round, designed to fit what looks like the interior of a UFO. Round tables and curved benches gleam silver and red. Tinted windows and strategically-placed mirrors reflect the room back on itself, making it seem twice as big as it is. A huge stuffed alien hangs on the wall. Owners Henry and Lillian DiCienzo, with their daughter Nicole, are out to entertain kids and adults alike. The menu is covered in space trivia, UFO sighting reports and tongue-in-cheek headings like Extra Terrestrials (sides) and Encounters of the Chicken Kind. The Flying Saucer offers such universal favorites as rib eye, chicken Parmigiana, sandwiches and pastas. The restaurant's renowned breakfast specials, including a 99-cent breakfast and a $2.99 edition, have earned the loyalty of locals and repeat tourists alike. Customers rave about the fast service, great coffee and generous portions. The restaurant is licensed. Have an out-of-this-world experience at the Flying Saucer Restaurant.

6768 Lundy's Lane, Niagara Falls ON (905) 356-4553
www.fallscasino.com/saucer

Flowers of Distinction at Patti Page's Tea Shoppe

When flowers and tea join together, it's a winning combination. Flowers of Distinction at Patti Page's Tea Shoppe invite you to leave your worries and cares at the doorstep. Sit awhile and enjoy lunch amid the orchids, violets and roses. Specialties include bacon and Gouda cheese quiche and mango chicken salad. You can choose from more than 30 varieties of loose leaf tea. Be sure to ask about the homemade desserts. On the floral side, designers Shirley Small and Bill Kroesbergen create masterpieces to enhance weddings, birthdays and other special celebrations. Kroesbergen, who is also the owner, has developed such a visually distinct and unusual flair for flowers that his creations are known as Bill's style. Mixed planters, cut flowers, exotic botanicals and dry arrangements are also available. Delivery is free from Owen Sound to Collingwood. The enchanting tearoom and florist is located in a 1938 Presbyterian Church. Come to Flowers of Distinction at Patti Page's Tea Shoppe, where you can sample delicious cuisine while feasting on nature's beauty.

52 Nelson Street W, Meaford ON
(519) 538-5942 or (800) 252-8150

Brooklyns Fun, Food & Bar

It's well known that Burlington Bowl (see its story in the Attractions & Recreation section on page 15) is a favourite gathering place and party destination in Burlington, and its guests boast that the restaurant inside, Brooklyns Fun, Food & Bar, is just as fun. Featured on Food TV's hit show, *Restaurant Makeover*, the new restaurant highlights a contemporary retro theme with colourful 1950s décor, black and white checkered floors, chromed-rimmed furniture and a retro jukebox. The renowned designer envisioned Brooklyns Fun, Food & Bar as "casual dining with 1950s fun and today's flair." Open 365 days a year. Expect great food and a great time. Reservations welcomed. Visit Brooklyns Fun, Food & Bar today.

4065 Harvester Road,
Burlington ON
(905) 681-1000
www.BurlingtonBowl.com/Brooklyns

Secrets From Your Sister

Owner Jennifer Klein and the staff at Secrets From Your Sister know that what you wear underneath your clothes affects your self-esteem. A bra fitting at this Toronto lingerie store is a painless and encouraging experience, where compassionate employees teach you the secrets of neck and back comfort and how to choose bras that complement your body type and outfit. Whether you are nursing, running a marathon or dressing for a formal affair, Secrets From Your Sister has the assortment you seek in sizes 28 to 44. Women who have trouble getting a comfortable fit are especially delighted by the store's selection and expertise. Expect to spend half an hour for a fitting. You can even make it a catered bra-fitting party at this enthusiastic store. In addition to bras, the store stocks briefs, knickers and pajamas, as well as garter belts, hosiery and sultry teddies. The staff takes special pleasure in helping men make purchases for their ladies. Men often feel intimidated in a lingerie store, but at Secrets From Your Sister, the staff knows just as much about making men comfortable as women. Discover sexy good looks with comfort underneath at Secrets From Your Sister.

560 Bloor Street W, Toronto ON
(416) 538-1234 or (888) 866-8007
www.secretsfromyoursister.com

Burlington Fairview Nissan/Burlington Toyota

Burlington Fairview Nissan and Burlington Toyota have been under the same ownership since 1981 and 1993 respectively. When acquired, Nissan and Toyota were two up-and-coming automobile brands and today their presence has grown in the industry. Over the years, Burlington Fairview Nissan and Burlington Toyota have grown in both sales and service volumes. Because of this growth, Burlington Fairview Nissan will soon become Burlington Nissan after a much anticipated move to a new state-of-the-art facility on North Service Road in 2008. Burlington Toyota will also under-go an extensive expansion and renovation in late 2007 in order to continue to meet its customer's sales and service needs. The renovations will be completed in 2008. Both of the new facilities will more than triple the size of the existing buildings, including increased number of service bays, a spacious showroom and a double lane drive-in service reception. The staff at Burlington Fairview Nissan and Burlington Toyota work hard everyday to meet and exceed customer expectations, and have a mission to build a lifelong relationship based on trust, respect and understanding. The dealerships are most proud of the MacLean's Dealer of Excellence award, which was awarded to the owner in 1999 for consistently demonstrating exemplary service to customers and commitment to the community. With a large inventory of new and used vehicle, you're bound to find a vehicle that meets your needs and a staff that will leave you assured of their commitment to service quality. They look forward to seeing you soon.

Burlington Toyota: 1249 Guelph Line, Burlington ON (905) 335-0223
www.burlingtontoyota.ca
Burlington Fairview Nissan: 3497 Fairview Street, Burlington ON (905) 681-2162
www.fairviewnissan.ca

Exotic Woods

Whether it's the desk where you sit, the soft acoustic guitar on the radio, or your favorite rocking chair, they're all made of wood—and Exotic Woods has just the right wood to make all those things and much more. The company began when John Hordyk, Sr. opened a small shop that sold quality hardwoods, softwoods and veneers from across the globe. The business has expanded greatly since then, and the shop stocks every kind of wood imaginable. It is now run by John's sons, John Jr. and Mel, along with a very competent staff. Exotic Woods stocks domestic hardwoods and softwoods ranging from oak to maple and beech. Imported varieties include such offerings as Brazilian bloodwood and African blackwood. Exotic Woods also stocks a variety of plywoods and veneers, including teak and birdseye maple. Craftsmen looking to create their own musical instruments will delight in options suitable for creating guitars, violins and mandolins. Exotic Woods also has unusual burls in stock. You'll find wood in all shapes and sizes, including wide natural-edge planks. The store also offers a large variety of hardwood flooring and decking options, as well as adhesives finishes. Whether you're looking for wood suitable for building a violin or flooring your home, you'll find it at Exotic Woods.

2483 Industrial Street, Burlington ON
(905) 335-8066
www.exotic-woods.com

The Country Pedlar Gift Shop & Tea Room

Whether you are seeking a delicious snack or an adorable gift, you will find it at the Country Pedlar, located at the West Lynde Plaza. Indeed, about the only things harder to resist than the scones, tarts and chocolates in the tea room are the plush Teddy bears and country treasures in the gift shop. Most visitors come by to eat and to shop, because the offerings are so good on both sides of the business. Mother and daughter owners Cathy Peel and Lorna Mugford deserve the credit for bringing everything together in such a delightful way. Lorna makes all of the baked goods daily, using recipes for some of them that only she knows. She is the person to compliment for the luscious chocolates and fudge as well. The gift shop has the feel of a well-stocked country store that has gone chic. Its shelves are full of gourmet foods, fashionable jewellery and fragrant candles. It also features a selection of tea pots and 40 varieties of loose tea. You won't stay a browser for long at the Country Pedlar, where everything is just too special to resist. Plan to spend some time there having tea, nibbling a snack and shopping for everyone on your list at the Country Pedlar Gift Shop & Tea Room.

965 Dundas Street W, Units 2B and 3B, Whitby ON
(905) 666-8000

Mickey McGuire's Cheese

Ask the father-son team of Mike and Paddy McGuire how their day is going, and they'll probably tell you that everything is just cheesy. They are the purveyors of fine imported and domestic cheeses who own Mickey McGuire's Cheese. Do you love the aroma and taste of cheese? Do you want to meet a couple of guys who are conversant on everything from the history of cheese to the perfect cheese pairing with a specific food or wine? If so, then their shop should not be missed. You will find their display cases full of handcrafted artisan cheeses, including fine Canadian cheddars, goat and sheep milk cheeses. Describe your perfect cheese to Mike or Paddy—perhaps something tangy on the tongue, creamy in texture and strong to the nose—and they will answer with a recommendation or two. In fact, everything has been cheesy in the McGuire family since 1975. Mike and Paddy run the business from the quaint downtown store with the old-fashioned ornate door. Step inside Mickey McGuire's Cheese and enter a world that will arouse your nose and make your mouth water.

51 King Street W, Dundas ON
(905) 627-1004
www.cheeseplease.ca

Jolanta Interiors

Jolanta Interiors is famous for its window displays, and this is no accident. The owner is a professional interior designer. In addition to her skilled artistic eye, Jolanta Sudnik ensures that her shop provides quality customer service and stands behind all featured products. Jolanta Interiors is the sole distributor for Universal Stone. This household cleaner is a polish and preservation solution from Germany that is biodegradable and completely free from toxins and acids. Jolanta also carries an impressive selection of amber jewellery, including many one-of-a-kind pieces made by an artist in Poland. Varieties of amber span a wide scope of colours and levels of translucency, and are prized for mystical and healing properties. Some pieces contain fossilized organisms, and each gem has its own distinct appearance. Jolanta also stocks an abundance of silver imported from Italy, Findland, Denmark and Poland. Jolanta carries numerous Alessi creations, which are functional works of art renowned for their decorative appearance and usefulness. Graceful Hoselton sculptures can also be found here, plus quality cookware, kitchen items and gadgets. Jolanta Interiors is a shopper's paradise for unusual and ornamental home decór. Stop by for an enjoyable exploration.

2368 Bloor Street W, Toronto ON (416) 762-9638
www.universalstone.ca

Birdwatch

Birdwatch is a birdwatchers paradise and offers one of the largest collections of unusual and inspired nature gifts in Canada. You can find everything you need to create a safe and inviting environment for a variety of birds as well as everything you will need to see and enjoy them. Give some birds a nice home with one of the many handcrafted birdhouses. Most of the houses are one-of-a-kind and are collectables as well as functional birdhouses. You'll find a large selection of hardware you can use to hang the houses, such as shepherds hooks and telescoping poles. Birdwatch stocks more feeders than you have ever imagined and has all of the necessary hooks and brackets for them. It has feeders to attract an array of different birds, making your bird watching experience exciting. The shop stocks premium quality wild bird seed as well as specialty and squirrel-proof mixes. Stop in for nature-inspired gifts for your friends or loved ones. You will find beautiful carvings, mailboxes, clocks, stone boxes and much more. The shop also displays some beautiful original artwork to add to your collection. Visit Birdwatch and enjoy all that nature has to offer.

1907 Avenue Road, Toronto ON (416) 785-9222 or (877) 785-9222
www.birdwatchcanada.com

The Travelling Musician

From an early age, Paul Harman loved music and you always found him playing in a local band. Then an opportunity comes in 1969 for him to teach piano and guitar in his parent's basement, and his teaching career started. Soon word got out and he began teaching about 24 students a week, which was enough for him to pay for his three university degrees. The problem was, that being a young male, as is typical, he never cleaned up after himself. So one winter his mother spotted all the melted snow from his student's boots and said that after three year of cleaning up after him that was over. His father said, "Why don't you go to the student's house instead?" The Travelling musician was born. After a few years of doing this he had a teaching staff of 14 and more than 400 students a week, teaching and selling all kinds of instruments. In 1981, an opportunity came to open up a music store in the old house across from the Beer Store. Photographs on the wall of his store illustrate his active musical life, and many of the people posing with Harman are music legends. Several famous Canadian musicians started their careers with The Travelling Musician and your chance of being a legend in your own right will go up immeasurably by taking lessons from the staff.

199 Queen Street E, Brampton ON (905) 459-1100

The Richter Group

Celebrating its 50th anniversary in 2007, the Richter Group now offers a wide range of vehicles, from small economy models to extra heavy trucks. The group, which started with Eastgate Ford in 1957, now offers vehicles from Saturn of Hamilton East, Hamilton Hyundai, Bay King Chrysler, Eastgate Trucks featuring Western Star and Sterling, along with a complete fleet of rental vehicles from Budget Rentals. Complete on-site collision centers are also part of the package. Founder Frank Richter was a stickler for hard work, honesty and integrity along with offering a superior product to his customers. Today, with a half-dozen franchises, the Richter Group scrupulously maintains these founding principals. Frank's sons, Lorne, Lowell and Ron Richter, along with grandsons Lance and Jamie and nephew David, who brought his Bay King Chrysler to the group, recently have continued the traditions set before them and have made the Richter Group one of Canada's leading transportation specialists. All dealerships offer state-of-the-art facilities and technology for all customer needs. The Richter Group recognizes the value of its customers and is committed to making each experience the best it can be. Serving the community as well as the customer base is also recognized as vital to the group. Active involvement with charities, volunteer work and local boards is part of its mandate. Come and experience the trust, dependability and accountability that 50 years has provided at any of the Richter Group stores.

350 Parkdale Avenue N, Hamilton ON
(905) 547-3211
www.therichtergroup.ca

Toronto at dusk

Bead Goddess

Gloria Browne understands the magic and power of beads. At Bead Goddess Bead Emporium & Gallery, Gloria can help you create a special bracelet that uses beads as totems to express who you are. Gloria's original bracelet kits help you select a perfect combination of colours, objects and symbols to manifest your vision. Combine a deep red carnelian with sultry green amazonite to begin a bracelet that affirms a spiritual journey or a future goal. Choose a clear aquamarine or dusky tiger's eye to move forward to a new adventure. Add a dragon charm to symbolize fortitude or a butterfly charm to symbolize change. Specialized beading classes and ongoing support from the staff at Bead Goddess will help you develop your beading skills. Schedule a beading birthday party and welcome your friends to string together a shared vision. If you're a beginner, the friendly staff will sit with you and show you the ropes. A wide selection of beads, supplies, tools, books and beading kits await you at Bead Goddess Bead Emporium & Gallery.

79C Dunlop Street W, Barrie ON (705) 734-2733

Scraps of Joy

Regular customers always know to check the calendar at Scraps of Joy, owned by Juanita and John Koole. The staff like to keep things busy at the scrapbooking supply store, filling the days with exciting sales and special events. On some days, they will do a good deed for the community by, for example, allowing customers to use the crop shop for free when they bring a donation for the local food bank. Classes are scheduled throughout each week, covering a wide range of topics. Are you new to scrapbooking? A beginner's class will teach you creative ways to start preserving your memories. For the more advanced hobbyist, there are classes on everything from how to take your stamping to the next level to how to create a double-page layout of your adorable pet. Juanita is a retired school teacher who just can't stop trying to teach. She makes a point of reaching out to kids by offering regular classes designed to show them how much fun it is to scrap. Shop for the papers, stamps and everything else you need for your scrapbooking projects at Scraps of Joy, and get the whole family in the act while you're at it.

304 Dunlop Street W, Barrie ON (705) 726-6287

The Purple Sock

An avid knitter with the surname of Stitchman opens a shop in a small town and introduces its population to the many benefits of knitting. Hundreds learn how to make their own mittens, socks and sweaters, while embracing knitting as a pleasant way to forget worries and reduce stress. This story may sound scripted, but it's fast becoming reality at the Purple Sock. The lady who owns this quaint knitting shop definitely knows her wool and yarns, and she is, indeed, named Lynn Stitchman. Since 2006, she has taught knitting to scores of newcomers, while supplying those already hooked on the hobby with everything they need to complete their latest projects. Though Lynn has been a knitter and spinner for years, she is anything but a one-dimensional person. Her business celebrates her other passion—namely, the one she has for tea—by offering 38 varieties of loose tea for sale, including her own Purple Sock brand, as well as an array of teapots and teacups. A positive thinker, Lynn regarded the collapse of the family barn in the winter of 2007 not as a disaster but as an opportunity. Her husband recycled the boards to build a counter and cabinets for the store. See for yourself how they add a nice touch when you drop by the Purple Sock and talk a little knitting with the owner.

13 Coldwater Road, Coldwater ON (705) 686-3455

Chez Bonbon

Chez Bonbon is the jewel of Hamilton. You need to experience for yourself this six room store and gallery of unique gifts, art, original paintings and furniture from the four corners of the globe. The shop also carries Joseph Schmidt and Max Brenner chocolates—these fine imported chocolates are second to none. Hannah and Ron Rozeneweig, a mother-and-son team, have been bringing treats to shoppers at their gift gallery for 26 years. The long corner building, accented with the bright red awnings, offers displays of jewellery, pottery, glass ornaments and antiques. Featured major talents include sculptors Boris and Richard Kramer and ceramics artist Jan Phalen. You'll see candles of all types, vases and abstract sculpture. Tiffany lamps are also scattered about. The knicknacks and baubles are endless. Chez Bonbon is the winner of the Excellence in Property and Business award for Westdale as well as the Excellence in Property award for the City of Hamilton. Come in and you'll see why.

1008 King Street W, Hamilton ON
(905) 525-7290

The Natural Bead

The Natural Bead is a jewel for those who love beads, jewels and gifts. Located near the lakeshore on Burlington's East Side, the store is owned by Sandi Tigchelaar and Julie Schaafsma. Sandi and Julie have made the store an eclectic joy to see. Upon entering, you're surrounded by beads and décor from around the world, from Africa, Thailand, the Philippines, Afghanistan and elsewhere. You'll find just the right items to use in creating your own jewellery, for example, beautiful Swarovski crystals. The store offers a variety of classes for those seeking to learn how to create beautiful beaded items ranging from necklaces to rings and Christmas ornaments. Looking for a fun way to celebrate a birthday, bridal shower or other special event? The Natural Bead offers a number of party options, including a pizza and beading party for kids and a Creative Girls Night Out, which includes the use of on-site tools. Those looking for ready-made jewelry will delight in the many creative pieces by Julie and Sandi, as well as several other local artists. You'll have the jewellery world on a string with skills you learn and the materials you pick up from the Natural Bead.

357 Brant Street, Burlington ON (905) 681-9249
www.thenaturalbead.com

Eagle Canvas Company and Marine Upholstery

Whether you need a top for your convertible or a boat cover, Eagle Canvas Company and Marine Upholstery does the job right every time. Since 1981, the shop has maintained a sterling reputation for its perfectly sized custom-made canvas products. Owner Greg Vola's clients include boat owners from Toronto to Niagara and northward. Eagle Canvas produces boat covers, cockpit covers and boat cushions, plus items such as interior trim seats, custom carpets and boat awnings. The shop also carries hardware for boat tops. Products for cars include convertible tops, travelling tonneaux, camper sets and custom carpets. Golf cart covers are another line. Restaurant clients such as La Costa Nova and Mexicali Rosa's come to Eagle Canvas for outdoor awnings. The Sun Stopper 2000 retractable awning, for example, is a premium quality awning with motor or hand-crank options. Grocery stores engage the shop for interior market-square area awnings. This family owned business offers friendly service and excellent craftsmanship. Canvas repairs are also a part of the business. For your next canvas or upholstery job, visit Eagle Canvas Company and Marine Upholstery.

2397 Industrial Street, Burlington ON (905) 335-9629
www.eaglecanvas.com

Mountainside Auto Tech

Fair and honest automotive services are not always easy to find. Once found, they collect a loyal following among the community. Mountainside Auto Tech is that kind of service center. Family owned by the Robinsons——Jim and Bette, along with their sons, Jamie, Scott and Jeff——Mountainside has a reputation for fairness and honesty matched with first-rate service that keeps customers coming back. The business has been serving Burlington for 40 years. Although Mountainside is primarily managed by their three sons these days, Jim and Bette are still active in the business they started. Mountainside Auto Tech staff maintain on-going technical training, and the Robinsons continue to invest in the latest equipment to keep up with technological advances in the industry. They can analyze your engine and align your wheels by computer. Customer service here is above and beyond the norm, including complimentary shuttle service. When your transportation needs a lift, take it to Mountainside Auto Tech, where you will always get a friendly smile with the service you deserve.

3097 Mainway, Burlington ON (905) 335-3878
www.mountainsideautotech.ca

Maggiolly Art Supplies

Maggiolly Art Supplies carries a full line of artist's supplies and materials, along with a colourful gallery of original art. The shop has a large selection of handmade papers and offers custom canvas stretching and framing. It stocks the popular Games Workshop by Warhammer as well as a line of funky jewellery pieces from New York City. Maggiolly Art Supplies offers a broad selection of art workshops and classes for adults and children. These classes are taught by professional artists throughout the year and range from once a week for an eight week period to intensive five-days-a-week programs. Art classes are offered in watercolour, oil and acrylic painting, portrait drawing and painting, landscape, still life, mixed media, *sumi-e* painting and comics and cartooning. Maggiolly Art Supplies originally opened in 1996 in Alliston and relocated to Orangeville in 2003. Owners Emilia Perri and George May are a husband and wife team, both graduates of the Ontario College of Art & Design and they exhibit their artwork in the local arts community. Their entire family is involved in the arts. Their son, Oliver May, has worked in the shop four years and is pursuing his studies in animation while their other son, Jordan, is attending the Ontario College of Art & Design. Their daughter Sara is involved in community theatre and acting. Others who work in the shop all have an art background, so they all know their stuff when it comes to art supplies. Come browse for supplies to create your next masterpiece, take a look at the splendid art collection or sign up for one of the excellent art classes offered at Maggiolly Art Supplies.

158 Broadway Avenue, Orangeville ON
(519) 942-9560

Keith's Stereo

Top-notch customer service and the best televisions and sound systems have been family traditions at Keith's Stereo for more than 25 years. Owner Keith Grafham has recently brought his son, Kent, onboard as a co-owner. Both men remain dedicated to the quality and principles that have made the store a favorite among those looking for audiovisual equipment in Burlington. If you're looking for the latest thumpin' stereo system for your car, complete with tweeters and subwoofers, you'll find it at Keith's, as well as remote car starters and security systems. Want to turn your living room into your own private movie theatre? Keith's Stereo offers a full range of options, including large plasma televisions and surround-sound systems, as well as satellite television options. You'll find an array of excellent brands to choose from, including Alpine, Pioneer, Kicker and Sony. Kent and Keith will answer any questions and help you find just the right system for your needs. Keith's Stereo offers a variety of installation and repair options, with quick turnaround times and all repairs done on-site. If you're looking for great sights, sounds and service, Keith's Stereo will be music to your ears.

3235 Fairview Street, Burlington ON (905) 637-2315

Computer Corner

Located in the heart of industrial Burlington, the experts at Computer Corner listen to your problems and determine cost-effective solutions. John and Jason Padgett, a father and son team, combine excellent customer relationships with 22 years of experience serving the community and its surrounding areas. No job is too small for this Canadian-owned family business. The firm supports both home and business computer systems and notebooks. It custom-builds is own systems and offers both in-house and on-site service for all makes of IBM-compatible computer systems including Acer, Compaq, Dell, Toshiba and many others. Highly-trained technicians install networks, servers and wireless network configurations, and also perform repairs. Computer Corner services all inkjet printers as well as HP and Lexmark laser printers. The store carries a full range of IBM-compatible hardware, cables and supplies. For your convenience, it also provides both notebook and desktop computer rentals and sells used systems. Burlington knows the specialists at Computer Corner. You should, too.

4391 Harvester Road, Burlington ON (905) 681-6585
www.computercorner.ca

The Wrapping Room

A three-part store in three rooms, the Wrapping Room is a must-stop on Hamilton's main shopping street, Locke Street S. Eric Thomson opened the business in 1998, modelling it after the high-style boutiques of Beverly Hills and Yorkville. The name comes from the room where gifts are personalized and gift-wrapped. The store also includes a salon-spa and fashion boutique. One of the things that makes the Wrapping Room special is its international influences. Eric shops for the boutique in Italy, France, England and Canada, handpicking each eclectic item. You'll find women's fashions, jewelry and accessories, including a popular collection of handbags. Baby products and home décor round out the selection. The salon-spa offers aromatic Swedish massage, European facials, cellulite treatments and waxing. A visit to the Wrapping Room is sure to distract in some way or another. You may even find the perfect gift for the woman in your life, and get it personalized and wrapped on the spot. Gift certificates make fail-proof, wrap-proof gifts. Whatever your pleasure, stop by the Wrapping Room when shopping in Hamilton.

237 Locke Street S, Hamilton ON (905) 529-1099

Finepoint Printing

Owners Mark and Jennifer Veenstra have a streamlined answer to all your printing needs under one roof. At Finepoint Printing, on-site designers create printed materials with a dynamic, innovative flair that's sure to give you an edge over your competitors. Brochures, pamphlets and white papers present a polished professional look. A new logo design and custom graphics can breathe life into your company's letterhead. Snappy signage attracts new customers and clients. Services such as image editing, desktop publishing, scanning and typesetting make light work for your overburdened staff. Finepoint Printing offers support for the latest versions of popular graphics and page layout programs. Highly-trained staff with detailed knowledge of the Mac and PC platforms are there to walk you through complex processes. When the printing is done, Finepoint can add finishing touches such as folding, binding, drilling, scoring and perfing. Let the experts at Finepoint laminate report covers and shrink-wrap all of your material into one, fashionable package that's sure to impress. Pick-up, delivery and world-wide courier services are also available. Bring your printing needs to Finepoint Printing, where excellence always comes first.

4028 Highway 6, Puslinch ON
(519) 763-1761 or (800) 774-7767
www.finepoint.ca

Crafters Paradise

Necessity really was the mother of invention for longtime crafter Karen Cooper. When two of the stores she shopped at for ceramics supplies closed, she was inspired to take matters into her own hands and created Crafters Paradise. Made For You, Or By You is the motto here, and accordingly, you'll find the shelves full of ceramics and other homemade crafts for sale. In addition to selling her own work, Karen rents space in the store to other crafters, who sell their own one-of-a-kind pieces. You'll find everything from ceramics to woodwork and homemade soap. Crafters Paradise carries a variety of frames and boxes, including some that can be fitted with a picture of your deceased pet and are suitable for storing its ashes. Want to learn how to make some of these items for yourself? Crafters Paradise offers classes in ceramics for both adults and children. You'll also be able to learn the arts of tole painting and loom knitting. Crafters Paradise offers a full range of supplies, including paints, threads and other necessities. Crafters Paradise is an Eden for those looking to buy and sell homemade crafts or to learn the art of making them.

109 S London Road, Unit 2, Sarnia ON (519) 383-6315
www.craftingsarnia.com

Forever Memories Photography & Gift Store

Forever Memories Photography & Gift Store is where people come for photography and gifts that become treasured memories. The shop's tranquil atmosphere is enhanced by owner Gabrielle Stringer's friendly, personalized service. Gabrielle is a longtime collector of angels, which became the inspiration for the gift section. The photography studio offers children's and family portraits. Wedding photography services are also available. The shop stocks the Willow Tree line of gifts and is an authorized dealer for Bradford Collectibles. You'll find gifts for all the sacraments and a variety of devotional items. The shop carries memory pieces for the garden, wedding picture frames and anniversary gifts. Be sure to check the lovely collection of jewellery. There are various plaques inscribed with inspirational messages. Gabrielle's favorite quote comes from Helen Keller: "The best and most beautiful things in the world can not be seen or touched. They must be felt within the heart." Forever Memories Photography & Gift Store reflects this sentiment perfectly.

1249 London Road, Sarnia ON (519) 337-9000

Rubies Candle & Gift Shop

Ruby Kennedy and her daughter Corrinne, the co-owners of Rubies Candle & Gift Shop, are in the business of helping you find just the right gift. They pride themselves on creating personalized mementos to please the loved ones in your life. Together, they have 20 years of engraving experience and believe that almost anything can be personalized. The shop offers laser engraving on wood, diamond scratch engraving on brass and laser engraving on glass. Weddings call for special gifts. An engraved beer stein or wine glass shows appreciation to bridesmaids and groomsmen. Non-melting Everlasting Candles are the shop's best sellers. Special sentiments can emblazon the candles, along with names and photos of loved ones. Select a beloved poem for inscription or create words of your own. Candles are often presented before a wedding so the bride and groom can incorporate the candle's special glow into the ceremony. In lieu of flowers, Everlasting Candles pay tribute to loved ones at memorial services. Special delivery services and a bridal registry make giving a joy. For truly special gifts, contact the experts at Rubies Candle & Gift Shop.

661 Grand Avenue E, Chatham ON (519) 351-1119

Lyn Bell Creative Sewing Studio

Marilyn Bell was a creative type from the start, but the sewing industry had bigger plans for her than just designing. At Lyn Bell Creative Sewing Studio, Marilyn does her part to inspire and assist creativity in others in order to keep the world sewing. Marilyn started designing clothes and selling at craft shows in 1991. When she opened her first small retail space downtown, she immediately became very busy. She hired local ladies to help with cutting and sewing and the rest is history. In 1999, she took the step of adding a retail sewing machine department and today, Lyn Bell Creative Sewing Studio is a virtual emporium of sewing and quilting supplies. In 2000, Marilyn closed the clothing portion of the business in order to devote all her energy to the sewing machine business. Marilyn employs her daughters, Linda and Lisa, and a talented staff of sewers and teachers. You'll find the latest in books, notions and patterns and one of the largest selections of quilting fabrics in the area. Marilyn offers demos and trunk shows to demonstrate what's new in the sewing world. Her highly skilled teacher's will train you on almost any sewing machine or serger model. They lead a full schedule of classes in everything from beginner quilting to machine embroidery. You can also come to Lyn Bell's for machine and serger repairs performed by her husband, Joe. Lyn Bell's Creative Kids program teaches children basic sewing skills to last a lifetime. Come to Lyn Bell Creative Sewing Studio and set your creative spirit loose.

48 Main Street S, St. George ON
(519) 448-3SEW (3739)
www.lynbelldesigns.com

Manhattan Bead Co.

Everything's A OK for Manhattan Bead Co. owner Anita Okada. A OK Beads is the name Anita chose for the line of handmade glass lampwork beads she produces. The beads have been juried in and exhibited at several shows and are sold across Ontario and North America. Anita's interest in beads was kindled in 2000 when she met a lampworker at an art show in Toronto. She began collecting beads and making jewellery. In 2001, she started making her own glass beads, and in 2004, she opened her store. Lampwork beads are made by melting soda lime glass onto stainless steel mandrels and manipulating them with special tools into the desired pattern before firing them in a kiln. Anita offers classes in beading and jewellery making, in addition to offering a selection of her own work. Bead and jewellery makers will find a splendid variety of supplies to work with at this shop, including imported Austrian crystals, freshwater pearls and a variety of beads from Europe and Japan. You'll also find an array of tools and supplies, including metal, sterling silver and vermeil findings. If you're a fan of jewellery and beads, you'll be feeling A OK at Manhattan Bead Co.

111 Broadway, Orangeville ON (519) 943-1299
www.manhattanbeadco.com

The Scrap Yard

The Scrap Yard began as an enjoyable hobby for Donna Foulger and her daughter-in-law Cecilia Foulger. By 2004, the two were ready to team up and open a shop—the Scrap Yard, a fun crafts shop dedicated to helping you preserve your photographs and other scrapbook memories in new and exciting ways. The Scrap Yard is friendly and inviting, with a comfortable and convivial atmosphere. You can come right in to the studio to assemble your scrapbook on the premises. Bring your current project, socialize and share ideas with other scrapbookers. All ages are welcome. It's a social event, a gathering of friends who come for classes and birthday parties alike. Making cards is a popular pastime. The Scrap Yard offers a variety of classes for both beginners and experts. Every other Friday, the shop hosts its popular Crop Night, an evening event that goes into the wee hours (or at least until midnight). The shop carries all the supplies you need to create scrapbooks and cards. Come in to browse and join the happy crowd of scrapbookers at The Scrap Yard.

169 Broadway Avenue, Orangeville ON (519) 941-7146

Holland Shop

Holland Shop in downtown Acton, is a genuine Dutch delicatessen with an inspiring history. For such a quaint little store, Holland Shop has a big reputation. Now owned and operated by Carolin Tolkamp, the shop has been owned by three generations of family members. Engel Huisman, Carolin's grandfather, immigrated to Canada in the 1950s. Soon after settling in Ontario, he began selling items door-to-door, mostly to fellow Dutch immigrants. After he'd secured a list of loyal customers, Huisman took a leap of faith. In 1955, he opened his own shop, which over time evolved into a well-known Dutch delicatessen. Most products in the shop are imported directly from the Netherlands and other European countries. You'll find smoked eel, Gouda cheeses and salted herring from the Netherlands. Hard-to-find foods, cheeses and gifts draw customers from all over Canada. The shop regularly serves people who come all the way from British Columbia and Alberta. Carolin is dedicated to running the shop as her grandfather and parents before her would have wanted. Holland Shop is truly the place to go if you are hankering for an authentic taste of Europe.

71 Mill Street E, Acton ON (519) 853-0950

Little Chloe's Chic Boutique

Little Chloe's Chic Boutique, as its name suggests, is bursting with adorable gear for Fido and Kitty alike. Owner Lyja Glanville, a pet style guru, stocks carrying totes, pet strollers and monogrammed lead and collar sets. Luxurious lounging beds, all-natural foods and grooming supplies help pet owners shower their small companions with love. Loyal owners of small and toy breed dogs can get together at Little Chloe's for a doggie play date and begin new friendships both canine and human. Put on the dog for a special occasion with Little Chloe's selection of pet jewellery and custom-knit sweaters crafted by Lyja's mother Ilona. The charm of Little Chloe's is enhanced by Lyja's artwork, which is displayed on the shop walls. A painter, Lyja commissions pet portraits that quickly become family heirlooms. From chewy to chaser and brush to bowl, Little Chloe's is where pet owners can return the love their pets give to them. Let your precious pet take you to Little Chloe's Chic Boutique, the most posh of pet outfitters.

128 Harbord Street, Toronto ON
(416) 923-PAWS (7297)
www.chicboutique.ca

Woolly's (from Ewe to You)

Woolly's (from Ewe to You), which opened two years ago to critical acclaim, offers one-stop shopping, with all of the tools of the knitting trade located under one roof. Comfy sofas and chairs beckon beginners who want to read about knitting before jumping in. You'll find well-trained employees ready to offer you assistance, advice and technical support. But most of all, you'll find a stunningly aesthetic array of yarn lining the shelves. Specialty wools encased in the glass display cases reveal the shop's history as a bakery. The wool comes from several suppliers and locations such as England and Italy. Auld Craft angoras and Polana Ranch alpacas are featured. Yarns now come in natural and synthetic materials such as cotton-nylon, acrylic or linen. Needles, patterns, books and even handmade buttons to decorate your finished masterpiece are on display. Cozy sweaters and baby blankets created by the expert staff are also for sale. Owner Maxine Walsh believes knitting is popular because it's easy, inexpensive and a hobby that is doable all year round. If the idea of "knit one, purl one" appeals to you, stop by Woolly's (from Ewe to You) and let the knitters who know the ropes get you started.

138 Main Street W, Shelburne ON (519) 925-6194

Gifts n' Such

A place to indulge your sense of magic and whimsy, Gifts n' Such features Celtic-inspired jewellery and resembles a land from your favourite fantasy novel with its fabulous collection of dragon, unicorn and fairy items. If earthly animals are more to your liking, you will enjoy browsing the bronze figurines of lions, zebras and other exotic wildlife. An ambition to bring items found in the big city boutiques to their little town of Strathroy drives owners Debbie and Larry Townsend. The business started with Larry selling birdhouses and garden décor out of their garage, but now their downtown store is large enough to hold everything that appeals to their imaginations. Since 2002, Gift n' Such has been a source for clocks, lamps and other home accents as well as everything from chess sets to spun glass collectibles. Its selection of indoor and outdoor fountains, many featuring medieval and mythical motifs, is particularly strong. To add some magic to your gift giving, try Gifts n' Such.

79 Frank Street, Strathroy ON (519) 245-9202
www.giftsnsuch.ca

Quilters Dream

Carol Dinsmore and Louise Girard are longtime friends whose passion for quilting eventually led them to participate in trade shows together for years. When Dinsmore aspired to open a quilt shop, it was a natural progression to recruit the talented Girard, and Quilters Dream was born. Besides selling quilts, materials and the equipment needed to create your own pieces, Quilters Dream offers technique instruction, camaraderie and adventures with fellow quilters. Quilt classes are taught by experienced quilters such as Girard. Her work is displayed and her patterns can be purchased at the shop. UFO Days allow time and space to complete your unfinished objects, while social events such as pizza and movie night combine quilting time with a fun night out. Quilting retreats such as Sisters of the Fold—a four-day group event that takes place twice a year in a church conference center—are enjoyable community events. The store also organizes Cruises for Quilting, where you can sew your way through the Caribbean. Just as in the process of quilting one thing leads to another, Quilter's Dream recently added Linda, alterations and dressmaking expert, to the team and expanded its services accordingly. Spend some time with your new friends amid the ample supplies at Quilters Dream.

252 Dundas Street E, Waterdown ON (905) 689-3434
www.quiltersdream.ca

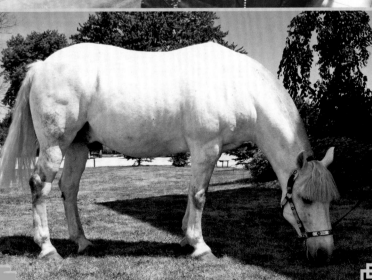

Wagner Orchards & Estate Winery

Harold and Janice Wagner planted their first apple trees in 1986 with a plan to start a pick-your-own apple farm. The current state of Wagner Orchards & Estate Winery far surpasses that original vision. After continuous expansion, the business has become a family destination, a place where folks can still pick their own fruits, though that's just part of the fun. There's a bakery producing homemade pies, strudels and desserts with varieties including apple, strawberry-rhubarb and peach. The winery is known for its fruit wines, such as its signature Saddlenotch, a dry apple wine that tastes very much like a Chardonnay. The Wagners also raise their own beef, pork and poultry, so you won't need to make an extra stop to shop for the meat that pairs well with the wines. Many folks leave the Wagner farm carrying a steak, a bottle of wine and an apple pie. The hams and mince meat pies around Christmas have become a holiday tradition. All of the food is grown in the healthiest way possible. Livestock is raised free of hormones, chemicals and antibiotics. The minimal amount of chemicals is applied to the fruit trees to produce a high quality fruit. Enjoy foods and wine fresh from the farm at Wagner Orchards & Estate Winery.

1222 8th Concession Road RR#2, Maidstone ON
(519) 723-4807
www.wagnerorchards.com

Smith & Wilson Estate Wines

Wine with a view. Smith & Wilson Estate Wines offers exceptional vintages rich in palate-pleasing pizzazz to sip while gazing at its picturesque panorama. Located on a gently sloping gravel ridge overlooking Lake Erie, the family-owned winery is blessed with sunshine and fertile soil. Owners George and Mary Jane Smith invite visitors to enjoy an afternoon of wine tasting and hiking around their 100-acre homestead. The tasting room lets you sip and swirl estate specialties. Try the award-winning 2006 Pinot Gris or the 2005 Ruby Tuesday, a playful blend of Chambourcin, Gamay and Merlot varietals. Originally, the century-old family farm was planted in fruits, vegetables and tobacco. Cherry, peach and apricot trees dotted the landscape where 17 varieties of grapes now grow. For more than 25 years, the Smith family produced grapes and sold them wholesale to neighboring vintners. Eventually, they were encouraged to open their own winery. On-site events include winemaker's dinners, seasonal fiestas, music performances and the popular Grape Jam, an acoustic blues festival held in September. Take the time to enjoy a guided walking tour of Smith & Wilson Estate Wines. You'll want to stop by the wine shop and buy a treat to add to your wine cellar.

8368 Water Street, Blenheim ON
(519) 676-5867 or (888) 676-5867
www.smithandwilsonestatewines.ca

Aleksander Estate Winery

As you travel west on the southwestern Ontario wine tour, one of the first wineries that you encounter has been earning praise for its Pinot Gris. Soft, silky and smooth with the aroma of apricots, pears and peaches, this wine alone makes a stop at the five-acre Aleksander Estate Winery a must. The vineyard, which sits atop one of the highest points in the county, grows such grape varieties as Cabernet Franc, Chambourcin and Riesling. Delicious fruit wines include award-winning peach and Cassis (black currant). Wine making at this small-batch winery is definitely a family affair. Alex Bemben, a wine industry veteran of more than 20 years, leads a team consisting of his wife, Genny, his daughter, Izabela, and his son, Lukasz. The Bembens regard their winery as the connection that brings family, friends, spirit, food and drink together. Choices abound after you have savored their Riesling. Try the Shiraz for a bold red or the Late Harvest Riesling for a sweet pleaser with the delicate fragrance of citrus fruit. Be sure to include the Aleksander Estate Winery on your tour itinerary.

1542 County Road #34, Ruthven ON
(519) 326-2024
www.aleksanderestate.com

Viewpointe Estate Winery

Nestled on the North Shore of Lake Erie, in the heart of Canada's oldest wine growing region, Viewpointe Estate Winery is the dream of John, Steve and Jean Fancsy of Colchester, Ontario. The Fancsy family shares a love of the land and Viewpointe has given them the venue to showcase some of the region's finest products and talents in a captivating setting. Viewpointe's architectural theme was inspired by a charming piece of the past: the Mettawas, a luxury hotel and casino founded by Hiram Walker in 1889. Viewpointe was built with exceptional detail and considers every aspect of its guest's enjoyment. The Fancsy's vision embraces a regional perspective, showcasing award-winning wines and food in a picturesque setting that makes for an ideal destination for any occasion. Viewpointe is a modern facility designed

to accommodate diverse groups, from friends and family to corporate clients. Activities range from a tour of the winery and vineyard to interactive cooking demonstrations, hosted in the Culinary Arts Centre. Viewpointe delivers the highest level of products and service to its guests. As demonstrated in every bottle, Viewpointe produces boutique wines from a special combination of place, process, expertise and passion. Featured wines include regional favourite Cabernet Franc as well as Barrel Fermented Chardonnay. Come experience Viewpointe Estate Winery and discover why it is more than a matter of good taste, it's winemaking from a different point of view.

151 County Road 50 E, Harrow ON
(519) 738-0690

Vineland Estates Winery

Niagara wine country is recognized as one of the finest wine-grape growing regions of the world. Situated on the slopes of the Niagara Escarpment, Vineland Estates Winery stands out among the wineries in the area. Not only is its location idyllic, complete with a view of Lake Ontario, but Vineland Estates Winery has established an International Exceptional wines reputation. Its fame can be attributed to Brian Schmidt, chief winemaker. Brian studied winemaking throughout Europe and brought his skills to Ontario in 1991, where he joined his brother Allan in running the estate winery. The estate itself dates to 1845, evident in the architecture of buildings such as the historic stone carriage house. Besides acres of vineyards, the grounds contain a private bed-and-breakfast cottage, an estate guesthouse, and a banquet building perfect for corporate events and weddings. The winery's restaurant is open year-round and has been featured as the quintessential wine country dining experience by *Gourmet* magazine and Zagat, to name just two. Tours are available through the vineyards, cellars and the production area. While you explore the grounds, you'll enjoy tastings of the winery's award-winning reds and whites, as well as its renowned icewines. For a premier wine and culinary experience plus palatial vineyard grounds, Vineland Estates Winery is a destination not to be missed.

3620 Moyer Road, Vineland ON
(905) 562-7088 or (888) VINELAND (846-3526)
www.vineland.com

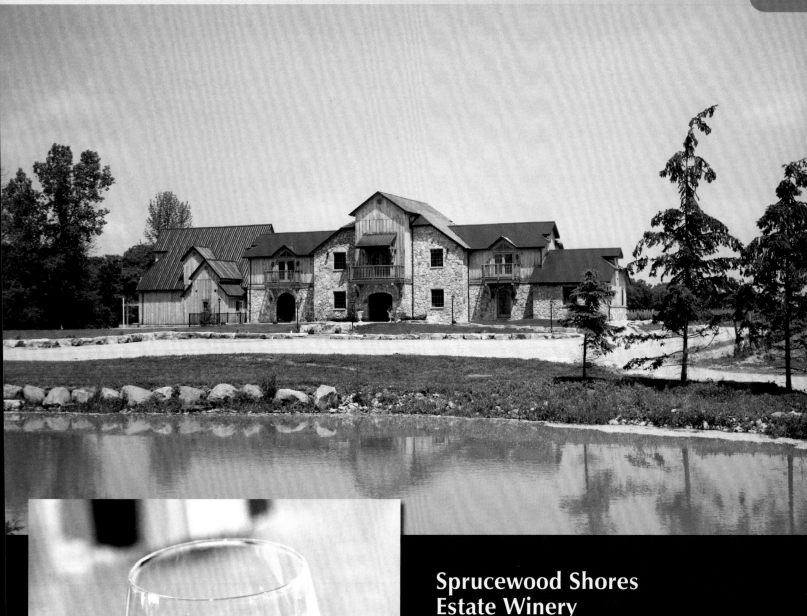

Sprucewood Shores Estate Winery

Sprucewood Shores Estate Winery offers a setting for tasting wine that is suitable for a postcard. The 35 acres of vineyard bordering Lake Erie supports a winery devoted to producing small, hand-crafted batches of Vitners Quality Alliance (VQA) wines. Gord and Hannah Mitchell's dream of having their own winery has been realized because of the help they have received from their children: Marlaina, Tanya, Steve and Jake. Each member of the family contributes his or her own particular skill to the team effort. Tanya, the wine maker, enjoys the challenge of producing something that everyone can unanimously agree is excellent. Her list of signature wines is quite lengthy, and includes a superb Cabernet Sauvignon and Pinot Noir in addition to a fabulous Pinot Gris and Chardonnay. The setting makes the estate popular for weddings. What could be more romantic than a beachfront toast, a stroll in the vineyard and a kiss on the balcony? This indoor and outdoor venue also meets the needs for corporate gatherings and other special events. With a four-room bed and breakfast on the premises, you can make your visit to Sprucewood Shores truly memorable by staying overnight. Enjoy wine with a spectacular view of Lake Erie at Sprucewood Shores Estate Winery.

7258 County Road 50 W RR#5, Harrow ON
(519) 738-9253 or (866) 938-9253
www.sprucewoodshores.com

TOWN OF HALTON HILLS

A delightful mix of urban and rural spaces, Halton Hills is an amalgamated community boasting unparalleled natural beauty, one-of-a-kind shops, recreational facilities, a cultural center and restaurants. The juxtaposition of town and country enables visitors and residents to enjoy breathtaking vistas and heart-pumping hikes along natural trails, while being moments away from modern conveniences. Halton Hills is comprised of two urban centres, Georgetown and Acton, surrounded by a natural rural area, including the hamlets of Stewarttown, Norval and Glen Williams, and settlement clusters of Limehouse, Hornby, Ballinafad, Ashgrove and Terra Cotta, all of which form an integral part of the rich history of Halton Hills.

The small town lifestyle of Halton Hills is one of its greatest treasures most valued by residents. To see friends and neighbours everywhere, from field to shop to arena, and anticipate a warm greeting is a cornerstone of this community's hospitality.

Throughout the year, festivals and events such as the Georgetown Farmers Market, the Highland Games, Canada Day Celebrations, the Leathertown Festival, and the Acton and Georgetown Fall Fairs draw visitors from all over Ontario. There are a number of local farms offering fresh produce, nursery products and recreational activities for the entire family. The sports clubs here offer thrilling entertainment for participants and fans alike.

Many residents and visitors treasure the natural beauty of the Willow Park Ecology Centre and Lucy Maud Montgomery Garden in Norval. They often choose to take a walk in the cool shade of the Bruce Trail through the Limehouse Conservation area or watch the children try to net small fish from Silver Creek as it meanders through Cedarvale Park.

Halton Hills is home to some of the friendliest and most fascinating people you will ever meet and they welcome you to visit and share the treasures of their community.

Main Street Inn

Relax in the luxury and timeless charm of the Main Street Inn, a bed-and-breakfast in a 150-year-old Victorian home. Located in the heart of historic, downtown Georgetown, the Main Street Inn is the result of the personal touch of owners Brian and Sharon Flood. With the loving restoration of the home, Brian and Sharon offer both a fine cuisine restaurant and upscale bed-and-breakfast nestled in beautiful Halton Hills. The two graciously decorated suites, the McLellen and the Bradley, ensure you will get the refuge and relaxation you deserve. Accommodations include stunningly appointed rooms with such amenities as oversized bathtubs, beautiful four-poster beds and wireless Internet connection. The restaurant invites you to indulge with its sumptuous smells and freshly made fare. With two beautiful dining rooms and an outdoor patio, you can enjoy a tasty, seasonally inspired meal in this beautiful environment. The Chef welcomes newcomers and locals to try delicious, fresh, seasonal dishes. Whether you're on holiday at the Inn or simply stopping in for a flavoursome meal, be sure to view the Main Street Inn's on-site art gallery. The gallery features gifted local artists and the exhibits change on a monthly basis. Whether you're in the area for a weekend getaway or just dropping by for a gourmet meal and a glance at the art, the Main Street Inn invites you to come, relax and enjoy.

126 Main Street S, Georgetown ON
(905) 702-5411
www.mainstreetinn.org

Elizabeth's Fashions & Bridal Boutique

What has kept Elizabeth's Fashions & Bridal Boutique at the top of the bridal industry for more than 25 years? Loyal customers know that it's the expertise of owners Elizabeth McNeilly, Cheryl Donoghue and Heather Burke, who have over 50 years of combined experience. Family owned and operated with the help of Elizabeth's husband, Robert, Elizabeth's Fashions offers personalized service, whether you're looking for wedding attire, formal wear or daywear. Elizabeth has a knack for finding the bride her dream dress. She knows that oftentimes, after viewing countless wedding dresses, the perfect one is overlooked and not even tried on. With stunning gowns from such designers as Alfred Angelo, Sophia Tolli and Justin Alexander, and companies such as Sincerity Bridal and Mon Cheri Bridals, Elizabeth's offers a wide range of choices for brides and their wedding parties. Bridesmaids, flower girls and mothers-of-the-bride are also warmly welcomed to the boutique. With as little information as wedding colours and basic measurements, the talented staff at Elizabeth's can locate a dress to suit almost any body type, style preference and budget. The shop also hosts off-site fashion shows within the community that benefit select charities. Enjoy desserts and coffee as entire collections of sportswear and day fashions are presented to you on the runway. Make Elizabeth's Fashions & Bridal Boutique your next stop for formal or casual wear and the best service around.

77 Main Street S, Georgetown ON
(905) 873-1470
www.bridalsplendor.com

Williams Mill Visual Arts Centre

Housed in three historic buildings in the charming hamlet of Glen Williams are the artistic creations of 35 distinguished Canadian artists. The Williams Mill Visual Arts Centre is home to a gifted array of painters, potters, quilt-makers, jewellery-makers, sculptors, photographers and artists who work in stained and blown glass, wood and fabric. The founders of the Williams Mill, Doug and Mary Lou Brock, purchased the property and restored the historic buildings to create studios and a gallery where artists thrive. The studios as well as the gallery are open to the public, and art aficionados frequent them to peruse constantly changing and evolving exhibits in almost every medium. From decorative art glass to ornate jewellery to stunning paintings, modern metal pieces and innovative sculpture in wood, clay or stone, the art featured at the Williams Mill makes the facility a destination for anyone wishing to experience the heart of old Halton Hills. The complex fosters an environment where the creative juices flow; it rejects the idea that artists have to work in isolation. At the Williams Mill, you can see both the creative process and the results. Whether you're simply passing through or you're on the hunt for some of the most innovative, affordable and beautiful works of art, make sure the Williams Mill Visual Arts Centre is on your list of destination spots.

515 Main Street, Glen Williams ON
(905) 873-8203
www.williamsmill.com

Ollie's Cycle & Ski

Ollie Tuchel isn't just the owner of Ollie's Cycle & Ski. He's one of the most seasoned local experts on outdoor adventure, namely cycling, skiing and snowboarding. Ollie's Cycle & Ski has been supplying the Halton Hills area with quality mountain bikes, road bikes and many brands and styles of skis and snowboards for more than 20 years. Located in the beautiful downtown area of Georgetown, Ollie's is a convenient stop for visitors and locals alike. The spacious interior consists of 2,400 square feet of carefully selected items. You'll find everything from Burton snowboards to Chariot Child Carriers to all-weather attire for the outdoor fanatic in you. Mountain bikes by Trek, Specialized, Rocky Mountain and Norco are placed throughout the store along with many high-quality road bikes. Ollie is happy to report that since the revitalization of snowboarding and skiing in the past decade, he's been able to carry more winter gear. Not only does this make the local skiers and mountain bikers happy, it keeps the shop an all-season supplier for gear and maintenance. In addition, if you're new to the area or looking for how to find the best bike trails or ski slopes, look no further. Whether you're in the market for a new bicycle or you're ready to finally pull your skis out of the garage and hit the slopes, make Ollie's Cycle & Ski your first stop for all your outdoor retail and repair needs.

30 Main Street S, Georgetown ON
(905) 873-2441
www.olliescycle.com

Heather's Bakery Café

Step into this cozy café in a charming country cottage and inhale the sweet aromas wafting from the kitchen. Heather's Bakery Café is the result of the baking and cooking genius of owner Heather Brownridge. After attending school and completing her pastry chef apprenticeship, Heather began decorating special-occasion cakes and creating gingerbread houses to sell at local craft shows. Her innovative designs and exquisite desserts lead her to expand into the world of retail in 2001. Heather's Bakery Café offers residents and visitors to Georgetown scrumptious home-baked goods as well as wholesome comfort foods, such as quiche, wraps, sandwiches and soups, for breakfast, lunch or dinner. Whether you're browsing the downtown shops and want to try a local's favourite, or you want a wedding cake with flowers cascading down the tiers, you're sure to find an array of mouth-watering, fresh-baked treats. Heather fires up the ovens at three in the morning and begins baking muffins, scones and other delicious delicacies. By 5:30 am, the bakery is open, fresh coffee is brewing and early risers are getting tasty warm-baked goods. Her special-occasion cakes and dishes are available upon order, and she's happy to consult with you to find just the right design for your dessert. Whether you're craving butter tarts, a flaky croissant or a cheesy seasoned soup, you'll find it oven-fresh and steaming every day at Heather's Bakery Café.

103 Main Street S, Georgetown ON
(905) 873-6569
www.heathersbakery.onlife.ca

The Olde Hide House

The home of Canada's Largest Leather Store is just one of the reasons why the small town of Acton is nicknamed Leathertown. In 1856, the Grand Trunk Railway arrived in Acton as did George L. Beardmore, who updated an existing leather tanning operation with newer buildings and machinery to create the most modern tannery of the time. By the turn-of-the-century, leather was the town's main industry and Acton housed the largest tanning operation in the entire British Empire. In 1899, Beardmore built the existing Hide House building as a tannery warehouse. Raw hides were brought in by rail and properly stored here to await transportation by horse-drawn carriages to the tannery for processing. President John Brison and Vice President Cathy Coles are proud to help preserve the history of the Hide House and the town of Acton itself. Today, after extensive restoration, the Hide House has been transformed into a flagship showroom that showcases Acton's leather industry heritage and presents a truly unique shopping experience, enticing visitors from all over the world. The 30,000-square-foot exposed brick and beam building creates a perfect backdrop for the company's unrivalled selection of high-quality leather and shearling coats, motorcycle jackets and chaps, gloves, hats, purses, accessories, gifts and classy leather luggage, plus the best collection of fine leather furniture you'll find anywhere. The company's popular slogan, "It's worth the drive to Acton," has become part of the local lexicon and fashion consciousness in Ontario and beyond. Visit Leathertown and experience some of its finest leather goods at the Olde Hide House.

49 Eastern Avenue, Acton ON
(519) 853-1031 or (877) 4LEATHER (453-2843)
www.HideHouse.ca

The Spa on Main

Located on Main Street in historic downtown Georgetown, The Spa on Main offers its clients an elegant, friendly atmosphere and many good reasons to keep coming back. Whether your day spa experience is about relaxation and being pampered and refreshed, or more about retaining a healthy, youthful appearance, you will find what you are looking for at The Spa on Main. The Spa on Main has assembled an experienced, well-trained staff that is committed to your health and well being. The beauty of your surroundings is only surpassed by the superior quality of the services and products used. Health and safety regulations are strictly adhered to. Let proprietors Greta Markus and Joan Scott and their team explain the benefits of their services or assist you in choosing the ideal spa package or gift certificate for your wedding party, personal or corporate needs. Bridal packages, including on-site make-up services, are also available. Among the many services available are basic and specialty facials, microdermabrasion, luxurious body treatments and massages. The Spa also offers complete hair removal services and professional make-up services. It also carries a complete range of Bioline skincare products for anti-aging and those targeting delicate and younger skins, and mineral skincare make-up by Jane Iredale. Call The Spa on Main to book your appointment or come in and browse the extensive spa boutique.

40 Main Street S, Georgetown ON
(905) 877-1500 or (866) 477-SPAA
www.thespaonmain.ca

McMaster's Meats & Deli

McMaster's Meat & Deli was started in 1999 by Robert Gordon McMaster, a direct descendant to Sam McMaster of Glen Williams. The timing was right; the residents of Georgetown wanted a Butcher who could combine quality meats and deli consistently with great service, yet still maintain a small town atmosphere. McMaster's Meats works as one with the community, hiring local students for staff and gives back to the community by sponsoring various charities, church groups, school lunch programs and sports teams. In the summer at the market, you will see a charity BBQ out in front of the store manned by volunteers giving their time for charity. Since January of 2007, Robert's Brother in law, Bill Bonnett, his wife Rose, and their children Amber, Tyler, and Spencer have been carrying on the family store after Robert's retirement. The store boasts the best steaks and roasts in town, and if you ask anyone in Georgetown, the freshest produce. If you are in the mood to cook Seafood, Perogies, Ontario Free Range Chicken, Ontario Beef, Ontario Pork and Ontario Lamb, this is the place to visit in Georgetown. McMaster's Meat & Deli is conveniently located downtown at Main and Church streets. If you are browsing the historic downtown area, the Bonnetts will welcome you to experience the charm and individual service of a small town butcher shop. McMaster Meats & Deli won the Favourite Butcher of the Year award for 2007, voted by the residents of Georgetown.

110 Main Street S, Georgetown ON
(905) 702-1274

Moxxi Boutique

You don't have to travel to the city to find the chic styles of contemporary fashion when you live in or visit Georgetown. Presenting stylish lines such as Kenneth Cole, InWear, LilliBleu and many more, Moxxi Boutique is the perfect place to enhance your wardrobe and get the latest modern trends. With designer fashions and accessories hailing from Canada, Europe and the United States, Moxxi Boutique can offer a wide selection of styles and brand names to a customer base with a variety of tastes. Moxxi opened in 2006 when owner Joanne Smith had been living in town for 10 years and realized the need for a fashionable attire shop in the downtown area. Patrons to Moxxi can find everything from casual weekend wear to formal gowns as well as accessories for every occasion. Joanne is proud to offer one-stop-shopping so you can find your perfect outfit and complement it with a trendy purse, scarf or shoes. In addition to carrying a wide array of modern fashions, Moxxi Boutique's constantly changing and updated inventory can be viewed in its periodic fashion shows, held right here at the store. Featuring some of Moxxi's best sellers and newest styles, the fashion shows allow newcomers and loyal customers to see what the shop offers. If you happen by during a show, you can enjoy tasty hors d'œuvres along with Joanne's contemporary styles. To find that distinctive look that sets you apart, visit Moxxi Boutique.

70 Main Street S, Georgetown ON
(905) 877-0111

Silvercreek Espresso Bar

If you ask for the best coffee in town, locals won't hesitate to promptly direct you to Silvercreek Espresso Bar. Located on the trendy downtown strip of Olde Main Street, Silvercreek is the perfect place to chat while enjoying your morning coffee and pastry with the newspaper. Order from the all day Lite Bites menu, which includes grilled sandwiches and panini, and feel yourself compelled to return for a leisurely afternoon or evening of people watching while being thoroughly mesmerized by your signature latte, mocha or macchiato. Silvercreek is in the middle of the town's cultural center, so you won't be far from the music, arts and theatre venues. Owners Gordon and Barbara Brown restored this downtown hot-spot, revealing a high ceiling and deep French windows overlooking a beautiful 120-year-old stone church. The interior of Silvercreek is furnished with leather sofas and chairs, marble tables and an extraordinary counter bar imported from Italy. The state-of-the-art espresso machine features the quintessential eagle and is nickel plated to evoke the silver of Silvercreek. This rich interior and the Main Street window offer a quiet retreat from the hustle and bustle of the neighbourhood, while the tables outside beckon you to appreciate the outdoors. While you enjoy this inspiring atmosphere, be sure to indulge in the Certified Fair Trade Organic coffees and espresso drinks customized to your taste. Silvercreek evokes that last trip to Europe.

112 Main Street S (at Church Street), Georgetown ON
(905) 877-5769

The Freckled Lion Children's Bookstore

Step through the doors of this downtown shop and prepare to be swept into a world of colourful fantasy. This whimsical bookstore fosters an encouraging reading environment with high-quality children's books and fun activities for kids. The Freckled Lion Children's Bookstore caters to young readers by placing books on kid-height shelves and offering various reading groups and story times. The vibrant walls and activity area, complete with a castle, inspire creativity and allow kids to visualize literature adventures. Harry Potter fans flock to the Freckled Lion for the array of books and accessories that are always in stock. Kids and parents alike will love Alivan's wands, which are certified authentic and made with the same woods featured in the Harry Potter books. On select days of the week, parents can bring their kids in to enjoy story time, where stories, crafts and puppet shows rule the activity area and are sure to delight preschoolers. One of the distinguishing features of the bookstore is its extensive collection of French books and resources, plus a specialist to assist you with all of your French reading needs. Native speakers can enjoy their favourite stories and special-order any books that are not available. If you are a French immersion student or just want to learn the language, these books are perfect to get your feet wet. No matter what you or your children's reading preferences are, come to the Freckled Lion Children's Bookstore for a wild ride through the world of literature.

56 Main Street S, Georgetown ON (905) 873-1213
www.freckledlion.com

Photography by: Lisa A Scale, Bella Photography Inc. Caledon, ON & Simon Burn, SDB Creative Group, Caledon ON

CALEDON

Farmland, country estates and conservation land forests surround several traditional communities in the Town of Caledon, population 57,050. The largest of these is Bolton, Caledon's shopping destination with its urban edge that complements its rural roots. Other communities include Caledon Village, Caledon East, Terra Cotta, Belfountain, Alton and Palgrave. Visitors looking for exceptional shopping opportunities will love Bolton, with its balance of independently owned boutiques and shops with the advent of convenience found in big box chains. Dotted throughout the Town of Caledon are picturesque communities with river valleys and large rural areas criss-crossed by both the Niagara Escarpment and Oak Ridges Moraine. In Caledon Village, you'll find the scenic and highly rated Devil's Pulpit and Devil's Paintbrush Golf courses, created by the now-wealthy authors of the Trivial Pursuit game, and in Belfountain, the famous Forks of the Credit, which offers a wonderful scenic adventure along winding roads. Caledon's more than 70 parks and 260 kilometres of trails are popular with day trippers from more urban areas of the Golden Horseshoe. Pleasant spots for a picnic include Dicks Dam and Mill Parks in Bolton. A bit further north in Palgrave is the Caledon Equestrian Park, home to Tournament of Champions, a national horse jumping show the third weekend of September. Palgrave's Albion Hills, Mono Mills' Glenn Haffy, Belfountain's Forks of the Credit and Belfountain Provincial Parks are Caledon's conservation areas popular for tobogganing, cross-country skiing, fishing, biking and hiking. Fall in love with nature and old-town charm in the Town of Caledon.

Caledon, brought to you by Bolton Merchant Association
www.ShopBolton.ca

Bolton

Caledon's
SHOPPING
DESTINATION

The Caledon Inn

The Caledon Inn began taking in travelers shortly after it was built as a farmhouse in 1830.
It's been a pub since the dawn of the 20th century and a restaurant for the last 40 years. Most
recently, it has been owned by Michael Olechno and Deanna Forder, who continue the pub
tradition on the lower level with fine dining upstairs. The inn offers several options for private
and corporate events. Chef Alan Coulter mixes European and Canadian cuisine for a menu
that is country at heart with sophisticated touches. Once you've discovered the Caledon Inn and
its picturesque 25-acre setting, you will want to make frequent visits, just 25 mintues north of
Toronto. Stopping in for a pint at McCarty's Pub is popular—you'll find classic pub grub and live
music two or three nights a week. When weather permits, fine dining spreads from charming
interior spaces to upper and lower patios plus an upstairs screened porch. A portable outdoor
structure offers pleasant dining in any season for up to 300 guests; a banquet room holds 60.
When you hold your wedding at the Caledon Inn, you get more than a place for a ceremony and
dining. You gain the help of a certified wedding planner who can arrange for flowers, invitations,
photographers and all the overwhelming details that add up to lifelong memories. Corporations
and private parties can make use of the inn's audiovisual equipment and enjoy a landscape
suitable for hiking or cross-country skiing. Discover the many charms of the Caledon Inn.

16626 Airport Road, Caledon ON
(905) 584-0033
www.thecaledoninn.ca

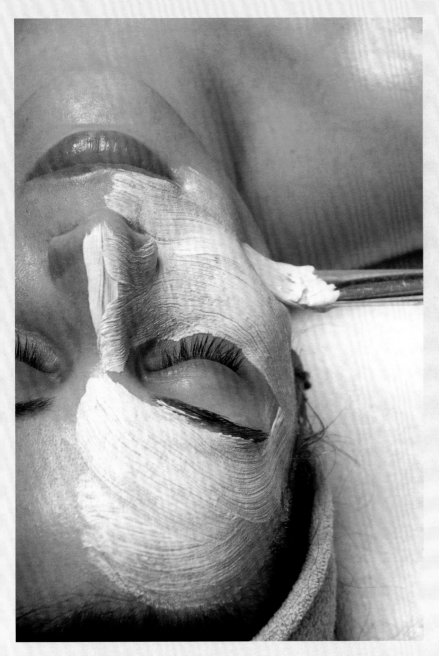

Jade Holistic Spa

Jade Holistic Spa seeks out the formula for wellness that works best for each individual client then offers the inspiration, information and tools you will need to attain balance and beauty. Tranquility begins with the soothing music and intoxicating scents you experience when you enter the Caledon spa. Owners Donna Pace and Daniel Lacoste believe the products that touch your skin should be free of synthetic substances. Daniel is an acupuncturist and registered holistic allergist whose work includes maintaining the body's natural energy, acupuncture-based facial rejuvenation and eliminating the symptoms of allergy with Bioenergetic Intolerance Elimination. Donna is a certified esthetician and holistic nutritionist who specializes in skin care. She uses such skin care lines as Jurlique and Eminence to soothe the skin with organically grown plants. Among the many signature facials is the Oxygen Facial, which nourishes the skin with oxygen, botanicals, trace minerals, enzymes and amino acids. Other treatments include laser hair removal, photo rejuvenation, anti-aging facial peels and non-surgical facelifts that employ microcurrents to firm and tone the skin while smoothing out wrinkles and stimulating cellular renewal. The spa uses organic wax, organic floral waters and mineral-based makeup that is good for your skin. All products and procedures have been extensively tested for safety and effective results. Discover your best self while experiencing individually designed treatments at Jade Holistic Spa.

25 Queen Street N, Bolton ON
(905) 951-8659
www.jadeholisticspa.com

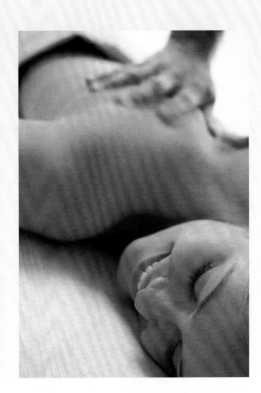

Photo by Lisa Scale, Bella Photography

Calm Waters Day Spa & Laser Clinic

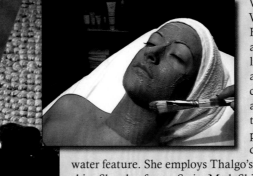

What living takes out of you, Calm Waters Day Spa seeks to restore. Carla Furfaro, her daughters Elise and Melissa and a professional staff provide every luxury to make your visit to the spa and laser clinic a relaxing time. Carla's career as an aesthetician has given her a perspective on the most healthful therapies. Facial treatments are performed in a soothing environment complete with candles and an in-room water feature. She employs Thalgo's marine algae formulas to heal the skin. She also favors Swiss Med, Skinceuticals and peels that contain anti-oxidants that reveal younger looking skin. The spa targets aging skin with microdermabrasion, chemical peels and nonsurgical facelifts that stimulate facial muscles. State-of the-art procedures include IPL Photo-rejuvenation used for treating redness, enlarged pores, sun damage, hyper-pigmentation and dilated capillaries. Accent Radio Frequency Technology tightens the skin to reduce double chins and jowls, contour fat pockets and smooth cellulite. Laser treatments remove unwanted hair and veins. Electrolysis and waxing offer other hair removal options. Opt for hydrotherapy, a body wrap or ion-detox cleansing. Registered massage therapists use Swedish or hot stones to elicit relaxation. The spa also offers Jane Iredale Mineral Makeup applications, manicures and pedicures. Take time out to revitalize, rejuvenate, relax, enjoy at Calm Waters Day Spa.

50 Queen Street N, Bolton ON
(905) 857-6466
www.calmwatersdayspa.com

Klementine Designs

Women who want to love the way they look seek out clothing and accessories at Klementine Designs. Sabrina Oliveri opened her store seven years ago, offering custom creations and alterations as well as clothing and accessories from designers in Canada, the United States, Denmark and Germany. Whether you seek casual cruise wear, business suits or formal wear for proms and weddings, Sabrina can help you. Her customers depend on her to find or create clothing that's right for a particular occasion and for the colouring and build of the person wearing it. Proof of her success pours in as customers send photographs and cards filled with gratitude. Sabrina can complete your look with Canadian-made jewellery as well as coats, scarves and purses. Few can resist the shape, function and decorative detail on handbags. By naming her shop after a grandmother who came from Luxemburg, Sabrina captures fond memories of a close relationship from childhood. Her mother, Barbara, is a vital part of day-to-day operations. Sabrina avoids clothing that needs dry cleaning as much as possible, preferring environmentally sound easy-care fabrics. For clothing that gets compliments, visit Klementine Designs.

19 Queen Street N, Bolton ON
(905) 857-7380

Hilltop Flowers

From the time she was quite young, Shelley Cormier knew what she wanted to do. Her passion for flower arranging has been benefiting customers at Hilltop Flowers since she purchased the shop eight years ago. She and her professional staff can capture the spirit of any occasion with flowers tastefully arranged in a vase or let you do the arranging with unique bouquets of the season's freshest blooms all wrapped up with complementary greenery. European dish gardens are the best choice for hospitals, offices and expressions of sympathy. The designers at Hilltop also create floral tributes for weddings and other special occasions. Funeral flowers are carefully selected with experienced designers to guide customers during their time of bereavement. For those who prefer the language of roses, Hilltop's staff will create classic bouquets of roses mingled with Baby's Breath. This Teleflora florist offers many lovely gifts, including wind chimes hand-painted glass panels and gifts especially for gardeners. Still other gift items include Webkinz, silk flower arrangements, tropical and flowering plants, fruit and gourmet gift baskets and bamboo displayed in artistic containers. When a floral designer puts the kind of love into projects that Shelley and her staff put into arrangements, that love shines through. Put some love into your gifts with a visit to Hilltop Flowers.

368 Queen Street S, Bolton ON
(905) 857-7440 or (800) 399-1594
www.a1florists.com/hilltopflowers

Bolton Florist

Personalized service, inventive floral design and a guarantee of satisfaction are the hallmarks of Bolton Florist, a florist shop that has served Bolton for 47 years. This FTD florist confidently meets your gift giving needs, and it has the knowledge and staff support to organize fresh flowers for such large events as weddings and funerals. Shelley Cormier owns Bolton Florist as well as Hilltop Florist. She and her staff pay close attention to their clients' visions and know how to coordinate their efforts for the ultimate effect. They excel in helping brides select flowers and stay within a budget. From the altar and the pews to the reception tables, Bolton Florist understands the importance of your special day. Its bridal bouquets and wedding party corsages and boutonnieres demonstrate a command of floral artistry and coordinated custom creations. The flower shop can even provide fresh blooms for the wedding cake. Bolton Florist has an antique ambiance and a large gift collection that includes glassware, vases and collectibles. Shelley's staff offers silk flower arrangements and makes corporate gift giving a snap with choices that include tropical plants and gourmet gift baskets as well as unique bouquets and flower baskets. Make sure your floral gifts carry the message you intend with a visit to the talented staff at Bolton Florist.

43 Queen Street N, Bolton ON
(905) 857-1596 or (800) 924-2609
www.boltonflorist.com

Hummingbird Flowers & Gifts

The residents of Caledon East find a good reason to visit the five-year-old Hummingbird Flowers & Gifts. "No occasion is too small or celebration too large for us," owners Carmela Gagliese-Scoles and her husband, Brian Scoles, say. On the flower side of the business, Hummingbird stands prepared to handle weddings, funerals and corporate events. It will deliver balloons to your girlfriend or a fruit basket to your favourite aunt. Carmela's ability to discern what you would like makes her an invaluable resource for any bride. Carmela has lived in the same house in Caledon East all of her life and shares her love of the town with everyone who walks through her doors. Her young sons Johnny and JoeJoe fill the shop with laughter and childish antics. Giftware includes jewelry, vases and stained glass. You will find mugs, baskets for the garden and potted plants along with worldwide delivery. During the holidays, the store brims with seasonal ornaments, cards and gifts. You can also place a *Sears Catalog* order at this location (www.sears.ca). Get help with your gift and flower selections at Hummingbird Flowers & Gifts.

15943 Airport Road, Caledon East ON
(905) 584-6192 or (888) 508-2687

Mirabella Gift Boutique

Once you meet Carmela Augello and her two daughters, Mary and Josie, you will be popping into their store on a regular basis, just to say hi, like so many patrons of Mirabella Gift Boutique. This five-year-old gift shop can help you find that perfect something for just about any occasion. Be it a wedding, bridal shower, engagement, baptism, communion or confirmation, these ladies can solve any gift-giving dilemma. Mirabella also makes the perfect Gift Basket—ideal for house warming and corporate giving at any time of the year. For formal flare, you will find fine china and exquisite crystal by Waterford and Royal Doulton and a wide variety of kitchenware to satisfy all styles and décor. If there is a specific china pattern or linen you seek, Carmela and her daughters will gladly source and order it for you. All that glitters in their front window is Swarovski crystal collections and jewelry—treasures that will be cherished forever, and just as vast is their extensive line of porcelain oil lamps from Lampe Berger. If you are in the Bolton area, Carmela, Mary and Josie would love for you to stop by Mirabella Gift Boutique—you will find that perfect gift!

1 Queensgate Blvd, Bolton ON
(905) 951-8165

A Scrapbooker's Dream Outlet

Elizabeth Nardella combined her university training in communications, fine arts, publishing and photography to open A Scrapbooker's Dream Outlet. This three-year-old superstore gives the crafter thousands of ways to arrange photos and mementos to capture special times in life. The store promotes the scrapbooking hobby as a way for individuals to express themselves and to touch base with other crafters during classes and private parties. Elizabeth has taken classes across Canada and the United States to stay on top of industry trends. She relies on her staff of expert scrapbookers who put every crafter at ease. You will find more than 10,000 products for scrapbooking and card making, including 4,000 patterned papers and 500 cardstock colours. Rubber stamps dominate one wall, while another showcases inspirational scrapbooks. The store brims with such embellishments as glitter and stickers. Classes require advance registration. When classes or private parties are not in progress, the spacious studio space is open to adult crafters. The room, which can accommodate 20 crafters, comes equipped with a die cutting machine. Embrace your memories with a visit to A Scrapbooker's Dream Outlet.

15 Allan Drive, Bolton ON (905) 951-9544
www.ascrapbookersdream.com

Kids Can Do

Knowing what kids can do is part of Kathleen Heron's job and the focus of her toy stores, Kids Can Do. She started her business in Orangeville in 1988 and expanded to Bolton in 2000. The store specializes in quality toys and activities for all ages from newborns to adults. Kathleen knows that what children do and learn during their early years can affect what they do for the rest of their lives. She offers toys that challenge kids to grow and learn, including games, CDs and DVDs, stuffed toys, puzzles and science and crafts projects. Recently, Kids Can Do has branched into toys for children with special needs. Besides the ability to teach, toys need to be safe and durable. The merchandise at Kids Can Do comes from such respected manufacturers as Playmobil and PlanToy. You can buy trikes made in Germany, wooden toys from Thailand, developmental toys from Manhattan Toy and WOW and puzzles from Ravensburger. Animal figurines from Schleich offer hours of creative play, while Brio and Thomas railway sets introduce youngsters to the world of miniature trains. Kids Can Do in Bolton offers children's parties, and the employees are experts on such events. They provide custom loot bags and other specialties that add flair to the celebrations. Kids Can Do makes shopping rewarding for you and fun for your kids. For a store that understands what kids like and what they need, visit Kids Can Do.

18 King Street E, Unit A2, Bolton ON (905) 951-9778

Gourmandissimo

When you hire Gourmandissimo to cater your party, you obtain the culinary artistry of husband and wife team Gilles and Adriana Roche. Gilles is a blue ribbon chef from Monte Carlo, and Adriana is a talented pastry chef. Together, they help people in the Caledon area celebrate the most important occasions in their lives, from intimate family celebrations to weddings and large banquets. The couple formerly had a Toronto restaurant, but following the birth of their first child, they switched gears. Gourmandissimo lets them pursue catering while still reaching out to Caledon on a daily basis with a storefront. You can stop by for cappuccino and a croissant, take home a gourmet meal or purchase specialty foods singly or in custom gift baskets. Look for fine olive oils and balsamic vinegars as well as Italian olives, sun-dried tomato sauce and hand-rolled pasta. An upstairs room allows groups as large as 50 to dine on one of Gilles' five-course dinners or something simpler, such as a Sunday brunch. The couple and their talented team also operate as exclusive caterer for the Best Western in Orangeville. For gourmet catering that offers big city flair without sacrificing small town joy, talk to Gilles and Adriana at Gourmandissimo.

16023 Airport Road, Caledon East ON (905) 584-0005
www.gourmandissimo.com

Photos by Simon Burn

Photos by Lisa Scale, Bella Photography

Howard the Butcher

Howard the Butcher, an 11-year-old shop, excels at parties, but also stocks everyday food that has earned the respect of Caledon's citizenry. From fresh fish and seafood to honey sliced hams, the shop spoils Caledon with fabulous party food 364 days a year. Owners Howard Beckett and Ann Dunbar, believe in supporting local farmers by carrying Ontario-raised pork, beef, chicken and lamb. The store also offers fresh local and Ontario produce when it is available. You might find some flowers to spruce up a party table. The store reaches beyond excellent butcher shop fare to offer fresh herbs and freshly baked bread as well as cakes, tortes and cookies. Prepared foods include sausages, dips, salsas, soups and meat pies like those Howard's mother used to make. Among the grocery items are steak sauces, oils and vinegars, cedar planking for grilling your favorite fish, Balderson cheese and frozen food. Howard and Ann are deeply involved in their community. They hold roast beef and spaghetti dinners to benefit Headwaters Healthcare, host barbecues in support of the Caledon Soccer Club and participate in Caledon eat local week. Whether you are planning a week of family meals or a party, bring your shopping list to Howard the Butcher.

15980 Airport Road, Caledon East ON
(905) 584-2934

Mercato Fine Foods Bakery & Deli

Sam Loiero grew up in the bakery business and wanted his family to enjoy a similar life. Four years ago, he and his wife, Rosanna, opened Mercato Fine Foods Bakery & Deli in the town of Caledon. Their children, Valentina and Massimo, and their nephew, Andrea, make valuable contributions to a business that involves a bakery, an espresso bar, a full deli, hot table and a grocery store featuring gourmet foods from around the world. Mercato's bakery specializes in fine Italian breads, European cakes, pastries and cookies, wedding cakes and freshly made gelato, a confection that features intense flavours, rich consistency and higher quality products. Mercato provides specialty oils, vinegars and preserves, as well as olives, pastas and an assortment of sauces, dressings and marinades that add a creative spark to home cooking. The store's cheeses represent small producers in Quebec, Italy, Switzerland and much more. A gift basket from Mercato is always meaningful. Baskets are available year-round, but are particularly popular at Christmas. Mercato inspires party plans and then turns those plans into reality with catering for such special events as communions, confirmations, graduations, birthdays and corporate meetings. Improve the quality of your meals and desserts with a visit to Mercato Fine Foods Bakery & Deli.

1 Queensgate Boulevard, Bolton ON
(905) 857-9040

Photos by Simon Burn

Chef Talk Bistro & Catering Inc.

Chef Talk Bistro & Catering Inc. has built a strong reputation for casual fine dining, banquets and catering services in Caledon. Chef Fab has been passionate about cooking since childhood when he would watch his grandmother in the kitchen. As he received an introduction to other cultures he began to appreciate international cuisine. Chef Fab graduated with honours from the culinary arts program at Humber College in 1989. He was the executive chef and operations manager for Peter & Paul's corporate catering division. He was also the owner of Mainstreet Diner and the Bourdeaux Café & Bistro. Dinner at Chef Talk is a sumptuous affair where diners indulge in flavours from around the world. The 70-seat dining room accommodates private functions such as weddings, birthdays and more. The catering service provided by Chef Talk is on the cutting edge of the culinary industry, which keeps it in high demand. Chef Fab has hosted celebrities such as Shania Twain, Lionel Ritchie, Robert Redford and Paul Martin. For a lighter lunch fare Chef Talk has recently introduced Soup Du Jour, located at 170 McEwan Drive in Bolton.

170 McEwan Drive, Bolton ON
(905)951-3555
334 Queen Street S, Bolton ON
(905) 857-6578
www.cheftalk.ca

Collins Bay Marina in Kingston
Photo by Jim Vance

Tulips in Ottawa
Photo by abdallahh

Eastern and Ottawa

Ottawa River and Parliament Hill
Photo by Michelle Tribe

Sam Jakes Inn

Overlooking the Rideau Canal, a UNESCO World Heritage site, Sam Jakes Inn provides a haven for those who appreciate the finer things in life. Named after Irish immigrant and original owner Samuel Jakes, the inn is located in a historic Merrickville 1861 building. Now a provincial heritage structure, this stone building has been added to and restored to its former grandeur. With graciously appointed suites and guest rooms, you'll never feel like a visitor. The classic 1860s décor and elegant restaurant, bar, library and on-site spa will make you feel like royalty. Since its purchase in 1988, the Clarke family has been proud to run an inn that offers sanctuary from the hustle and bustle of busy urban life. Sam Jakes Inn has seasonal views from the rooms, where you may admire the colours along the misty canal. Chef Thomas Riding and Innkeeper Lisa Clarke offer the best of local food, wine and beer on the menus. Scrumptious meals are served in the Dining Room, on the garden patio and verandah. The Inn is within an hour's drive from Ottawa, so you can escape to your refuge. Whether you need a weekend refresher, a mid-week escape, holding a special function or planning a business retreat, Sam Jakes Inn invites you any time of the year.

118 Main Street E, Merrickville ON
(613) 269-3711 or (800) 567-4667
www.samjakesinn.com

Cedar Shade Campground

Years ago, *Le Droit* newspaper called Cedar Shade Campground "a small paradise." Spend some time there and you'll soon understand why. When Jeannine and Jacques Péladeau acquired the land 30 years ago, they began a love affair with the lakeside haven. The affair continues today as they pass along their legacy to the next generation. Casual, friendly and enjoyable, the pristine campground and surroundings offer a family getaway for guests of all ages. The 170 sites for RVs and tent campers head the list of offerings. Water, sewer and electricity are provided for a small additional fee. Cottages are available as well with well-equipped kitchens. Picnic tables and fire rings are in ample supply. You can stay for a night, a week or the entire season. An on-site restaurant provides guests with an alternative to campfire cooking. The campground has Wi-Fi Internet access. Activities include a heated pool with two wading areas and a spa, an artificial lake, a beach and a playground. There's a petting zoo, billiards and an arcade for those who crave video games. Washrooms, showers, laundry facilities and telephones are plentiful. Ice and wood are delivered to your RV or tent. Dances, wagon rides, bingo, horseshoes and various ball games head the extensive list of organized events. You can even get a professional massage by the pool. You'll experience many pleasures when you reserve a spot at the Cedar Shade Campground.

530 Peladeau Road, Alfred ON
(613) 679-4447
www.cedarshade.com

Hatton House Bed & Breakfast

Paul Bullied was a police officer who wanted to cook. He always had a passion for preparing food for others and he and his wife Laurie decided that when he retired they'd make that dream come true. Hatton House Bed & Breakfast is the realization of that dream—and a chance for you to experience Paul's gourmet three-course breakfast after a night of sweet dreams in the bed-and-breakfast's elegant accommodations. Hatton House features three luxurious guest rooms, each with its own charm. Whether you're in the Rooftop Suite, with its four-poster bed and whirlpool bath, the Victorian Room, with its antique furniture, or the bright, airy Garden Room, you'll delight in the décor and amenities. Particularly popular among the guests here is the indoor swimming pool and sauna, which is just the thing for relaxing after a stroll through Carleton Place or a day in nearby Ottawa. The bed-and-breakfast, with its large gardens and ample accommodations, is an ideal place for weddings and other celebrations. Come enjoy the gourmet food of a cooking cop and the gorgeous, comfortable accommodations at Hatton House Bed & Breakfast.

242 High Street, Carleton Place ON
(613) 257-5201
www.hattonhousebb.com

Evergreen Camping & Resort

Evergreen Camping & Resort answers the call for a safe and peaceful place where families can play while enjoying nature. A small swimming lake with a sandy beach is at the heart of it all and is the scene of much action during the day. The kids will love the slide that delivers them straight into the water. Take a dip in the heated pool as well, or stroll the many trails that wind through the wooded resort. Other attractions include an arcade, rec hall and sports courts. You can enjoy badminton, volleyball, basketball, horseshoes, petanque, shuffleboard or croquet. Evergreen has 106 seasonal sites and 36 sites for transients or weekenders. Several sites are right on the lake. If you prefer a cabin, you have a choice between a small unit that sleeps four or a larger one with a loft. The cabins and campsites may be reserved for a day, week or month. Freshen up in the wash rooms. A store, restaurant and boutique offer other hints of civilization during your stay in the outdoors. Renee and Luc Desormeaux, your friendly and courteous hosts, speak French and English. Frolic in the lake by day, and then watch the stars come out at night at Evergreen Camping & Resort. It's open May 1 to October 1.

5279 County Road 17, Alfred ON
(613) 679-4059 or (888) 679-4059
www.evergreencamping.ca

Quality Hotel Royal Brock

Let elegance surround you when you visit Quality Hotel Royal Brock. This hotel has a
big city feel in a historic location. The Hotel Royal Brock wants you to feel as comfortable
as you would at home. Each of the 72 spacious rooms is equipped with solid hardwood
furniture, triple sheeted beds and bathrooms with deluxe towels and imported amenities. In
addition, the hotel offers a sports club with an indoor pool, hot tub and squash courts, as
well as an amazing spa. The Quality Hotel Royal Brock is one of the only hotels in the city
with a fully functioning spa. Massage your cares away or simply get your nails done for a
night out on the town. The hotel is conveniently located in downtown Brockville so you'll
waste no time getting to where you want to go. You'll find fine dining, theatre, shopping
and tours of the 1000 Islands at your fingertips when you stay at the Quality Hotel Royal
Brock. If you'd prefer a quiet night in, let the friendly staff at the hotel's Wild Vine Restaurant
serve you. The Quality Hotel Royal Brock also offers a wide array of business services.
Whether it be a wedding, party or seminar, let the hotel's first class banquet facilities cater
to your every whim. Don't forget to check out the Rose Garden, a beautiful abotanical
paradise perfect for a spring wedding or engagement party. Whatever the occasion, make
your visit to Brockville a memorable one when you stay at Quality Hotel Royal Brock.

100 Stewart Boulevard, Brockville ON (613) 345-1400 or (800) 267-4428
www.qualityhotelbrockville.com

Robertson House Inn Bed & Breakfast

Jun and Kazuko Hosogoe are your hosts at the Robertson House Inn Bed & Breakfast and its on-premises Kazuko Restaurant. Robertson House Inn, a fine example of early Loyalist Georgian architecture, is an Ontario Historic Landmark. It was originally erected around 1810 and may be the first building constructed in Brockville. The inn is now renovated and refurbished with 21st century updates. Guest quarters are furnished in a romantic, 19th century flavour. One of the three accommodations is a two-bedroom suite; all have private baths. Modern-day amenities include air conditioning, satellite television and Internet access. Enjoy the Continental breakfast, served according to your schedule. Check the special rates for weekly, monthly and extended stays. At the Kazuko Restaurant, Jun is the master chef. He trained in his native Japan, then honed his skills in France. His wife, Kazuko, manages daily operations and serves as guest liaison. Try the famous Dim Sum lunch or the specialty crêpes, wraps and sandwiches. The restaurant offers seafood, steak and chicken for dinner in a fine dining atmosphere, as well as theme nights. For a truly gracious experience, come to Robertson House Inn Bed & Breakfast.

10 Broad Street, Brockville ON
(613) 345-5164
www.robertsonhouseinn.com

Pine Street Inn B & B

Guests are treated like royalty at the Pine Street Inn Bed & Breakfast. The royal treatment comes naturally to co-owner and Chef Michael Dunn, who is a former chef to her majesty, the Queen. Michael and his wife, Francine, have created a haven that feels like home for their guests. Built in 1870, the inn has been featured in Lonely Planet publications and in *History Detectives* on PBS. It's just minutes from the St. Lawrence River—you can see it from the balcony. There are four bedrooms to choose from, each equipped with a plush bathrobe and slipper. Michael serves a full gourmet breakfast in the sunny breakfast room. His food is dependably delicious, his sauces light and flavorful. By request, he and Francine will prepare a picnic basket for your day's excursion, or dinner with advance notice. The couple also offers catering services for your events. Internet service is available, and the inn does accommodate children. From the fantastic front porch, you can easily walk to the river, downtown, and to the Arts Centre, making it a convenient home base for all your explorations in Brockville. Find great food, comfortable lodgings and beautiful scenery at the Pine Street Inn B & B.

92 Pine Street, Brockville ON
(613) 498-3866

The Carleton Heritage Inn

Larger than a bed and breakfast but more intimate than most hotels, the Carleton Heritage Inn offers old-time grandeur coupled with modern elegance in the heart of downtown Carleton Place. Victorian touches abound in the 15 standard rooms, each named after a renowned poet. All rooms come with private bath, cable television and high-speed Internet access. The four-room Imperial Suite, the inn's most spacious accommodation, is decorated with period antiques and accented with a four-poster bed and two fireplaces. It's easy to find a place to eat with two restaurants on the premises. Catch the game on the big screen at Main St. Suds while feasting on pub fare and quaffing an ice-cold draught on tap. If you prefer something a little fancier, then try the Mississippi Grill for steak and the chef's own special creations, served in a casual fine dining atmosphere. The Sunday brunch is famous all over the Ottawa Valley for its more than 50 feet of delicious food, including an omelette station. The Carleton Heritage Inn hosts many special events for groups of up to 150 people. Bring your tiniest glimmer of an idea to the in-house event staff, and they will make it a reality. Engagement parties, bridal showers and weddings are specialties. Find a perfect blend of modern sparkle and yesteryear's splendor at the Carleton Heritage Inn, one of the oldest hotels between Toronto and Montreal.

7 Bridge Street, Carleton Place ON (613) 257-2525
www.thecarletonheritageinn.ca

A Rose on Colonel By Bed & Breakfast

In 1999, Ann d. Sharp took a 1925 English cottage and enhanced its beauty with mirth, colour and conveniences. The result is A Rose on Colonel By Bed & Breakfast—the only bed-and-breakfast on Ottawa's famous Rideau Canal, which was designated a UNESCO World Heritage site in 2007. Two of the inn's airy rooms overlook the canal, built in the 1830s under the leadership of Colonel John By as a military waterway. A third room is shaded by a century-old oak tree. Visitors bike along the canal in summer and skate upon it in the winter, when it becomes the world's longest skating rink. Beautiful surprises at the inn include the Hand of Fatima knocker on the massive oak door modeled on the first known door bell. The front garden becomes a wonderland of roses each year, and the ground floor boasts more than 30 leaded-glass windows. A Rose on Colonel By was chosen as one of the Best Places for Relatives to Stay by the *Ottawa XPress*. Local publications and television stations have featured the bed-and-breakfast, and it is one of only four Ottawa bed and breakfasts included in *Michelin's The Green Guide, Canada*. For romantic accommodations on the south shore of the canal, stay at A Rose on the Colonel By Bed & Breakfast, minutes from downtown.

9 Rosedale Avenue, Ottawa ON
(613) 291-7831
www.rosebandb.com

Ashbury House Bed & Breakfast

Based on the comments that guests leave behind at the Ashbury House Bed & Breakfast, you will be pleased that you chose this place from the moment you arrive. There is usually warm apple pie and coffee waiting in the dining room. Innkeepers George and Charmaine Neufeld will greet you immediately, ask you how your trip went and before you know it, you will be chatting away. It's remarkable that so many people thank their hosts for the interesting conversations as often as they praise the beautiful rooms, comfortable beds and blueberry pancakes for breakfast. Each of the three guest rooms at the Ashbury House has its own special charm. All are furnished with period antiques in keeping with the character of the stately 100-year-old Edwardian house. The inn is located within walking distance of downtown Ottawa and many tourist attractions, including the Canadian Parliament buildings, the Canadian Mint and Byward Market. "Why do you think we always return to this house?" wrote Hans and Gisela from Germany. "It's like being at home. We are already looking forward to coming back next year." Enjoy appetizing food and peaceful slumbers, as well as stimulating conversation, at the Ashbury House Bed & Breakfast.

308 First Avenue, Ottawa ON
(613) 234-4757
www.ashburyhouse.com

Cedar Shade Campground

Years ago, *Le Droit* newspaper called Cedar Shade Campground "a small paradise." Spend some time there and you'll soon understand why. When Jeannine and Jacques Péladeau acquired the land 30 years ago, they began a love affair with the lakeside haven. The affair continues today as they pass along their legacy to the next generation. Casual, friendly and enjoyable, the pristine campground and surroundings offer a family getaway for guests of all ages. The 170 sites for RVs and tent campers head the list of offerings. Water, sewer and electricity are provided for a small additional fee. Cottages are available as well with well-equipped kitchens. Picnic tables and fire rings are in ample supply. You can stay for a night, a week or the entire season. An on-site restaurant provides guests with an alternative to campfire cooking. The campground has Wi-Fi Internet access. Activities include a heated pool with two wading areas and a spa, an artificial lake, a beach and a playground. There's a petting zoo, billiards and an arcade for those who crave video games. Washrooms, showers, laundry facilities and telephones are plentiful. Ice and wood are delivered to your RV or tent. Dances, wagon rides, bingo, horseshoes and various ball games head the extensive list of organized events. You can even get a professional massage by the pool. You'll experience many pleasures when you reserve a spot at the Cedar Shade Campground.

530 Peladeau Road, Alfred ON
(613) 679-4447
www.cedarshade.com

Brockville Arts Centre

The show earning raves this weekend at the Brockville Arts Centre might be a tribute to the legends of country music. Next weekend, it might be a Broadway revue. Beloved for its large stage and excellent acoustics, the centre offers some of the finest stage entertainment in Ontario, encompassing drama, music and dance as well as children's theatre. The facility annually hosts the Thousand Islands Jazz Festival in May and features a Fall Classical Series to complement its Fall Review Series and Summer Music Review Series. Expect a thrilling yet intimate show in this house with a seating capacity of 802. The crowd is large enough to energize the performers with its enthusiasm, while a good seat with a great view is always guaranteed. The list of recent and past performers include big bands and crooners as well as folk acts and classic rockers. Back in the early 1900s, famous comedian George Huntley became disgusted with conditions at the opera house and inspired a group of local citizens to form the Brockville Operatic House Co. Boasting the third largest stage in Canada when it opened in 1911, this predecessor of today's auditorium was gutted by fire in 1937. Catch an exuberant performance at the Brockville Arts Centre.

235 King Street W, Brockville ON (613) 342-7122 or (877) 342-7122
www.brockvilleartscentre.com

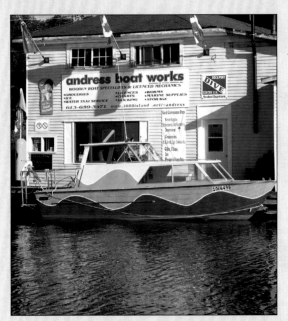

Dive Brockville Adventure Centre

As the warm waters of Brockville continue to attract diving enthusiasts, the staff at Dive Brockville Adventure Centre stands ready to serve them with daily dive charters, rentals and instruction. Water temperatures reaching 80 degrees with no thermo-clines have earned Brockville the nickname of the Canadian Caribbean. Perhaps the most popular diving destination in all of Canada, this stretch of the St. Lawrence River boasts great visibility and many fascinating shipwrecks. Scuba charters run from Dive Brockville Adventure Centre seven days a week from April to November. Be sure to ask about package deals combining a dive charter with overnight accommodations. Dive courses for novice divers are available at flexible dates as well. Continental breakfast at the hotel and lunch aboard the boat are included. Rent a kayak from Dive Brockville to enjoy the nature up close and to see some of the 1000 Islands yourself. Choose between sit-in or sit-on kayaks, both available by the hour or day. Kids can enjoy fun summer activities at the adventure centre's summer camps, which are available all summer or for a day or a week. Owned by Helen Cooper, Dive Brockville Adventure Centre has been making life more exciting since 1995. Keep it in mind as you plan your Canadian Caribbean holiday.

12 Water Street E, Brockville ON (613) 345-2800 or (877) 982-2827
www.divebrockville.com

Absolute Comedy

Jason Laurans, owner of Absolute Comedy, warns that if you arrive late for the evening's entertainment, you may have to sit in the kitchen and watch the show on a 14-inch black and white screen with no sound. On top of that, he will spit in your drink. We think he's only kidding, but you never know with edgy comedy. The stand-up performers who appear on the stage at Absolute Comedy, the only independently owned comedy club in Ottawa, know how to make people laugh. Their takes on life, love and the pursuit of happiness might make you squirm a bit, too. Open Wednesday through Sunday, the club attracts touring professionals who have played major venues in New York, Montreal and Los Angeles and gigs for Comedy Central. Come just for the show or combine the show with dinner. The food is delicious, and the prices will make your wallet laugh with relief. Do you know how to spin a party with your wit? You might want to try your jokes on the Wednesday crowd at Absolute Comedy. That's the night when the amateurs take the stage before the pros. Laugh until it hurts at Absolute Comedy, and remember don't be late.

412 Preston Street, Ottawa ON (613) 233-8000
www.absolutecomedy.ca

Tait's Bakery & Deli

Fine food has been the family business at Tait's Bakery & Deli for nearly a century. The Tait family founded the bakery in 1908, earning a reputation for excellence and service. The Mazurek family, which purchased the bakery in 1957, has built upon that tradition. Tait's is currently owned and operated by brothers John and Stephen Mazurek, the sons of Bruce Mazurek, who purchased the bakery from the Taits. In 2006, the family was able to open a second location. The secret for success at Tait's today is the same as it was in the beginning: quality products made using the finest ingredients, offered at an affordable price. Baked goods at Tait's include homemade bagels, muffins, cakes and pies, created according to the original Tait family recipes with no preservatives or fillers. Stop by the deli for one of the delicious sandwiches that use the bakery's fresh bread. Whether you'd like a simple salami or a deluxe model with roast beef, turkey and ham, you'll find something to tempt you. At your next event, treat your guests to a delicious meal catered by Tait's. From sub platters to cheese trays and fresh fruit, there's something for every taste. Come enjoy the family tradition of fine food at Tait's Bakery & Deli.

31 King Street W, Brockville ON (613) 342-3567
2123 Parkdale Avenue, Brockville ON (613) 342-3061
www.taitsbakery.com

Main Street Creamery

When the summer sun gets high in the sky, folks start showing up in droves at Main Street Creamery to seek some ice cream relief. Among the 30 flavours of hard ice cream are such exotic tastes as cotton candy and peanut butter cup. You are not alone if soft ice cream is your preference. Indeed, the favourite item in the shop, the Hurricane, features soft ice cream with chocolate bits. For owner Leslie Mayville, life took a turn from software to soft and hard ice cream when she left her computer job in Toronto to open the Main Street Creamery. "I like being in the happiness business," says Leslie, who definitely knows how to keep her customers smiling. Her milkshakes are thick, her waffle cones are made on the spot and her banana splits are loaded with lots of good stuff. Main Street Creamery received a certificate of appreciation from the Bath Canada Day Committee for its contribution and dedication to making Bath Canada Day a success. Enjoy a creamy treat at Main Street Creamery, a community gathering place with a friendly vibe.

176 Lodge Street, Bath ON (613) 352-3357

Pasticceria Gelateria Italiana Ltd.

In business since 1979, Pasticceria Gelateria Italiana is more than just a pastry shop. Situated in the heart of Ottawa's Little Italy, the European-style pastry shop is a place for the whole family and serves some of the best espresso and cappuccino you can find, as well as homemade gelato, chocolate truffles, cannoli and other wonderful pastries. The shop is well known for their beautiful cakes and desserts. Pasticceria also serves breakfast, and their lunch menu offers a choice of daily hot pasta, grilled panini sandwiches, gourmet pizzas, salads and more which can be enjoyed with Italian wine or imported or domestic beer. Everything is made from scratch on the premises, including the gorgeous wedding cakes and sugar or chocolate sculptures on display upstairs. This gallery of edible art is designed to help brides and grooms pick a cake for their special day. Award-winning Chef Joe Calabro, a member of the Canadian Culinary Federation of Chefs & Cooks and Les Toques Blanches — to cite just a few of his many professional credentials—invites you to visit Pasticceria Gelateria Italiana to treat yourself with a sweet that attains the level of art.

200 Preston Street, Ottawa ON (613) 233-2104
www.pasticceria.ca

Cup After Cup

Cup After Cup earned an Eat Smart Award of Excellence in 2007 for its menu promoting healthy eating choices. Clearly, the food at this coffee shop isn't merely an afterthought, but a source of immense pride for owner Krista King-Holmes. Her soups, such as Chick Pea Chowder and Hearty Tomato Vegetable, are creative, wholesome and satisfying. Fresh baked goods and hearty sandwiches make her place the perfect spot for breakfast or lunch. For a snack, try a famous date square with a fresh cup of crème brûleé coffee. A complete range of espresso and cappuccino drinks are also available. The locals return over and over to Cup After Cup, appreciative of its relaxing atmosphere, friendly service and bright artwork on the walls. When they can't stick around, they count on Krista and her staff for prompt take-out. Cup After Cup caters as well. You, too, will fall in love with this downtown Prescott charmer, which offers seating on the front patio in summer. It's a rare day when Krista isn't present, cooking, baking and running the show. She started the business from scratch in 2004, fulfilling her dream of being her own boss. Eat well while enjoying your coffee and meeting the locals at Cup After Cup.

179 King Street W, Prescott ON (613) 925-0503

Downtowne Ice Cream & Candy Shoppe

Exotic flavors are a tradition at the Downtowne Ice Cream & Candy Shoppe. Are you adventurous enough to try a scoop of the lemon honey garlic? Shelley Innes serves up 28 different flavors of ice cream on any given day. Not all are as unusual as chili chocolate and chai tea latte, but each is homemade from the finest ingredients available. Many different flavors of gelato complement the choices of ice cream. You can smell waffle cones being made as soon as you step through the door. The other half of their enterprise, an old-fashioned candy counter, features Shelley's own chocolates and suckers. The *tourtière* made by her husband, Serge, has become very popular. A line of locals and visitors alike often forms at this shop, where a spirit of friendship and community reigns. Shelley runs this true family business with her husband and their daughter Heather Massie. In July 2007, the owners held an ice cream festival and donated all proceeds to the local daycare center and youth group. Discover flavors to tantalize your taste buds and bend your imagination at the Downtowne Ice Cream & Candy Shoppe.

165 St. Lawrence Street, Merrickville ON
(613) 269-2168

Photo by Harrison Smith

Novellino Clothing & Accessories

Novellino Clothing & Accessories' dedication to delivering the latest and greatest in trendy apparel is reflected in its name—*novellino* is Italian for new, young and fresh. Though Novellino caters to the clothing needs of all women, its primary customers are the fashion-conscious 15 to 35-year-old women who have made the store their shopping destination. Novellino's owner, Tammy Godefroy, prides herself on offering such trendy women's clothing lines as Guess, Billabong and Killah, as well as a variety of smaller labels from around the world. Novellino will begin offering its own line of clothing in the near future. Whether you're looking for jeans or a cocktail dress, you'll find it here. The store carries a small run in sizes and generally doesn't order the same thing twice, so there's always something new to see and all of the items are extremely desirable and exclusive. Finish off that perfect outfit with a gorgeous handbag and some sparkling jewellery. The store offers a fun, upbeat environment, with a southern Mediterranean theme. Let Novellino Clothing & Accessories outfit you in the freshest fashion.

286 Princess Street, Kingston ON (613) 541-0219
www.novellino.ca

Fancy That Group

In 1974, Inger Sparring-Barraclough opened a trendy accessory store which eventually grew into the Fancy That Group. The Group's three fashionable shops, Limestone and Ivy, Fancy That and the Roundstone, have a boutique atmosphere where customers are encouraged to work with personal fashion consultants. While each store has a style and ambience of its own, they all sell quality European, Canadian and American designs. Limestone and Ivy, a casual clothing store for women and men, offers practical and affordable attire with comfort and style. The chic ladies clothing and shoes at Fancy That are always the latest in fashion and present new styles and designers each season. The Roundstone's clothing offers customers a sophisticated look and provides an array of items from elegant dresses to comfortable shorts. With over 32 years in business and a true passion for fashion, the staff at the Fancy That Group continues to supply the fashionistas of Ontario with the newest trends and latest in chic and casual style. You can find location information as well as links to all three shops on the Fancy That Group website. Be sure to stop in to each distinctive store to complete your well-rounded wardrobe.

48-50 Princess Street, Kingston ON (613) 549-4489
www.fancythatkingston.com

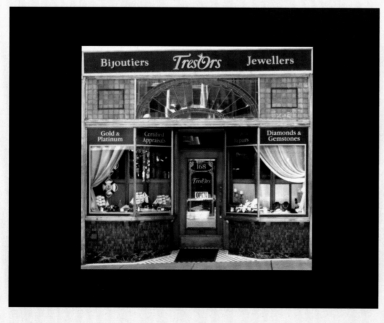

Tres Ors Jewellers

If you're looking for a jewellery shopping experience in an elegant European atmosphere, Tres Ors Jewellers is the place for you. With 35 years of experience, second-generation jeweller Alain Filion took over the store in 2004, but the building it occupies has been home to a jewellery store for much of Kingston's existence. French by birth, Alain specializes in elegant European styles, with some items imported from Italy and elsewhere in Europe. Alain delights in custom-making pieces to your exact specifications in 18-karat gold, silver and platinum. He stocks an impressive variety of gemstones, including the rare Canadian polar diamonds, as well as South Sea and Tahitian pearls. The store also handles estate jewellery as well as repairs, engraving and re-plating. Make time to check out the store's beautiful wall and grandfather clocks. Tres Ors glitters with old-time elegance, including the 1900-era cherry wood cabinets in which the jewellery is displayed. Tres Ors Jewellers is your golden opportunity to find elegant European-style jewellery.

168 Princes Street, Kingston ON (613) 542-4492

River Myst

Looking for clothing that flatters the female form? River Myst is the clear choice. "Magic happens" in this store, say owners Catherine Howard and Ron Pawlinski, explaining why their store draws women of all ages looking for fine fashion. Whether you're looking for contemporary casual clothes or elegant evening wear, this store has it. Catherine and Ron proudly feature mostly Canadian designers in the store, including the renowned Frank Lyman lines of dresses, sweaters and other fine garments. The clothing at River Myst is tastefully displayed in sections that highlight each piece's beauty. River Myst also carries a wide variety of gift items, including the Canadian Enchanted Meadow line of soaps, scrubs and bath products. The store is the only one in Kingston to offer the beautiful Alexandria fragrance lamps, which fill the air with the gentle scent of aromatherapy oils. River Myst also carries delicate Franz Porcelain vases and sculptures. Flattering fashion and great gifts await you at River Myst.

56 Brock Street, Kingston ON (613) 544-1230
125 Water Street, Gananoque ON (613) 382-1289

Frontenac Jewellers

For Frontenac Jewellers owner George Dafnas, owning his own jewellery store was like clockwork—literally. After immigrating to Kingston from his native Greece, George spent much time outside Frontenac Jewellers, watching as the previous owner repaired watches and clocks. Eventually, the owner invited George to come in and learn the trade. In 1976, George bought the business, which is now managed by his daughter, Natasa. Frontenac Jewellers has always been known for its quality watches and watch and clock repairs, but in the past decade, its focus has shifted more toward gems and jewellery. In addition to the gorgeous pieces on display, including beautiful rings, pendants and other items, customers can have their own designs created. Work with the expert jewellers to create the ideal piece for any occasion in gold, silver, platinum or paladium, with real Canadian diamonds. Frontenac Jewellers also carries elegant Swiss watches from Tissot, which are renowned for their utility and beauty. George and Natasa pride themselves on their high level of service and loyal customer base. For elegant jewellery and watches, there's no time like the present to come to Frontenac Jewellers.

75 Princess Street, Kingston ON (613) 542-4666

Pauline's Lingerie

Rediscover romance with gorgeous lingerie that just can't be found anywhere else. Pauline's Lingerie, established in 1976 by certified corsetiere Pauline Marshall, offers its clients professional bra fittings and fabulous lingerie. Whether you're looking for the perfect undergarments or for a special sensual something, Pauline's is certain to have the products and expertise to help you find it. In addition to selling the finest lingerie, Pauline's carries a variety of swimwear and accessories. Many customers come in for a bra fitting and leave with a new favourite handbag or robe as well. Owner Pauline Marshall has built a reputation and a clientele that stretches from Montreal to Toronto and into the United States. Pauline's granddaughter, recently certified corsetiere Catherine Howley, has been involved with the business since she was 14 years old and continues with a passion for her job. Pauline's offers quality brands such as Felina from Germany and Chantelle and Passionata from France. Even the seasoned lingerie buyer will find something special at Pauline's, with styles from Frou Frou, GayLure, Blush and Dreamgirl. Visit Pauline's Lingerie in historic downtown Brockville and find that special item you never knew you needed.

156 King Street W, Brockville ON (613) 345-2244

Inch of Gold

Gary and Shelley Campbell welcome customers new and old to Inch of Gold. True to its name, the shop sells gold, silver and crystal jewellery chain by the inch, and it specializes in customizing the length of each chain to meet its customer's exact desires. A company founded in 1982, Inch of Gold in Merrickville is Canada's flagship store, with over 100 chains to choose from and a wide selection of clasps and pendants from which personalized pieces of jewellery are created. Its jewellery is complemented by locally made woodcraft, cast iron pieces, and original one-of-a-kind gift ideas sure to be remarked upon as conversation pieces. In a store filled with whimsy and humour, you will be sure to find the perfect present or momento of your stay. Canadian distributorships available.

135 St. Lawrence Street, Merrickville ON
(613) 269-4232
www.inchofgold.com

Starlet

Starlet is a fun and funky boutique that features primarily Canadian jewellery as well as hilarious greeting cards, fantastic handbags, delicious body care products and so much more. In this shop you will find something for every style and budget. Owners Cat and Jefta Monster opened Starlet in an old bank building and now it shines as one of the most outstanding shops in the area. Awarded in 2006 for business of the year and for the inspiring restoration of a downtown building, Cat and Jefta have made Starlet a destination for local shoppers and tourists. The interior is artfully decorated with classic white moulding, pale yellow walls and a signature coral wall branded with the Starlet logo. The shelves are lined with an amazing jewellery selection equivalent to that of boutiques in larger cities such as Montreal, New York or Los Angeles. In addition to the eye-catching jewellery, Starlet offers the latest in handbags and hats for every season. No matter what you find, because of the exceptional customer service and quality of products, you're sure to leave Starlet feeling like a star. For more information and pictures please visit the website.

32 Dundas Street E, Napanee ON
(613) 354-3665
www.starletboutique.ca

Photo by Windflower Photography Ltd

Fabulous, The Shoppe of Gorgeous Things

Artist and entrepreneur Andrea Fabricius opened this trendy shop in 2003 with a knack for discovering distinctive and hard-to-find items. Fabulous, the Shoppe of Gorgeous Things is the realization of Andrea's dream to provide an exciting shopping experience for residents and visitors to Almonte. With an East Indian flair and a colourful, cozy atmosphere, Fabulous beckons to those looking for something different. When you enter, you might be struck by the walls adorned with bright scarves, the vintage and original jewellery or the fragrance of locally made soaps and perfumes. Bohemian and fine silk garments hang about the shop, while funky gifts such as mini djembe drums, chic headbands and knit hats are placed artistically throughout. Andrea's artistry is also displayed on the walls; vibrantly coloured oil paintings and mosaics can catch the eye from any vantage point. In addition to offering customers these extraordinary items, Andrea also provides mosaic creation courses, set designs for local music venues and runs a kids art camp. Whether you're looking for an uncharacteristic gift or just happen by the lively little store, let Fabulous, the Shoppe of Gorgeous Things inspire your next shopping trip.

63 Mill Street, Almonte ON
(613) 256-1955

Kehla Jewellery Design Studio

When you wear Michaela Wolfert's originally designed jewellery, don't be surprised if you suddenly become the center of attention wherever you go. Upon entering Kehla Jewellery Design Studio, you'll see why. These truly one-of-a-kind pieces come from the creative mind and skilled hands of Michaela herself and are the product of a lifetime of study, apprenticeship and passion. She first discovered her love for the craft when she watched a goldsmith at work. Many awards and 28 years later, Michaela's handmade, precious metal jewellery and sculptured pieces have made her a legend. In addition to making jewellery for her studio and creating custom pieces, Michaela teaches jewellery making courses and workshops. Each piece of jewellery combines traditional craftsmanship with simple and elegant designs. Your eyes might be drawn to the brushed gold rings with a sparkling pink oval diamond or a dramatic silver necklace reminiscent of an Egyptian queen. Michaela's delicate floral and leaf lines flatter dainty necklines while the crinkle designs offer a more contemporary look. Be sure to check out all of Michaela's funky and flattering creations when you visit Kehla Jewellery Design Studio.

7 Mill Street, Almonte ON   (613) 256-7997
www.kehladesign.com

Excitable Fashions

Can you pick out the woman in the crowd wearing Excitable Fashions? If she has that look of confidence and feels desirable then she is, because that's the effect that this line of intimate apparel and dancewear has on any woman who wears it. Women who wear Excitable Fashions can be found anywhere, from campuses and offices to the supermarket, symphony or for a hot night on the dance floor. There is no surer place to find an Excitables girl then at the Excitable Fashions retail store in Ottawa. Set free in a store full of exotic lingerie, dancewear and sexy shoes, she becomes the daring person she has always desired to be. Even the woman seeking something more subtlety alluring will find plenty of options. Merchandise includes garter-belts and hosiery, dancewear and shoes, exotic lingerie and swimwear. Couples love shopping together at Excitable Fashions, too. In fact the men's novelty briefs, thongs and swim-briefs have been known to turn smiles and raise eyebrows. Shop Excitable Fashions today for underclothes that are as much fun putting on as they are taking off.

186 Preston Street, Ottawa ON   (613) 237-1669
www.excitablefashions.com

Stone Monk

Brand names and good fashion at low prices are what you will find at Stone Monk. College students, teenagers and adults on a budget will appreciate the affordable selection, which ranges from casual to evening wear. Jacqueline Austin was originally an employee and model for Stone Monk. Fashion is her passion, so when the opportunity arose to purchase the business, Jacqueline was ready. Personal service is more than a byword at Stone Monk. Jacqueline easily slips into the role of consultant when working one-on-one with customers to assemble an outfit. When she buys for the store, she keeps her regular customers in mind and always includes items she knows will work for them. This kind of service and selection has caused the word to spread. There is now a second location in Tweed, and Jacqueline plans to franchise in the future. Jacqueline and her daughters, Ashley and Taylor, extend their invitation to come and browse Stone Monk in Napanee or Tweed, and start working on the wardrobe of your dreams.

130 Richmond Boulevard, Napanee ON (613) 354-4997
340 Victoria Street, Tweed ON (613) 478-2249

Desert Jewel

In the short time that Desert Jewel has been open, owner Anne and Stephen Hull have found that women will travel a long way to get what they sell. As an authorized dealer of Desert Diamonds, this store attracts shrewd customers from near and far who appreciate excellence at an affordable price. Set in 18-karat gold, Desert Diamonds are diamond simulants whose brilliance, fire and longevity rival that of natural diamonds. The only dramatic difference between the two is price. Often the best-dressed women in town can be found at Desert Jewel, because Anne encourages women to bring in their formal gowns and accessorize from her showcases for that perfect complement. Anne and Stephen's daughter, Stephanie Hamilton, is a top distributor in the United Arab Emirates (Dubai) for Desert Diamonds and inspired her parents to open a store for the community. Every now and then, Anne will close the store to hold a Sparkler Party, an occasion to serve guests coffee, tea and treats while bedazzling them with a private showing of Desert Diamonds jewellery. Desert Jewel also carries fresh water pearls, as well as rhinestone and crystal jewellery. Truly special jewellery for women of all ages. Own the closest thing to diamonds without spending a fortune by shopping at Desert Jewel.

27 Dundas Street W, Napanee ON (613) 354-4882
www.desertdiamondsco.com

Rowland Leather

Quality leather is always in fashion. These days, Rowland Leather is leading the way with original designs by Michael Rowland. Michael started out selling his work at craft shows. Today he supplies his own three stores in Ontario with the highest-quality leather bags and briefcases, gloves and slippers. Michael's passion for fine craftsmanship shows in his work. He challenges customers to detect a difference between a high-end fashion bag by Coach and one of his own. With over 30 years of experience backing him up, Michael is devoted to enduring quality and exquisite style. His award-winning designs are nothing short of excellent. Michael works with a rich colour palate, including sage green, deep red and chocolate browns. He invites you to stop in one of his shops and engage your senses. Experience the smell, touch and beauty of leather when you visit Rowland Leather.

159 St Lawrence Street, Merrickville ON (613)269-3151
1095 Bank Street, Ottawa ON (613)526-1954
103 Clothier Street E, Kemptville ON (613)258-7763
www.rowlandleather.com

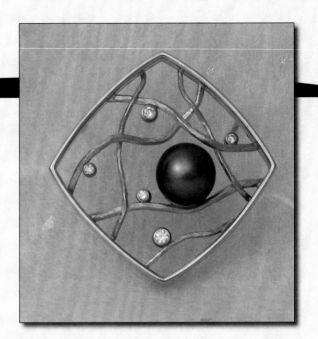

Sandra Whitton Gallery

The Sandra Whitton Gallery is a place of rare distinction; its walls come alive with the paintings of award-winning artists and its showcases filled with stunning pieces of handcrafted jewellery in gold, platinum and silver, set with a variety of gems. The jewellery studio is on-site, making it simple to talk with the owner, Sandy Whitton, if you would like to have a ring or another piece of work custom designed and made to your precise specifications. A highly talented goldsmith with an excellent sense of design, Sandy began her career in 1985 and worked in a Yorkville studio for a number of years before returning to Kingston. In 1995 she opened her first gallery, which featured her own jewellery exclusively. After establishing an impressive customer base, Sandy decided to expand and opened the new gallery in May of this year. Sculpture, paintings and multimedia work from artists both local and international fill the bright and elegant space. The displays are changed every six weeks or so, ensuring there's always something new and interesting to see when you visit. Whether you are looking for a distinctive piece of jewellery or a work of art to bring a room to life, you will find a wealth of beauty and choice at the Sandra Whitton Gallery.

253 Ontario Street, Kingston ON
(613) 531-0968
www.sandrawhitton.com

Chameleon Nation - Creative Emporium

Looking for local art in Kingston became a lot easier when Chameleon Nation - Creative Emporium opened its doors. Ashleigh Fortune is the woman behind the scenes. A Kingston native, she wanted to create a nourishing, stress-free environment in which to display the art of emerging and established artists. Chameleon Nation features the work of four to six artists each month and reserves a community section for Canadian charities. Chameleon Nation hosts special events to introduce the work of various artists. All mediums and ideas are welcome in the Emporium, which operates as a multi-media creative art space and commercial gallery. Part of the space is allocated to ceramic and functional art pieces. Chameleon Nation provides certified art appraisals, installation and consultation services to the general public. Make an appointment to bring your art for appraisal, or come to spend some time viewing the ever-changing exhibits at Chameleon Nation - Creative Emporium.

112 Princess Street, Kingston ON (613) 545-0832
www.chameleonnation.com

Photo by Kelly Cookson

Kingston Glass Studio & Gallery

Looking for one-of-a-kind art that'll blow your mind? Kingston Glass Studio & Gallery offers beautiful and functional glass art that's guaranteed to add sparkle to any setting. The studio's four artists include Susan Belyea, who helped to found the business in 1998, Mariel Waddell, Alexi Hunter and Cheryl Dunsmore. Those who like a little function with their form will enjoy the variety of beautiful, useful objects they'll find at Kingston Glass, such as paperweights and candlesticks. Serve up some art at your next party on plates and bowls as well as wine and martini glasses from Kingston Glass. The studio also features a variety of experimental pieces and sculptures that add character to any room. Everything is made on-site, and guests, including school groups, can watch as art is created with the use of a 2,100-degree furnace that holds 300 pounds of glass. Want to make your own glass art and jewelry? Take one of the classes offered at Kingston Glass. Come to Kingston Glass Studio & Gallery studio for art that will light up any occasion.

56 Queen Street, Kingston ON (613) 547-9149

The Studio at Greyweathers

The Studio at Greyweathers is home to the creative souls of Holly Dean and Larry Thompson. Delighted to be among the few lucky individuals that do what they love for a living, Larry and Holly spend much of their time creating beautiful hand-made ornaments for Cirque du Soleil. Holly is a gifted artist and calligrapher who creates art rich in mood and mystery. Her mixed media art can be found all over the world including an original collection of paintings designed for the Cirque. Larry finds his heart in letterpress printing, creating breathtaking books with hand-set type and spirited illustrations. He says, "the romantic in me holds letterpress sensuously: the smell of the ink, the landscape of set type or cut blocks, the feel of type imprinted into beautiful papers and the thrill of pulling that perfect impression." Larry operates most of the technical aspects of the printing press, from setting of type to binding of books, while Holly contributes design advice, calligraphic embellishments and inspiration. They share a deep love of their creative way of life. Both Larry and Holly welcome you to visit them in the Studio at Greyweathers where you can enjoy their work first hand.

606 Elgin Street, Merrickville ON (613) 269-3714
www.greyweathers.com

Claudette Hart Pottery & Gours

Step into this light, airy studio and take a moment to marvel at the creations of Claudette Hart, the Gourd Lady of Merrickville. Claudette Hart Pottery & Gourds is set in a charming country cottage where visitors and art aficionados can gather to admire one-of-a-kind designs. The earthy tones and asymmetrical lines of Claudette's gourd art adorns the walls and shelves, each distinctly different from the next. You'll also see her pottery, funky vases and original sculptures. As one of the only gourd artists in Canada, her work is treasured among collectors. The gourds can be transformed into decorative functional items such as masks, baskets, lidded containers and even purses and jewellery. Claudette's love of nature and culture shines through in her creations, just ask the proud owners of her playful greenmen. These ceramic faces are perfect to watch over your garden and welcome buds to bloom and plants to flourish. If you're looking for a way to personalize your home, check out Claudette's handmade dishes. Using her watercolour skills, Claudette originally designs, creates and glazes the vibrantly coloured pieces. Stop into Claudette Hart Pottery & Gourds today and see the inspiration for yourself.

123 Bruce Street, Merrickville ON (613) 269-2580
www.merrickvilleartists.com/claudette

Geraldine's Gallery

While she's an artist and avid art lover, Geraldine Query spends a lot of her time promoting art in the Ottawa community and helping artists find their voice in Canada's art culture. At Geraldine's Gallery, local artists get top billing and Geraldine knows how to promote their work outside of the gallery's walls. In addition to featuring artists, Geraldine has a gift for finding artists exhibitions and commissions. Previously working as a curator, gallery manager and an arts administrator, Geraldine knows the ins and outs of the art scene and how to work them. In addition, her passion for the city and mystical connection with nature inspires her own work, which often depicts the local environment. She believes that art is about memories and the human emotion connected with memories. When you walk in the gallery, you'll see how her work and the work of the featured artists are an expression of the spiritual connection humans have with their surroundings. With a variety of mediums including prints, mixed media, oil and watercolour paintings, and various installations, Geraldine's Gallery offers a number of perspectives. Come in today and let the stunning works inspire you.

701-A S Gower Drive, Kemptville ON (613) 258-0033

Anika Arts & Flowers

To experience a living work of art, visit Anika Arts & Flowers, where the flowers and gifts glorify any room. From original artwork to unusual gifts and floral arrangements, anyone who appreciates a personal touch is sure to find something at Anika. Owner Duska Maric began Anika Arts & Flowers after a lifetime of artistic influence from her family in Serbia. Duska dreamed of creating a flower shop that resembled a gallery of fine art where she could make irreplaceable gifts infused with feeling and love. In addition to creating vibrant and original flower arrangements, Duska focuses her artistic vision on glass, pottery and painting. She also employs her imaginative abilities to create some of the most exquisite wedding arrangements and centrepieces. The store flows from one room to the next in a graceful display of flowers, glassware and fine gifts. The atmosphere is serene and personable, and the quality of service complements the quality of merchandise. Be sure not to miss this welcoming oasis when you visit Ontario.

8–3570 Strandherd Drive, Ottawa ON (613) 825-7811
www.anikaartsandflowers.com

Beauty Escape Day Spa

Whether you are slipping in a beauty treatment after work or are on vacation, you are sure to enjoy the services owners Jennifer and Dean Coulter and their staff provide at Beauty Escape Day Spa. The Spa opened its doors on May 20, 2003 and is situated on two acres overlooking beautiful Baptiste Lake. Jennifer and Dean moved back to the Bancroft area in 2001, purchasing the 8,000-square-foot house that Jennifer's parents had built as their dream home in 1992. After some research, they felt that Bancroft needed an economical day spa. Jennifer has nine years of experience in the cosmetic field and specializes in make-up applications for brides and their bridal parties. Beauty Escape offers full spa services in a quiet relaxed environment. It caters to men, women, and even the future generation of spa enthusiasts. You will feel like you are at a home-away-from-home with a good book and a warm cup of tea while being pampered. You will find its services quite informative and will receive many helpful tips to take home with you. Beauty Escape guarantees that you will receive friendly quality service at prices you can afford.

1458 S Baptiste Lake Road, Bancroft ON
(613) 332-6714 or (888) 254-7821
www.beautyescape.ca

The Spa Royal Brock

Look and feel 20 years younger when you visit the Spa Royal Brock. This Brockville treasure offers the only full-service spa and massage parlour inside a hotel. Featuring holistic treatments and all-natural products from Switzerland, the Spa Royal Brock's goal is to revitalize body and mind. Owner Linda Smith opened the spa with a passion for aesthetics and a desire to provide a calming atmosphere for today's busy client. Offering various facials, massages, Reiki and hot stone massages, the spa is the perfect place to relax and rejuvenate. If you're looking for a day of pampering, get a manicure, pedicure or wax treatment. Dip your hands in a warm paraffin bath and feel the healing moisture soak into your skin. Close your eyes and inhale the botanical herbs as they awaken your senses and invigorate your skin. Now offering micro-dermabrasion, Linda can slough away old skin cells, scars or fine lines to reveal a fresh, new complexion. No matter which treatment you choose, the Spa Royal Brock is dedicated to making your experience a memorable one. Enjoy the lifestyle of royalty when you indulge at the Spa Royal Brock.

100 Stewart Boulevard, Brockville ON
(613) 345-5687
www.sparoyalbrock.com

Photos by Barbara Simpson, Brockville, Ontario

Diva Salon & Day Spa

Whether you're here for a quick haircut or a luxurious day of massage, you're the center of attention at Diva Salon & Day Spa. "Our goal is to exceed your needs and expectations," says owner Paula Foster. "We strive to create an environment where knowledge, beauty, comfort and personalized attention combine to create a memorable experience." Foster and her highly trained staff have been providing memorable experiences to guests since 1995. Your hair is in good hands in the 12-chair salon, which offers everything from a simple haircut for men and women to foil highlights, colour correction, straightening and many other services. Relax in the capable hands of one of Diva's talented massage therapists. Choose from a variety of techniques, including hot stone and aromatherapy massages. Ayurvedic therapy, a system of healing from India believed to be more than 5,000 years old, is also available. Diva offers a variety of spa packages, facials and body treatments, in addition to massage and hair styling. The spa is proud to offer the Aveda line of hair and body products. The atmosphere is fun and relaxing and the surroundings provide the atmosphere of a luxurious 1920s grand hotel. Despite the high quality, Diva is affordable. Let the talented stylists and therapists at Diva Salon & Day Spa treat you like the star you are.

336 Princess Street, Kingston ON
(613) 544-4067 or (800) 957-DIVA (3482)
www.divasalon.ca

The Old Tin Shed

Folks around Bancroft watched with curiosity to see what Dagny Musclow, her six-year-old daughter Moryah and her mother Janis Whitehead would make of an old and neglected building sitting in the pines just six kilometres from town. In 2003, the Old Tin Shed opened its doors and customers discovered a store that warranted frequent visits and time for browsing. The inventory is a delightful assortment of new, antique and one-of-a-kind objects that bring country appeal to homes and gardens. Before you enter this treasure trove of gifts, you will want to take a good look at the gardens the three generations of women planted around the building. Once inside, you will find bath products, folk art and picture frames along with farmhouse primitives, lighting and linens. Dagny loves creating new things from salvaged materials. She stocks Burt's Bees products as well as Babywrappers and Peepee Teepee. Talented employees, including a floral designer and an artist, add their skills to the mix. Janis was a retired schoolteacher when Dagny recruited her for the store. Moryah has grown up serving customers, wrapping gifts and doing her homework in the shop. The three will make you feel like old friends when you visit the Old Tin Shed.

29681 Highway 62 N, Bancroft ON (613) 332-6565
www.theoldtinshed.com

Mirick's Landing Country Store

Linda Nash looks at an old wooden step ladder and thinks that it would make a nice floor lamp. She takes pieces of tattered quilting and uses them to create Santa Claus suits for primitive Santas. Her business, Mirick's Landing Country Store, serves as a showroom for her latest recycling projects. You will find birdhouses and frames that she has fashioned from pieces of 19th century furniture, plus coffee tables made from windows and mirrors. Look up to see the teapot chandelier. Owning four homes, including a bed and breakfast, gave Linda plenty of decorating ideas. Encouraged by her success at crafts shows, she set up shop in May 2006, trusting that her friends would continue to give her things they don't want anymore so that she can turn them into wholly original pieces of furniture and home décor. So far she has suffered no shortage of supplies. Mirick's Landing supplies locally as well as far away customers with the famous Thermohair socks, which are locally made. A baby section is stocked with everything from books to booties. Through the sale of Baby Knee Pads, Linda has generated enough money to inoculate the children in a small village in Africa. Drop by Mirick's Landing Country Store, where recycling is taken to artful heights.

106 St. Lawrence Street, Merrickville ON (613) 269-3559
www.mirickslanding.ca

Windsor's Courtyard

Lush greenery and fragrant flowers surround the doorway of this artsy shop. At Windsor's Courtyard, you can find something to truly set your home and garden apart from the rest of the neighborhood. Located in a charming 100-year-old brick building in historic Merrickville, Windsor's features a funky and eclectic collection of home décor, artisan metalwork and garden accents. You may just find the perfect piece to accentuate your style or inspire you to redecorate. Owners Elaine and Bruce Windsor opened this artsy shop in 2003 with the goal to bring original and distinctive pieces to the area. The in-house artisan, Bruce, replenishes the stock with his garden creations, making Windsor's Courtyard a destination for original art. The exquisite metal daylily, a Bruce original, stands at 30 inches and will brighten any garden or large potted plant. Elaine does the purchasing for the store, often traveling around the world with her sister Dorothy to find the perfect items. Upon entering, you might find a wide array of hummingbird feeders, ornate clay pots, aged metal wall hangings and vibrant decorative tiles. Elaine and Bruce are proud to see their inventory constantly moving, and guarantee something new every time you visit. Stop in to Windsor's Courtyard today and discover your newest decorating muse.

211 St. Lawrence Street, Merrickville ON (613) 269-2999
www.windsorscourtyard.ca

The Melon Patch Home & Garden

At the Melon Patch Home & Garden, the new look of modern country is reflected in beautiful eco-friendly décor. Owner Elizabeth Sarich-Harvey has always been concerned with the health of the environment, and when she and her late husband purchased the building that became the Melon Patch's first home, she took advantage of the opportunity to do something about it while still offering the interior designs she was known for. Thus, you'll find a range of items to beautify your home, including brilliant fragrant Soya Candles, made with products native to the area. The Melon Patch also sells a popular line of coasters made from local stones. Nature Clean products offer a scent-free biodegradable alternative to chemical-filled cleaning agents. The store also offers a line of gourmet foods and framed mirrors made from recycled tires. These beautiful, functional items can be easily integrated into any home—and Elizabeth can help with that, too. The store offers a full range of interior consulting services, including color consultation and furniture reupholstering. Elizabeth is proud of the level of customer service offered here, as well as the fact that the store has become a destination for out-of-towners. Look for the latest in environmentally friendly décor and home accents from the Melon Patch Home & Garden.

357 Main Street, Bath ON (613) 352-9977 or (877) 227-1115
www.themelonpatch.com

Allegro Ristorante

Owner Vito Scaringi invites guests at his four-star Italian restaurant, Allegro Ristorante, to sit back and let the evening unwind. "The essence of fine cuisine is achieved only by allowing time for preparation," he says. A meal at this Little Italy location builds like a dramatic performance, each course bringing new tastes and aromas to your table. Begin the parade of artistically presented dishes by choosing something from the antipasti menu, the Gamberi Allegro, perhaps—shrimp in a Grand Marnier cream sauce. Still ahead is the soup and salad course, with a popular minestrone and a spinach salad with gorgonzola and mascarpone. A third course requires a basic decision before you consider the options in depth. Will it be chicken or veal? A pasta dish brings the meal to a grand crescendo, before the dessert, like a brief comic coda, provides a joyous finale. Keep spirits high throughout the performance by selecting something from the outstanding wine list. Spend a special evening at Allegro Ristorante, experiencing why *En Route* magazine placed it among the Top 100 Restaurants in Canada three years in a row.

422 Preston Street, Ottawa ON (613) 235-7454
www.allegroristorante.ca

Bella's Bistro Italiano

Indulge your taste buds with New World Italian when you dine at Bella's Bistro Italiano. A family run business with a devoted following, Bella's down to earth atmosphere and superior food will keep you coming back for more. This restaurant has been a standout in Ottawa since it's inception in 1995. You'll know the difference when you taste the home-made pasta, the fresh picked vegetables and the tangy sauces, all perfected by Chef Raffaela (Bella) Milito. The vast menu includes enchanting dishes such as linguine con frutti di mare, which is linguine with black tiger shrimp, mussels and sea scallops in a spicy tomato balsamic sauce. When dining, make sure you leave room for the dessert menu, with luxurious treats such as zuccotto, an Italian pound cake shell marinated in dark rum and marsala, filled with chocolate and vanilla mousse, almonds and chopped chocolate. Bella's is a friendly neighborhood gathering place with soft lighting and classic décor finishing off the classy tone of the restaurant. A one-of-a-kind find in Ontario, Bella's Bistro Italiano invites you to experience genuine Italian cuisine.

1445 Wellington Street W, Ottawa ON (613) 724-6439
www.bellas.ca

Som Tum Fine Thai Cuisine

Ottawa residents with a sense of history recall that Art Akarapanich opened the city's first Thai restaurant in 1983. Those with a love for fresh spring rolls, savoury curries and spicy beef dishes hope that it continues doing its thing for many years to come. Art, originally from Thailand, notes that a lot of care and love has gone into the creation of each dish on the menu. Ask him to explain the appeal of Thai cuisine, and he'll tell you that it stretches the limits of the palate with tastes ranging from sweet and tangy to sour and blazing hot. "The food we serve is truly authentic Thai," says the owner, "prepared using ancient recipes with ingredients flown in from the Far East weekly." Order any number of dishes, such as the chicken in pandanus leaves or the crispy chicken salad with mango, to sample the marvelous Som Tum way with poultry. The lightly battered fish with sweet basil sauce is also a winner. All dishes are prepared when you order, so let your server know how spicy you like your food. Enjoy a flavourful lunch or dinner at Som Tum with Ottawa's own Art of Thai restaurants.

260 Nepean Street, Ottawa ON (613) 781-8424
www.thaitaste.ca

Juniper Kitchen and Wine Bar

The experience of Juniper Kitchen and Wine Bar is one which tempts the imagination and delights the senses. One of Ottawa's top tables, Juniper continues to be innovative and evolve. Juniper's menu is one that reflects the bounty and produce of the region as well as the foods and flavours of the seasons. Drawing on the diversity of the Canadian culinary community, Juniper's menu interprets new and old world flavours, creating a new contemporary Canadian cuisine. As distinctive as the menu is the award-winning and continually changing wine list. The wines are chosen to represent their terroir, the outstanding taste and sense of the place in which they are grown. An extensive selection is offered by the glass, allowing for food and wine pairings with each course. Once having dined at Juniper Kitchen and Wine Bar, you will promise yourself to return again into the delight and creativity of Juniper's dining experience.

245 Richmond Road, Ottawa ON
(613) 728-0220
www.juniperdining.ca

Siam Bistro

Cold days in Ottawa often chase folks into Siam Bistro for a steaming bowl of chicken coconut soup called Tom Kha Gai. Since 1996, this popular Thai restaurant just west of the Somerset Strip has served up tasty and creative nourishment for every season and disposition. Owner Montha McGinnis believes that the variety in Thai cuisine is one of the main reasons why people like it so much. "You can take a particular vegetable or meat and prepare it so many different ways," she explains. To prove her point, she notes that the dinner menu at Siam Bistro features more than a dozen shrimp dishes. Try the red curry with shrimp and pineapple called Gang Kour Sapparot. You will also find plenty of options if you are in the mood for a chicken, beef or vegetarian dish. Montha has taught Thai cooking on a part-time basis in the Ottawa area since 1990. This knowledgeable and articulate spokesperson for Thai cuisine describes the perfect dish as one in which "the taste spreads out in your mouth; the flavours are strong but well balanced." Savor the true meaning of these words by enjoying lunch or dinner at Siam Bistro.

1268 Wellington Street W, Ottawa ON
(613) 728-3111
www.siambistro.com

Sacred Garden

The stream of customers to the Sacred Garden has been steady since this vegetarian Thai restaurant first opened its doors in 2006. It seems that Ottawa had been waiting for just such a place to come along. Among the stand-outs on the menu is a softly fried eggplant and tofu dish, served with chilies and vegetables in a hot, sweet and salty sauce. Recipes deftly substitute fermented soy products to imitate the tastes of fish sauce, oyster sauce and shrimp paste. Some dishes offer soy-protein renditions of chicken, beef and seafood. The only complaint that food critic Lucy Rest had about the hot and sour shrimp soup with coconut milk, for example, was that it "was almost too pretty to eat." Reacting to the chef's flair for presentation, she notes: "White-on-white, the creamy broth and snowy knot of vermicelli comes in an eggshell-coloured bowl with one bright red 'shrimp', a ring of 'squid' and tender brown mushrooms." Be sure to try the crispy spring rolls with sweet chili sauce or the rice paper roll-ups stuffed with vermicelli, herbs and tofu. For dessert, you'll love the deep-fried banana in a sauce of butter, honey and freshly squeezed lime. Join the hosts of others who have declared Sacred Garden not just their favorite vegetarian or Thai place, but their favorite restaurant overall.

1300 Bank Street, Ottawa ON
(613) 733-8424

Brockberry Café & Suites

For classy and personal dining in a beautiful historic limestone villa built in 1832, visit Brockberry Café & Suites. Owner Josie Groniger prides herself on running one of the only historically-set casual dining restaurants in Brockville. A relaxing atmosphere and pleasant music accompany a creative menu overseen by head chef Seth O'Hara. Each item is fresh and has a global influence. One of the signature salads, the Mandarin Poppy Seed Salad, is a favorite among locals. The signature dressing at the café is Seth's famous poppy seed salad dressing. In addition to a classy repertoire of food, Brockberry offers full-efficiency suites available for overnight stays or corporate rentals. Don't miss the evening entertainment or the personal touches all over the restaurant. Located within walking distance of the waterfront, shops and theatre, Brockberry's location is prime for experiencing old town Brockville. Visit Brockberry Café & Suites and find out why this Canadian treasure is a treat for any traveller.

64 King Street E, Brockville ON (613) 498-2692
www.brockberry.com

Buds on the Bay

Begin your journey through Brockville, the gateway to the 1000 Islands, with a mouth-watering meal at Buds on the Bay. Offering one of the best steak dinners in the area, Buds on the Bay wants you to leave satisfied. Try the tender juicy New York striploin or the hearty T-bone and you'll be hooked on Buds. Not ready to brave the steak menu? Try a crisp salad or some of the expertly prepared seafood. In addition to delectable dishes, the ambiance at Buds on the Bay is hard to beat. If you're looking for a laid-back, fun-loving restaurant and a bar that will keep you engaged with entertainment, quality food and beautiful views, this is the place. The restaurant features one of the city's largest outdoor patios overlooking the beautiful St. Lawrence River and features live entertainment during warm summer evenings. For a softer, gentler evening, the rooftop dining room can host any special event and is a beautiful place for a romantic dinner. Don't forget about O_2 Nightclub, one of the hottest places to dance the night away in the city. For an all-in-one experience, visit Buds on the Bay.

17 Broad Street, Brockville ON (613) 345-4341
www.budsonthebay.com

The Locks Italian Restaurant

Seeing nothing around Merrickville that fit his idea of an Italian restaurant, Josef Zsofnyak and partner, Jean Nark Robinson, decided that this was the place where they could make their culinary mark. Since opening the Locks Italian Restaurant in 2006, Chef Josef gained legions of loyal customers for his pork tenderloin scaloppini with gorgonzola pear sauce and other fabulous dishes. Though born in Hungary, he has lived most of his life in Italy, where he trained and worked as a chef. Begin your experience at the Locks by getting warm by the fireplace and enjoying a glass of wine from the extensive wine list. For an appetizer, Chef Josef recommends the bruschetta with smoked salmon and goat cheese. Setting a lofty standard for his restaurant, he insists on the highest quality meat and chicken, as well as the freshest fish and seafood. The vegetables come from local farms and Josef's own garden. The sauces are created when you order, including the exquisite Rose Cinzano sauce that tops the lime-marinated shrimp and sea scallops. Josef has infused the 1837 building that houses the restaurant with a rich European character. Consider the Locks Italian Restaurant when seeking creative Italian cuisine in an Old World atmosphere.

229 Main Street W, Merrickville ON (613) 269-4444
www.thelocksrestaurant.com

Ballygiblin's Restaurant & Pub

"Come for the food. Stay for the fun," reads the business card of Roger Weldon, owner and chef of Ballygiblin's Restaurant & Pub. Since November 2006, that's just what the residents and visitors to Carleton Place have been doing, enjoying a quaint meal in the front end of the restaurant before heading back to the pub for fun with friends. If you feel a family vibration, there's a good reason—Roger co-owns the restaurant with his brother-in-law Derek Levesque, who manages the dining room while Roger cooks up a storm in the kitchen. To be sure, Ballygiblin's offers traditional pub grub, including the ever-popular fish and chips. Those looking for something a bit more adventurous will also find plenty to please their palate. Indian and Thai dishes fill out the menu, along with sandwiches and quesadillas. Roger's commitment to using the freshest ingredients extends even to changing the wine list with the seasons. The atmosphere is upbeat, with friendly attendants ready to take care of your needs. Enjoy the artwork of local painters and photographers that lines the walls—it's available for sale. Ballygiblin's Restaurant & Pub invites you to come enjoy good food, good drink and good friends.

151 Bridge Street, Carleton Place ON
(613) 253-7400
www.ballygiblins.ca

The Good Food Company

Petra Graber began the Good Food Company with nothing but a passion for fine cuisine and a knack for entertaining. Today, she offers international dishes, delicious desserts, take-out and catering through her trendy café. Located in a charming historic building, the Good Food Company is abundant with fresh, made-to-order delectables that will tantalize your taste buds. Organic coffee and espresso drinks, creative salads and tempting entrees ensure that you'll find a favorite on the menu. The eggs Benedict is particularly popular. If you're craving something sweet, look no further than the Good Food Company. Many visitors return to the café just to get another taste of the heavenly dessert they had last time or sample the newest treat. Perfect for a weekend brunch or a casual meeting, the Good Food Company offers an eclectic mix of tried-and-true recipes and invention to satisfy customers of all walks of life. The friendly staff is dedicated to providing the best dining experience in the area. Stop in to the Good Food Company today and discover the good food you've been missing.

31 Bridge Street, Carleton Place ON
(613) 257-7284

Thyme & Times Past Inc.

Thyme & Times Past—the unofficial museum shop in the nation's capital. Combining antiques, vintage and traditionally made items, Thyme & Times Past has created an unexpected, eclectic feast for the eyes. International pottery, textiles, paper, teas, candles, Christmas ornaments, jewellery and soaps beautifully combine with the arts of nature. Throughout the spring and summer months, pots of herbs and flowers spill out on the doorstep and onto the surrounding walkway. Handmade and Fair Trade products add to Thyme & Times Past's captivating nouveau traditional charm. For 2008, a new collection of Jane Austen-inspired gifts and mementos will be specially featured and sold exclusively in the store. Come take a stroll through this inspired collection of one-of-a-kind gifts, traditions, thyme and times past.

**25 Beechwood Avenue, Ottawa ON
(613) 744-4732**

V.O. Sugarplums

An eclectic shopping experience awaits you at V.O. Sugarplums, where each separate room is focused around a different theme and features a different colour scheme. A piece of antique Italian brass might grab your attention in one corner, while a cute purse might strike your fancy in another. Among the assorted merchandise, you will find Colonial Candles of Cape Cod, Myka Jewellery from Vancouver and Camille Beckman body products. Owner Gail Jackson's fondness for all things Victorian is reflected in her selection of lace, decorative lamps and reproduction candle holders. She even carries a line of Victorian nighties. From teas and teapots to wall prints and iron ware, the merchandise is as varied as it is delightful. A back room displays Christmas items throughout the year. Gail set up shop in this 100-year-old Heritage home in 2001. Because she selects all the merchandise, the store is definitely an extension of her tastes and personality. However, she is deeply indebted to her faithful employee, Sharon O'Neill, for hard work and dedication through the years. Gail and Sharon make guests feel welcome with their hospitality and are eager to share their insiders' knowledge of the area with folks visiting from out of town. Find something special for everyone on your gift list at V.O. Sugarplums, and pick out a present for yourself as well.

**118 Brock Street W, Merrickville ON
(613) 269-2957**

Photo by Windflower Photography Ltd

Design by Destination

You can travel the world looking for exotic gifts or you can let the world come to you at Design by Destination. Owner Victoria Derksen used her love of traveling and her background as a travel agent to open her own Almonte imports store in 2004 following three years spent overseas. Her shop fills with the aroma of freshly brewed coffee while customers delight in such hand selected accent pieces as rugs and pottery. Japanese lanterns allow you to create unusual indoor and outdoor effects. A watering can shaped like a pig will please the world-savvy gardener. You can find personal adornment, such as purses and jewellery. Textiles hold particular interest for Victoria, which means you will find silk scarves and cashmere shawls from Tibet. Women from Bangladesh sew bedspreads for the shop. Victoria always has her eye out for Fair Trade items. She uses lovely ribbon to package gifts and invites her customers to mark their favorite places in the world on a laminated world map that hangs on the wall. For chic merchandise that celebrates ethnic variety, visit Design by Destination.

96 Mill Street, Almonte ON (613) 256-0035

Curiosities

This eclectic antique and collectible shop will satisfy even the most inquisitive shopper. With a wide array of antiques, heirlooms and various historical collectibles, Curiosities has something for every visitor, whether it be old military items, such as bayonets and medals, or aged linens and lace. Upon entering, you might be struck by the amount of merchandise in the store, which comes from years of browsing auction houses and estate sales. In 2003, owners Jack and Marian Elgood and Maureen McPhee and Peter Blenkarn combined their divergent interests to create Curiosities, where visitors can spend countless hours browsing the ever-changing items. Friends and longtime collectors, Jack, Marian, Maureen and Peter joined together and Curiosities soon became the phenomenon it is today. With items ranging from traditional silver tea sets and antique kitchenware and dishes to old cameras, quilts and military uniforms, each item holds a fascinating history behind it. Be sure to check out the books, where tattered covers and yellowed pages tell stories of ages of readers. Take a look at the antique irons and hand-sewn linens to see the handiwork of generations gone by. Stop in today and get lost in the past at Curiosities.

30 Mill Street, Almonte ON (613) 256-7943
www.curiosities.ca

Mrs. McGarrigle's

From its humble beginnings creating mustards, preserves & savouries after hours in an 1830 city jail-turned-youth-hostel, Mrs. McGarrigle's has evolved into a gourmet food, fine kitchenware and home décor retailer. Since it opened in historic Merrickville in 1993 where it occupied 400 square feet, the business has undergone several expansions. It now occupies over 3,000 square feet in a beautiful 1888 general store and includes two floors of upscale home, kitchen and bath décor as well as shelves of ingredients and tools coveted by any cook worth their salt. Testing and tasting is one of Mrs. McGarrigle's distinguishing characteristics. Patrons are greeted by tempting aromas wafting through the store—sometimes the result of delicious demonstrations and sometimes originating from the kitchen where production runs 5 days a week to keep up with the constant demand generated by nearly 300 retail outlets across the country stocking Mrs. McGarrigle's mustards, preserves and condiments. There's always something new cooking at Mrs. McGarrigle's, it's an experience worth the drive; an epicurean destination in the National Capital area and an undeniable lure for those who enjoy fine cooking, fine dining and gourmet living.

311 St. Lawrence Street, Merrickville ON (613) 269-3752 (877) 768-7827
www.mustard.ca

Rideau Creek Landing

You can guess what Lynda Robeson does at her store, Rideau Creek Landing, when she isn't busy with customers. The loom is your clue that the beautiful hand-woven items that you see for sale are made right on the premises. Indeed, guests to historic Merrickville often enter Lynda's shop to find her at work on another gorgeous shawl or jacket. She has been weaving for over 30 years. A little more than a decade ago, she moved her shop into Merrickville from the surrounding countryside, where it had been open for years in a handsome 19th-century farmhouse, and she has loved the pleasant atmosphere of the village ever since. Linda enjoys making home accessories and kitchen items. Her handwoven placemats and table runners are especially popular. Apart from the numerous items crafted personally by Lynda, her shop carries a wide variety of crafts made by countless other artisans from around the world. You will want to drop by and browse through her selection of handmade stained glass table lamps, handmade jewelry from a number of skilled artisans and a wide variety of scented candles. Lynda has participated for years in craft shows across Ontario, though what she loves best is being at her shop, where she can create at her loom and chat with customers. Visit her at Rideau Creek Landing.

230 St. Lawrence Street, Merrickville ON (613) 269-4455

Creative Gifts & Baskets

Mabel Gurnsey, owner of Creative Gifts & Basket, loves helping customers put gift baskets together. With so much in her store from which to choose, you will have no problem filling a basket with the favourite things of the lucky person who will be receiving it, plus a few surprises. From garden décor to gourmet delights, the merchandise at the heart of this shopping experience is wonderfully distinctive. Along with lovely amber and silver jewellery, pick out something nice for yourself from the selection of ladies' clothing, and then browse the baby apparel to find something that will look cute on your latest child or grandchild. Mabel has years of experience performing her specialty of creating gift baskets for all occasions. She started the business by selling gift baskets from her home. Eventually, merchandise began taking over the dining room and family room, so she needed a retail location just so she would have space in her house to live. Mabel thanks her girls for their tireless dedication and help making the store a friendly and helpful environment to visit. The store is located on the shores of Lake Ontario. Drop by Creative Gifts & Baskets and let the shopping excitement begin.

6 Speers Boulevard, Amherstview ON (613) 389-1862

Heritage Point Antiques & Gifts

From the best glass cleaner in the country to a huge selection of Burt's Bees products, Heritage Point Antiques & Gifts represents a little bit of everything. Owners Jo-Ann McGraw and Paul Reinke both attend gift shows to purchase the items sold in their store. Humorous cards and magnets provide fun gifts for friends. Books for the library and a baby corner for the littlest member of the family are only a few of the items they are known for. Jo-Ann loves Angels and Teddy Bears. Candles and antiques lend a cozy air of distinction to any dwelling place. Proceeds from their used books go to the Fairfield-Gutzeit House, and they are involved in the Bath Cancer Walk. The couple reduces the price on approximately 600 store items and donates the proceeds to cancer research. Jo-Ann and Paul also own the Bayshore Bed & Breakfast in town. The B&B is located across from the lake, with two rooms and a honeymoon suite. Guests appreciate the full breakfast and comfortable accommodations. Stay at the Bayshore Bed & Breakfast and then make your way to Heritage Point Antiques & Gifts for a true Bath experience.

384 Main Street, Bath ON (613) 352-9938
www.bbcanada.com/bayshorebb

Seasons' Promise

Owners Leigh Barnum and Susanna Davis merged their individual talents into Seasons' Promise, a gift store and wellness shop that offers meaningful, eco-friendly gifts, health products and advice. Susanna, a registered nurse, heads up Willowood Health in the wellness section of the shop, where you can find a full range of nutritional items and receive personalized health consultations. Leigh runs the gift shop, where visitors can find cards, jewellery, candles and Fair Trade foods. Holistic healers will delight in the healing stones, dream catchers and wish stones. Native American art hangs about the shop and nature lovers will enjoy the vibrantly coloured T-shirts with environmental scenes. The eco-conscious shopper will love the artistically designed Tree-Free Greetings brand cards and gift bags, decorated with art from world-renowned artists and made with a clean, preserved environment in mind. Susanna and Leigh are happy to share in this vision to create a peaceful ambiance where shopping is a nurturing experience. Come to Seasons' Promise and bask in the warm, centered atmosphere where you can find anything from health advice to expressive gifts, clothes and artwork.

1440 Princess Street, Unit 7, Kingston ON (613) 544-5853 or (800) 489-9884
www.seasonspromise.com

Marie's Place Music Emporium

You don't have to go to Los Angeles to find the musical instruments that the stars use. Visit Marie's Place Music Emporium for all the big-name brands as well as a large selection of hard-to-find brands, instruments and accessories. Whether you're a musical genius or new to the world of sound and rhythm, let Marie's Place give you the personalized service that only a small-town music store can offer. Marie's Place is located in Napanee, a town famous for producing musical performers such as the world-wide pop star Avril Lavigne. Avril purchased her first guitar at the Emporium and was often found wandering the isles of Marie's Place. At Marie's Place, you can find the perfect guitar for your first lesson or find a rare collectible Fender for your collection. Either way, owner Brad Wright knows you'll leave the store happy. For the beginner, Marie's Place has a wide array of books to assist you on your musical journey. If you're in need of speedy and efficient instrument repair, Marie's Place repairs all instruments on-site. Find virtually any instrument or learn how to play one when you visit Marie's Place Music Emporium.

62 Dundas Street W, Napanee ON (613) 354-5368
www.mariesplace.ca

Trousdale's General Store, est. 1836

This historic gem, one of Canada's oldest continuously family run general stores, is full of nostalgic charm and contemporary treasures. Ginny and John Trousdale and their children are the fifth and sixth generations to operate Trousdale's General Store, which opened in 1836. Back then, it doubled as a bakery, and you can still see the original horse-drawn bread wagon parked in the back. The store also retains its marble-countertop soda fountain, tin ceiling and creaky wood floors. Vintage products from 1836 mingle with the eclectic assortment of modern merchandise that Ginny hand-picks for the store. You'll find handmade crafts, including quilts and pottery, body care products, toys and jewelry. Practical goods are represented too, including fine foods and kitchenware, men's work wear and garden accessories. The store's 3,000 square feet allow for several distinct departments, including the original apothecary and a delightful selection of vintage candy. It's a charming place to browse by any standards and full of unexpected finds. Even if you're just after an old-fashioned Chocolate Cow, don't miss Trousdale's General Store.

4395 Mill Street, Sydenham ON (613) 376-7622
www.ruralroutes.com/trousdale

Photo by Randy deKleine-Stimpson

Del-Gatto Estates, Bella Vineyards

Del-Gatto Estates, Bella Vineyards offers hand-crafted, distinctive and affordable wines, with a focus on rare varieties such as Geisenheim, Frontenac and Leon Millot. Canada's *Tidings* magazine awarded the winery's Bella Vigne Geisenheim 2005 a score of 89 in a field of wines from all over Canada. In April 2005, the Opimian Society, Canada's largest and oldest wine society, awarded the winery a Silver Medal for its Geisenheim 2004. Winemaking is deep in the heart of owner Pat Del-Gatto, fourth-generation vintner with roots in Italy. In 2002, Pat and Heidi quit their corporate jobs and purchased 74 acres south of Picton. Pat's parents, Giacomo and Maria, are an integral part of the vineyard's success. Giacomo laid out the grid of the vineyard. Both Giacomo and Maria continue to help maintain the vines. The winery building was completed in 2006, with the tasting room and retail shop slated to open in 2009. Until then, Del-Gatto Estates, Bella Vineyards wines are available at Black Prince Winery in Picton. The Del-Gatto family are generous supporters of community theatre and arts groups. You owe it to yourself to try some of Del-Gatto Estates, Bella Vineyards outstanding wines soon.

3633 County Road 8, Cape Vesey ON
(613) 476-7455 *www.del-gattoestates.ca*

Science North in Sudbury

Killarney Provincial Park
Photo by Florin Chelaru

Central and Northern

Canadian Geese
Photo by C. J. Ryan

Touchstone on Lake Muskoka

Touchstone on Lake Muskoka puts the dream of owning a piece of beautiful waterfront property within reach by offering fractional ownership options that let you join with others to buy a beautiful vacation cottage here. You'll pay only an amount proportional to the amount of time you'll spend here each year, splitting the expenses of owning the home with the other owners buying in with you. At Touchstone on Lake Muskoka, your fractional ownership also saves you money on home repairs and maintenance. These three and four-bedroom cottages and villas offer all the luxuries of home, including gourmet kitchens and spacious living areas, plus private hot tubs and amazing views of the lake and forest. You'll enjoy all the amenities of a large resort, gorgeous lakefront acreage, docks, beaches and boating. Head indoors to relax over a fine meal or enjoy time in the spa and fitness center. For a fraction of the normal cost, you can enjoy all the luxury and convenience of your very own vacation home at Touchstone on Lake Muskoka.

1869 Muskoka Road 118 W, Toronto ON (905) 762-0293
www.touchstoneonlakemuskoka.com

Muskoka Gateway Inn

There's a lot more to the Muskoka Gateway Inn than meets the eye as you drive by on Highway 11. This 18-room motel may initially look like any one of the hundreds that line the highways, but if you linger a little, you'll see that there's a lot more to it than that. Prior to purchasing the Muskoka Gateway Inn two years ago, Mark and Lynne MacDonald worked in the construction and medical trades, buying the inn as a way to retire, while still enjoying the opportunity to serve the public. It's that level of customer service that distinguishes the Muskoka Gateway Inn from the rest. The motel is also distinct in that no two rooms are alike. From the flowery Monet Room to the rustic Cowboy Room, each room has its own tasteful décor. Serving everything from an early-morning breakfast to a delicious dinner, the restaurant features delectable food any time of day in a comfortable dining room. Take-out service is also available, and if you don't find your favourite food on the menu, feel free to ask the chef to make it for you. Enjoy the distinctive charm, service and comfort of the Muskoka Gateway Inn.

2408 Highway 11, Gravenhurst ON (705) 687-9511 or (888) 687-9511
www.muskokagatewayinn.ca

All-Season Cottage Rentals

While enjoying the exciting ski slopes or the stunning vistas of Eagle Lake in the hills of Haliburton, stay in a cozy country cottage in the woods. All-Season Cottage Rentals can help you complete your vacation with a warm place to settle in at night. Whether you're looking for a winter weekend stay for snowshoeing at the nearby slopes, or summer hideaway where you can sun yourself on the lakeshore, owner Janice Bishop, a Haliburton local, has the connections to find you the location, style and size cottage to fit your needs. Not only does All-Season Cottage Rentals offer wonderful locations, but a large variety of choices for renters. With a wide array of lakefront estates, quaint homes and cabins, you can experience Ontario's Northwoods in the fashion you're accustomed to. If you're looking for a winter cottage stay, ski chalet, or a quiet winter getaway, Janice knows where it is. You'll know you're getting a real home with all the amenities, too, because all of the cottages, cabins and luxury homes are rented from owners who take pride in their space. Inspected and approved to high standards, you can expect a peaceful stay with All-Season Cottage Rentals.

Haliburton ON (705) 754-1506
www.haliburtoncottages.com

Cranberry Cove Muskoka

Bala is known as the cranberry capital of Ontario, so Cranberry Cove resort and spa is aptly named for its location. The resort and spa are on 43 acres in Bala, overlooking Sunset Bay and Lake Muskoka. Cranberry Cove offers spa services, yoga classes, fitness facilities, meeting space and an array of recreational activities. Upon arrival at the spa, a Holistic Health Care Practitioner will work with you to personally tailor your spa experience. Treatments, workshops and classes, including seven kinds of yoga, allow you to focus on particular issues or general fitness. Specialized packages emphasize Holistic Anti-Aging, Rest & Rejuvenation or Healing & Transformation. The resort provides a spectacular setting for events, with a reception room that looks out on gardens, a waterfall and a pond. With award-winning catering, Cranberry Cove can wine and dine up to 100 guests. Corporate retreats will benefit from the on-site business centre with audio-visual services. Suites, treetop cottages and an executive townhouse provide restful retreats for parties of two to eight. Activities are abundant, including indoor and outdoor pools, a paved roller blade track, a 9-hole executive challenge mini-golf course and numerous game courts. You can hike local nature trails, canoe on the lagoon or ice-skate on the marsh in the winter. Plan your next event or spa retreat at Cranberry Cove Muskoka, voted Best Accommodations in Bala by *The Muskoken*.

3571 Muskoka Road, Bala ON
(705) 762-5501
www.cranberrycove.net

Best Western Great Northern Resort and Conference Centre

Planning a wedding, a business conference or a family getaway in Sault Ste. Marie? Best Western Great Northern Resort and Conference Centre knows how to meet your needs with 212 guest rooms and suites, many on-site recreation opportunities and the largest conference and meeting facility in Northern Ontario. Along with standard guest rooms, the resort offers family suites with bunk beds, business-class rooms with king-size beds and specialty rooms with private whirlpools or wheelchair access. The newly renovated Skyline Suite gives occupants a panoramic view. Your pets are welcome in selected rooms. Groups enjoy theatre-style seating for 1,400 or a banquet setting for 800 along with nine private meeting rooms and an exceptional catering staff. You will find casual comfort and pleasurable meal choices without leaving the hotel at Dixon's Restaurant, while the lobby lounge invites socializing. You can opt for room service, take advantage of wireless Internet access and take advantage of a shuttle to the airport or casino. Kids not only stay free, but their dreams come true with indoor and outdoor swimming pools and a five-and-a-half storey indoor water slide. The entire family will appreciate the 24-lane bowling centre. A sauna and the services of Greenhouse Day Spa will ease stress, while the fitness centre lets you continue your workout routine. It's not far to golf, skiing, museums, shopping and tours of locks or the Agawa Canyon train. Find your personal answer for relaxation and entertainment at Best Western Great Northern Resort and Conference Centre.

229 Great Northern Road, Sault Ste. Marie ON
(705) 942-2500 or (800) 563-7262
www.bestwesternsault.com

Sir Sam's Inn & WaterSpa

Sir Sam's Inn & WaterSpa offers luxury, plus the benefits of an outdoor experience. With an outstanding chef on-site, you may dine on elk, salmon or venison and then enjoy a dip in the mineral pool before heading to your suite or chalet to watch the flames dancing in the fireplace. Most accommodations have Jacuzzi tubs as well. Daylight brings with it the opportunity for water sports on the lake just outside your door, plus hiking and mountain biking. There are ski slopes adjacent to the inn, and your choice of dogsled or snowmobile tours for some winter fun. Wedding facilities are also available. Sir Sam's Inn & WaterSpa is open throughout the year, so you can enjoy all of the seasons in a perfect blend of adventure and comfort. The story leading up to the inn starts with a famous Canadian. Sir Samuel Hughes was the decorated government minister who led Canada's military through WWI. In 1919, he chose a site deep in the woods to build his retreat. Two years later, he passed away. In 1930, the inn became the Glen Eagle Fishing Lodge. After a later period of latency, the inn finally became Sir Sam's Inn & WaterSpa. This transformation provides a generous degree of enjoyment for the community and the public at large. Whatever else he did in history, you must give him credit for this: Sir Hughes picked an excellent location for Sir Sam's Inn & WaterSpa.

1491 Sir Sam's Road, Eagle Lake ON (800) 361-2188 *www.sirsamsinn.com*

Auberge Du Village Bed and Breakfast

In the heart of Sudbury, Auberge du Village Bed & Breakfast occupies a charmingly restored building on Durham Street. Accommodations include two elegantly inspired suites for a romantic getaway or to add comfort and convenience to a business trip. Each suite has its own private floor, the Bordelais occupying the second floor and the Campagne taking the third floor.

A complimentary freshly baked baguette, a selection of fruit and cheeses and a bottle of wine are placed in the room to greet you upon arrival. Each morning, a deluxe continental breakfast is brought to your suite. The suites are designed with an eclectic mix of bistro and Old World charm. Each suite includes a luxurious king-sized bed, romantic fireplace and a kitchen with microwave and refrigerator. The rooms are beautifully decorated and feel like a home. Elegant dishes and stemware are provided in the room, as is high-speed Internet and access to cable television. There is an in-room ironing board, iron and hair dryer, making it easy to look as if you were never travelling at all. Down the stairs from the suite, La Boulangerie du Village artisan bakery and deli serves freshly baked artisan bread, soups, sandwiches and desserts. The bed-and-breakfast is close to Science North, Dynamic Earth, downtown, art galleries and the theatre. These are just a few reasons you will want to make the Auberge Du Village your home-away-from-home each time you are in Sudbury.

104 Durham Street, Sudbury ON
(705) 675-7732 or (888) 675-7732
www.aubergesudbury.com

Bonnie View Inn

The Bonnie View Inn opened in 1924 with three quaint cottages and the same warm, peaceful atmosphere that it has today. Now with eight cottages and an elegant main building with six rooms, the inn offers an upscale retreat perfect for a romantic getaway, a business conference or even a classy wedding. Owners Andrea Hagarty and Monte Miscio are proud to offer a refined haven along the pristine shores of Lake Kashagawigamog. With tranquil surroundings and a number of seasonal activities, there's something for every visitor. Summer guests can enjoy sun-bathing on the sandy beach, swimming or sailing, boating, waterskiing and fishing on the lake, while the scenic winter grounds are perfect for ice skating, tobogganing and skiing. The inn also rents out snowmobiles and cross country skis so you can hit the trails. Adventure seekers will want to check out the nearby dog sled tours, where they can take anything from a quick two-hour tour to a mystical moonlit run. Golf fans will appreciate the five nearby courses as well as the driving range. If you're visiting to soak up the serenity, be sure to check out the spa, where you can get pampered to your heart's content. In addition, all your meals are included with your accommodations. Enjoy chef Monte's hearty breakfasts and delicious entrées. Whether you're staying in one of the private lakefront cottages or in the welcoming main house, you'll savour every moment at the Bonnie View Inn.

2713 Kashagawigamog Lake Road, Haliburton ON
(705) 457-2350 or (800) 461-0347
www.bonnieviewinn.com

Holiday Inn Sudbury

Conveniently located near the business and production centers of the city, as well as many fun and educational facilities, the Holiday Inn Sudbury is the city's new landmark for hospitality. Recently renovated, the hotel is an ideal place for business and social events, especially weddings. The hotel's experienced wedding planners can create the dream wedding you've always wanted. Planners can also assist you in planning a successful business event. Holiday Inn Sudbury offers a variety of room configurations for vacationers and business travellers. Whether you're looking for a conventional room, a business-class room or a luxurious suite, you'll find it here. Guests receive a variety of amenities including duvets and feather pillows, free wireless high-speed Internet access and a free morning newspaper. Enjoy a brisk workout in the hotel's fitness and exercise room, followed up with a swim in the spacious indoor pool. Treat yourself to a delicious meal at the hotel's elegant restaurant. Other business traveler features include free printing and e-mail service, as well as expansive meeting rooms and equipment, plus free parking for your clients and customers. Whether you're traveling for business or pleasure, you'll feel right at home at Holiday Inn Sudbury.

1696 Regent Street, Sudbury ON
(800) 465-4329
www.hisudbury.ca

Stouffer Mill
Bed & Breakfast Getaway

Repeat guests at the Stouffer Mill Bed & Breakfast Getaway have something in common with the migratory birds at the nearby Haliburton Forest and Wildlife Reserve: they keep coming back to a beautiful place. Nature lovers are particularly drawn to this 12-sided circular home, using it as a base camp for forays into the wildlife preserve and Algonquin Park. There's wildlife viewing a-plenty right on the 130-acre property, much of it centered around the 10-acre active beaver pond. To encourage guests to roam the forested estate, hosts Don and Jessie Pflug provide complimentary walking sticks, maps and snowshoes. Their home sits atop a hill, and the panoramic view from the rooftop solarium with hot tub is spectacular. Featured in *Canadian Homes & Cottages* magazine, Stouffer Mill offers three guest rooms, all with a private bath and deck. Enjoy a refreshing swim in the pool, and then relax in the deck chairs while your steaks are sizzling on the barbecue that all guests are welcome to use. Fireplaces cast a mellow glow on the main level and upper levels, while keeping the place cozy when it's cold outside. Days begin with a four-course gourmet breakfast. Escape again and again to Stouffer Mill Bed & Breakfast Getaway.

17359 Highway 35, Minden ON
(705) 489-3024 or (888) 593-8888
www.stouffermill.com

Sudbury Association of Bed & Breakfasts

The Sudbury Association of Bed & Breakfasts represents seven of the finest year-round bed-and-breakfasts in Sudbury. Members adhere to the highest standards of cleanliness, comfort and amenities. You'll find a variety of lovely settings, including lake shore locations and breathtaking gardens, and amenities that include hot tubs and spas. Great packages range from romantic getaways to wedding events. All facilities afford easy access to the Science North and Dynamic Earth, summer festivals and autumn's Cinefest, as well as to other exciting festivals offered throughout the year. Visitors marvel at the array of tourist activities, the crystal-clear lakes and the fascinating nature trails just a step away. With cruises, sailing, windsurfing, fishing and swimming on Lake Ramsey, 23 area golf courses and five boating and flying clubs, Sudbury is an exciting destination. Skiing, snowmobiling and snowshoeing are popular winter activities. Skate on a groomed one-kilometre skating track. Take in a symphony or enjoy one of five museums, theatre group productions and art galleries. Browse the fine shops. For information and reservations, contact these top-flight bed and breakfasts directly. Make Sudbury your next vacation destination.

A1 South Bay Guesthouse B & B: (877) 656-8324
Amy on the Lake B & B: (705) 677-0295
Artisan Upstairs Guesthouse: (705) 674-4387
Auberge-Sur-Lac B & B: (888) 535-6727
Fenton's B & B (in Lively): (866) 613-8582
Millwood B & B: (866) 307-7702
Sudbury South Suites Plus B & B: (866) 523-0511
www.bbcanada.com/associations/sudbury

Clevelands House

Standing proudly along the Lake Rosseau shoreline, Clevelands House is a grand old-fashioned family resort. The resort offers a variety of accommodations, including terrace and woodside suites, cottages and rooms in its lodges and main hotel. Brightly colored Muskoka chairs sit in a row along the beach, inviting you to relax between rounds of fun on the lake. Paddle boat, canoe and kayak rentals are available. The grounds feature everything from golf and tennis to the one-acre Cleve's Playworld for the kids, guaranteeing that you won't run out of things to do. A restaurant and live entertainment complete the experience. Founded in 1874 as a single guest room in the home of Charles and Fanny Minett, Clevelands House grew to become one of Canada's largest owner-operated resorts. Under ownership of the Cornell family, the resort has tripled in size and added many of its star attractions, including a nine-hole golf course, 16 tennis courts and four swimming pools. Bob Cornell began as a bellhop at Clevelands House in 1949 and worked his way up to manager. Along the way, he fell in love with dining room server Fran Lees, whom he married in 1958. In 1969, Bob and Fran became owners of the resort. Their children and their children's spouses have played key roles at Clevelands House through the years. Look to Clevelands House for good times on Lake Rosseau.

100 Main Street, Minett ON
(705) 765-3171
www.clevelandshouse.com

Sunset over Lake Simcoe
Photo by cadmanof50s

The Inn at Christie's Mill

The German count, Graf Von Goertz, wasted no time in putting his mark upon the Inn at Christie Mill when he bought it in 2002. An entire new wing with 15 deluxe suites, called the Count's Wing, was added, as were the 7,000-square-foot Avalon spa and a meeting room. Experience classic luxury by staying in the Count's Suite, decorated with the owner's private furniture, dating back to 1830. The spa offers a blend of therapies, combining the traditional with trendsetting wellness techniques from around the world. Take a rejuvenating dip in the indoor salt-water mineral pool. A place where sophisticated ambience meets country hospitality, the inn is a picturesque Lake Country destination, ringed by water and granite outcrops. The surroundings are spectacular in all four seasons and can be savored as you dine at Twigs, the inn's lakefront dining room that looks out upon the lovely scenery. The suites in both wings of the inn are elegantly appointed and include a fireplace. Some suites boast a whirlpool bath and patio overlooking the Trent-Severn Waterway. The site of the Inn at Christie's Mill has seen much change since 1830, when the first sawmill on the Severn River was built here. The mill was destroyed by fire in 1869, rebuilt and then destroyed by fire a second time in 1896. Serving as a campground for fishermen next, the land was not developed again until 1920, when a lodge was built. Consider the Inn at Christie's Mill for a romantic getaway amid nature's splendor.

263 Port Severn Road N, Port Severn ON
(705) 538-2354 or (800) 465-9966
www.christiesmill.com

Oakview Lodge & Marina

How many country getaways come with a gourmet restaurant attached? At Oakview Lodge & Marina, you can wake to a tranquil morning on Little Hawk Lake, spend the afternoon boating and then dine in the evening at Krenar's Vineyard, the domain of Chef Krenar Kulla. He flashes Mediterranean and Asian influences in his superb dishes, all of them lovingly prepared from the freshest ingredients. Various meal

plans are available for guests who stay at the lodge, which offers six romantic suites, all with private baths, as well as a two-bedroom luxury cottage called the Loon's Nest. You'll enjoy warming yourself by the fireplace, watching satellite television and enjoying a spectacular view of the lake. A sandy beach invites guests to while away the hours reading a good book and gazing at the scenery. Boat and canoe rentals are available. Open year-round, the inn is popular with snowmobilers and Nordic skiers in winter. Valerie Kulla manages Oakview, while her husband prepares the exquisite meals. Which will you consider the main attraction, the food or the beautiful setting in the heart of the Haliburton Highlands? Enjoy fine dining in a casual cottage atmosphere at Oakview Lodge & Marina.

2029 Little Hawk Lake Road (County Road 13), Minden ON
(705) 489-2463 or (866) 292-6125
www.oakviewlodge.com

Severn Lodge

In the early days of Severn Lodge, guests slept on cots in canvas tents or treated themselves to the deluxe comfort of a bed in a room with a pitcher and a bowl for washing. The demands of vacationers have grown steadily since the 1920s, and the Severn Lodge has kept pace, though it has never had to add lavish attractions to draw guests. The natural beauty of its setting was, and always will be, its best selling point. The

lodge is nestled on the northern shores of Gloucester Pool, part of the historic Trent Severn Waterway in the famous Muskoka-Georgian Bay lake district. It is situated on more than 2,000 feet of private shoreline surrounded by hundreds of acres of pristine woodlands. Enjoy a breathtaking view of pine-clad islands and sheltered bays as you sit back in your deck chair. Fishing, waterskiing and hiking are just some of the activities that may get you out of your seat. A cruise on the lake in the resort's 1922 mahogany motor launch is always fun. The main lodge and several out buildings—all made of clapboard and sporting white paint and red roofs—form a pretty campus, complete with an outdoor heated swimming pool, cobblestone sidewalks and boat docks. The Breckbill family has run the lodge since 1936. Come join current owners Rick and Sue Breckbill, along with Rick's brother, Ron, and their families for a vacation amid the classic ambience of the Severn Lodge.

116 Gloucester Trail, Port Severn ON
(705) 756-2722 or (800) 461-5817
www.severnlodge.on.ca

Parker House Inn & Restaurant

The Parker House Inn & Restaurant, a Sudbury institution, is housed in two impeccably restored estate homes. Seven rooms, including three suites, are tastefully furnished with lovely antiques plus all the modern amenities. All rooms provide air conditioning, cable television, VCR, telephone, high-speed wireless Internet access and en suite bathrooms. You'll enjoy a comfortable sleep on beds of superior quality. Suites variously feature gas fireplaces, Jacuzzis, Provencal linens and fully-equipped kitchenettes. Relax with a rejuvenating massage or spa treatment. The informal, warm and upscale décor is inviting and comfortable. Choose from six dining areas, designed to suit your mood. Browse the inn's library of daily periodicals. The inn's European-style café provides a casual, bistro-style atmosphere for breakfast, lunch or dinner. All dishes are prepared from scratch with fresh, local ingredients. Even the coffee is roasted on-site—the café is famous for its coffee and scrumptious desserts. You can host cozy parties, meetings or weddings in the inn's two banquet rooms, which accommodate groups of up to 20. Catering services are also available. When visiting Sudbury, make the Parker House Inn & Restaurant your home away from home.

259 Elm Street, Sudbury ON
(705) 674-2442 or (888) 250-4453
www.parkerhouseinns.com

Rawley Resort

The lighthouse-type tower at the end of the building beckons the mariner and landlubber alike to come and experience the comfortable luxury of the Rawley Resort. Getting onto Georgian Bay is easy from the nearby launch ramp, while a sandy beach affords guests with opportunities for splashing in the water, sunning and building sand castles. Whether you choose to stay in a suite or loft, a full breakfast, complimentary evening hors d'oeuvres and use of the outdoor heated pool are yours. All suites are one bedroom with living room and dining areas. Rich in warmth, the rooms feature fireplaces, French doors and fine furnishings. The oversized balconies are perfect for relaxing and taking in the waterside views and the beautiful sunsets. The marble bathrooms with large glass showers and rainforest shower heads spell luxury. Some include whirlpool baths. The Waterside Lofts are two storeys with one bedroom and two bathrooms. They boast the best water views in the resort and have the advantage of a first-floor private deck and a second-floor balcony overlooking the water and dock. Guests are entertained by cooking demonstrations and wine and scotch tasting events. In addition, the staff can customize and arrange a package to include anything from golf and fishing to casino gaming and sightseeing by helicopter. Sit back by the waterside or on the balcony at the Rawley Resort and take a breath of fresh Georgian Bay air.

2900 Kellys Road, Port Severn ON
(705) 538-2272
www.rawleylodge.on.ca

40 Bay Street Bed & Breakfast

Each room at 40 Bay Street Bed & Breakfast offers another reason to plan a visit to this century-old home on Parry Sound's waterfront. Susan Poole and her son, chef Simon Poole, opened the bed-and-breakfast in 2006 with your comfort in mind. All rooms are air-conditioned, have king or queen-sized beds, en-suite baths, and access to two cozy sun porches, a guest refrigerator and wireless Internet. Susan assures a good night's sleep with a pillow collection that covers every sleeper's need. Each guest room offers a memorable feature that sets it apart from other rooms. The Bay Room treats you to views of the waterfront and the Georgian Bay, while the Garden Room offers a sun-drenched private deck. For a visit with a spa-like feeling, consider the Retreat Room with a two-person shower that contains a rain head and body jets. Chef Simon's breakfasts would be reason enough to stay in this lovely home. His professional training and dedication to fresh organic ingredients and Fair Trade products show in everything from the coffee to such house specialties as cheddar and chive scrambled eggs, French toast with maple syrup and smoked salmon with brie quiche. Come feast your senses at 40 Bay Street Bed & Breakfast.

40 Bay Street, Parry Sound ON   **(705) 746-9247 or (866) 371-2638**   *www.parrysoundbedandbreakfast.com*

Sir Sam's Ski/Snowboard Area

Nestled in the highlands of Haliburton is a gem of a ski and snowboard resort called Sir Sam's Ski/Snowboard Area, located just two-and-a-half hours northeast of Toronto. Since 1965, this family run business has offered a first-class getaway for the outdoor enthusiast. Experience great snow conditions, a variety of challenging runs from beginner to expert, and fantastic panoramic views. Let the friendly and courteous staff look after your needs whether you require rental equipment, ski lessons or food and beverage service. Twelve main ski runs and six lifts guarantee no waiting to experience the fresh powder. This resort has something for every skier, from the daring expert to the shaky toddler. With breathtaking vistas of the countryside and lake from the tops of the hills to the gentle, tree-lined slopes of the beginners runs, you're sure to enjoy every moment. If you'd prefer to take it slower, Sir Sam's provides snowshoeing trails and equipment. Trek through the scenic snow-covered hills and breathe in the fresh crisp air. After a day of snow-romping, cutting it up with your snowboard or swishing through the evergreens on skis, enjoy a warm welcome back to the chalet where you can sip hot cocoa and watch the sunset from the picture window. It's hard to find a place where you can feel the rush of adrenaline and the calm of nature together. Visit Sir Sam's Ski/Snowboard Area to take it all in while you cruise it, carve it, climb it and love it.

1054 Liswood Road, Eagle Lake ON
(705) 754-2298
www.sirsams.com

Bala's Museum

Lucy Maud Montgomery, the cherished author of the Anne of Green Gables stories, based one of her best books, *The Blue Castle*, on a holiday she spent in Bala. Fans of the author can explore her life and work at Bala's Museum, inside the restored Victorian house where Montgomery spent that holiday. Owners Jack and Linda Hutton have gathered together a collection of her books, including first editions of each of the Anne books, and many other artifacts and memorabilia pertaining to Montgomery. The gift shop has hard-to-find editions of L.M. Montgomery books, Anne movies, toys and Green Gables china. Children can choose their own Avonlea costumes to wear during their visit to the museum. There is an old-fashioned lawn party in the summer to re-enact Montgomery's arrival to Bala, complete with music, free popcorn and skits. The museum also hosts other events of interest, such as the historical display by Ontario artist Nancy M. Green that chronicles *The Forgotten War Effort: Knitting*. Owner Jack, an international rag-time pianist, often entertains visitors with a sing-along. Those who know the Anne stories will find this ode to Montgomery's world irresistible. Those who have not yet been introduced will find Bala's Museum a fine place to start.

1024 Maple Avenue, Bala ON (705) 762-5876
www.bala.net/museum

Muskoka Lakes Museum

Marion Catto had a dream of opening a pioneer museum in Port Carling, an enjoyable and informative tourist attraction that would serve the community and preserve the area's history. In 1961, the Port Carling Historical Society commenced at Catto's cottage on the Indian River. Plans progressed until, in 1967, Catto cut the ribbon for the grand opening of the Muskoka Lakes Museum on Island Park. The Muskoka Lakes Museum offers a fascinating look at the cultural history of the region. You'll see an 1875 log cabin filled with period artifacts of the pioneer life. The Marine Room chronicles the rich marine heritage of the Muskoka Lakes region through a history of the regional wooden boat building industry. Other exhibits feature Indian artifacts and Victorian furnishings. The Catto Art Gallery represents local artists, landscapes, flora and fauna. You'll have fun browsing the gift shop for Victorian-themed keepsakes such as tea sets, nightgowns, boat clothing and pioneer children's toys, as well as Inukshuk giftware. Guided and self-guided tours of the museum are free during the open season, which lasts from May through October. Check the website for periodic events that may coincide with your visit.

100 Joseph Street, Port Carling ON (705) 765-5367
www.muskoka.com/tourism/mlm

Sudbury School of Dance

It's called the Sudbury School of Dance, but many Sudbury residents know it as the Home of the Earthdancers. Since 1990, the Earthdancers have promoted environmental awareness in the community and have raised funds for local, national and international environmental causes through benefit dance performances. Folks in the area are rightly proud of this group of young dancers for winning an Ontario Youth Achievement Award from Osprey Media. Denise Vitali runs the facility, where children from ages six and up learn to express themselves through movement, while doing important work for Mother Nature. Overall the school has been operating since 1986. Watch your child develop into a confident and graceful Earthdancer at the Sudbury School of Dance.

165 Pine Street, Sudbury ON (705) 674-0190

Charles W. Stockey
Centre for the Performing Arts
& Bobby Orr Hall of Fame

For three weeks every summer, some of the loveliest music ever composed floats to the rafters at the Charles W. Stockey Centre for the Performing Arts. Connoisseurs of chamber music flock to this building in the heart of Parry Sound's waterfront district for the world-renowned Festival of Sound. With its rich acoustics, the intimate 480-seat auditorium is beloved by fans and performers alike. The festival is the highlight of a diverse schedule of year-round entertainment. Part of the centre is a hockey museum dedicated to Parry Sound's favourite son, Bobby Orr, who starred for the Boston Bruins. The Orr family has handed over a large collection of memorabilia for display at the Bobby Orr Hall of Fame. The facility celebrates the achievements of this legendary athlete using the latest interactive technologies. The complex that houses the museum and performance hall incorporates two reception rooms, a fully equipped state-of-the-art kitchen, dressing rooms and a bay-side outdoor performance desk. The auditorium can be configured for raked seating or flat floor for receptions, weddings and conferences. To reflect the natural beauty of the area, the building was designed to resemble a Georgian Bay cottage. Beams from indigenous pine and granite from the local quarry add a special intimacy to the interior of the concert hall. Enjoy heavenly music at the Stockey Centre and celebrate one of hockey's greatest at the Bobby Orr Hall of Fame.

2 Bay Street, Parry Sound ON (705) 746-4466 or (877) 746-4466 *www.stockeycentre.com*

Haliburton Forest & Wildlife Reserve

There are so many things to see and do at the Haliburton Forest & Wildlife Reserve that the hardest part of a visit is deciding which one to do first. The beautiful reserve was purchased from a German baron, who kept it for a year before selling it to Adolf Schleifenbaum. Adolf's son, Peter, and his family are the proprietors today. The reserve preserves a wildlife habitat, including wolves. The Wolf Centre, located on-site, is a wolf museum that celebrates and sheds light on these magnificent creatures. The multi-use forest also shelters a recreational and educational research facility. Things to do include dog sledding, cross-country mountain biking and the Walk in the Clouds rope trail. The rope trail leads to a landing high in the trees, a truly inspiring destination for a picnic lunch. A restaurant, visitor's centre and Heritage Museum are also located on the property. Haliburton Forest is a snowmobiling wonderland and you don't have to worry about whether it has snow or not. The Schleifenbaums have developed their own impressive snow-making equipment, revolutionizing snowmobile adventures with better, consistent snow conditions. The Schleifenbaums also build and sell eco-friendlly log homes using locally grown wood. Choose the service or activity that appeals to you most, and unwind at the Haliburton Forest & Wildlife Reserve.

1095 Redken Drive, Haliburton ON
(705) 754-2198
www.haliburtonforest.com

Medeba

Outdoor adventures build leadership skills, a strong set of values, and change peoples lives—important reasons why Medeba has offered specialized adventure programs with a Christian perspective for more than 50 years. This non-profit ministry, located in a near wilderness setting in the beautiful Haliburton Highlands, uses adventure programming and activities to challenge and encourage young people. Medeba boasts of adventure activities such as white-water kayaking, ice and rock climbing, ropes courses, a double giant swing and a double 700-foot zip line to name a few. Programs designed to provide learning and growth, meet rigid safety standards and continue a tradition started by founders Stu and Jackie Wilson in 1952. Medeba offers summer camps and outdoor education programs that welcome everyone. Many Christian church retreats take place on the grounds along with gatherings of clubs involved in outdoor adventure activities. You won't have to stay in a tent at Medeba, because the sprawling campground on 200 acres can house up to 170 guests in year-round cabins, accompanied by a dining hall, several meeting rooms, and many other program buildings. Medeba also has a vision to develop authentic Christian leaders through its 10-month Leadership Development Program where participants are inspired to develop lives of adventure and faith while acquiring transferable leadership skills. Medeba has also won an award as one of the best Christian workplaces in Canada. Engage in life-changing programs at Medeba!

Box 138, West Guilford ON (705) 754-2444 or (800) 461-6523 *www.medeba.com*

Don's Bakery

Since 1947, Don's Bakery has been the only bakery in Bala. It is the only one the town has ever needed. One fine day, Allison Davidson got a job at Don's, and she never left. Allison and her husband, Ross, have owned the bakery since 1979, changing the location only once, in 1997. Don's makes rich fudge brownies, delicate puff pastries, date squares and cinnamon buns, as well as fresh bread, but it is its scones that are its towering triumph. No one has been able to reproduce them, and they are notoriously big-sellers. Don's also capitalizes on Bala's magnificent cranberry product with delicious cranberry brie puffs, loaves and muffins. The bakery makes everything from scratch, weighing, blending and baking on the premises. If you call ahead the day before, Don's will have your specialty order waiting for you when you stop by. Don't miss Don's Bakery, a long-term neighbor to the Mill Stream Deli & Café.

3119 Muskoka Road N-169, Bala ON (705) 762-3937
www.donsbakery.on.ca

The Blue Willow Tea Shop

Located near the sparkling waters of Lake Muskoka, the Blue Willow Tea Shop offers a relaxing place to enjoy a cup of steaming tea and the breathtaking views of the rocky shore and distant islands. After immigrating from England, owner Sue Barrett opened the Blue Willow Tea Shop with a desire to bring the fine teas and flavours of Europe to this artistic town. With selections of black, green, white and herbal teas served in ceramic blue willow tea pots, the shop has become a popular destination for tea lovers and sightseers alike. The aromatic Earl Grey and smoky Lapsong Souchong are two favourites among the black teas, while the antioxidants in the tangy green teas give a healthful kick. The flavourful herbal teas, such as the cranberry apple, are naturally soothing, and can warm even the chilliest customer. First-time visitors can enjoy Sue's entertaining tea presentations, which tell the history and culture of tea. Afterwards, listeners are invited to an informal tea-tasting and afternoon tea. Finish off with a sandwich or a delicious cake, or stay for one of Blue Willow's dinner nights. Make your next stop the Blue Willow Tea Shop and taste the comforting effects of tea for yourself.

900 Bay Street, Unit 2, Gravenhurst ON (705) 687-2597
www.bluewillowteashop.ca

Bill Hill's Ice Cream Shoppe

Travel 13 kilometres to the end of Honey Harbour Road and you will find an old-fashioned ice cream shop right out of a storybook. Bill Hill's Ice Cream Shoppe dates back to 1947, when Bill, a small-town grocer, founded it on the shores of Lake Ontario in Bronte Harbour. His granddaughter, Suzy Pallo, inherited the shop in 2001. By then, Bronte Harbour was no longer the close-knit fishing village it had once been. Suzy decided to move the store north in order to preserve its original spirit as a community gathering place. "Honey Harbour has all the feelings of a small-town atmosphere an ice cream shop needs to survive," Suzy found. The friendly townspeople welcomed her with open arms. Many of them remembered the well-loved grocer, Bill Hill, who believed in giving every kid in the neighborhood a job. "We found a place with fresh air, where kids still swim in the lake, and great-grandchildren are doing much of the scooping," Suzy says. "I know Bill Hill would approve!" Enjoy the outdoor patio, homemade waffle cones and 25 flavours of ice cream at Bill Hill's Ice Cream Shoppe.

2636 Honey Harbour Road, Honey Harbour ON (705) 756-5051

Muskoka Roastery Coffee Co.

Douglas Snell's great-grandfather was a Muskoka pioneer who worked the rugged land to make a life for himself and his family. As the first coffee roaster in the region, Douglas has inherited that pioneering spirit. He and his wife, Patricia, own Muskoka Roastery Coffee Co. and Seven Main Café in downtown Huntsville, Ontario. Starting with the highest quality Arabica coffee beans, Doug then developed a unique line of distinctly Canadian blends. To name but a few, try the bestselling Muskoka Maple, which features the truly Canadian taste of Maple or the Black Bear Roast, a full bodied dark roast, a taste with a growl! Everything that Muskoka Roastery Coffee Co. produces tastes great in the wilderness. See for yourself by brewing a pot of the Lumberjack over a campfire in the heart of Algonquin Park, or take a cup of the Howling Wolf out to the deck of your lakeside cottage. At Seven Main Café, in downtown Huntsville, you can sip your coffee while munching on a delicious dessert. This café sells all 22 of the famous Muskoka Roastery Coffee roasts and blends by the bag and by the cup! Muskoka Roastery Coffee can be found in many grocery stores and gift stores throughout Ontario. True to their Muskoka heritage, the company continues to roast and hand-package to order. Inhale the aroma of coffee from Muskoka Roastery Coffee Co. Taste the spirit of the wilderness in every sip.

7 Main Street W, Huntsville ON
(705) 789-9592 or (866) 521-9592
www.muskokaroastery.com

Carissa's Ladies Wear

Carissa's Ladies Wear is a quaint boutique in Downtown Sudbury where service is the key to the shop's 25 years of success. The owner is Gale Prosperi and since the shop opened, her vision of dressing sophisticated women who need a put-together look from head to toe has become a thriving reality. Gale named the store after her daughter and believes that the personal touches make all the difference. Competing with the big chains is not easy, but with her consistent professional staff and personal service, her loyal customers have been shopping here since the doors first opened. A hands-on owner, Gale does all the buying herself, supporting local designers and importing specialty lines from Canada, Italy, Germany and Holland to name a few, in order to have a unique blend of versatile style for all women. Carissa's Ladies Wear also tries to give back to the community and contributes to Sudbury's growing downtown culture. Fundraising, events and community involvement have always been a part of the stores agenda. If you are looking for a dynamic, unique and most of all personal shopping experience, come to Carissa's.

125 Durham Street, Sudbury ON
(705) 671-9756

Shine Jewellery & Accessories

Owner Kelly McBride knows how to get the attention of Bracebridge shoppers—she changes her window display at Shine Jewellery & Accessories every two weeks, luring you inside to take a look at the new items she has added to the inventory. Beyond a large jewellery collection, expect to see many Canadian handicrafts. You might find a purse, baby clothing or a gift for a young child. The inviting space uses chandeliers, wood flooring and exposed brick from the original building for a pleasant shopping environment. Goods sit in glass wall cabinets, and a large jewellery display case dominates the centre of the floor. Kelly opened the Bracebridge shop in 2006 when her jewellery making hobby outgrew her dining room table. Her creativity also extends to photography, and she specializes in photographing people. Her creative photos of families, weddings, children and pregnant mothers won her Best Photographer awards in 2006 and 2007 from *Muskoka Magazine* and a 2006 award from the *Bracebridge Examiner*. Not only does Kelly keep shoppers in the Bracebridge shopping district on their toes, she offers a second store on Main Street in Huntsville. For enjoyable shopping and a constant influx of new merchandise, visit Shine Jewellery & Accessories.

15 Manitoba Street, Bracebridge ON
(705) 645-9700

Country Pickin's

In 2007, Laurie and Rennie Bonfield celebrated the 25th year of business for their shop, Country Pickin's. Laurie lived in this very building until she was eight years old. After she moved away, it went through many transformations, including a boarding house and antique store, but when she bought it and moved it down the street, everything came together. The Bonfields expanded the rear of the house and stocked it with gifts and brand-name clothing. It sparkles with country charm through the large pane-glass windows. There is a beautiful view of the lake from the rear windows. Among the women's fashions, you will find Not Your Daughter's Jeans, as seen on Oprah. There is a generous selection of sizes and styles, plus accessories to finish your look, including hats, shoes and jewellery, and a section for men, too. If you are planning a vacation, stop at Country Pickin's first, because it carries sandals, cruise-wear and swim suits all year for just such an event. Half of every dollar spent on FDJ French Dressing jeans is donated to a worthy cause. On top of all of this, Country Pickin's has some great gift ideas. Next time your in Haliburton, visit Country Pickin's.

163 Highland Street, Haliburton ON (705) 457-2726

Reg Wilkinson Men's Fine Clothing

Upon entering Reg Wilkinson Men's Fine Clothing, customers find soft music and a vintage atmosphere that takes them back to an era when business success was based on quality products and personal service. At this family-owned Sudbury store, the old-fashioned values remain, while the clothing lines keep up with current styles. The shop's collection changes every six months and includes everything from smart casual to custom-made suits in hundreds of imported fabric options. The shoe selection will please your boss or the woman in your life. Reg Wilkinson opened the store in 1948 as the culmination of a career in the retail clothing business. As the youngest of 12 children, he had worn more than his share of hand-me-downs and vowed "only the finest would be sold." In 1962, his son Bob joined the enterprise and helped keep it in touch with modern trends. In 1994, Reg's grandson Todd joined the firm after graduating from Laurentian University and working for six years as a manufacturer's representative. He is the third generation of Wilkinsons at the store. For old-fashioned quality in modern men's apparel, visit Reg Wilkinson Men's Fine Clothing.

118 Durham Street, Sudbury ON (705) 675-6710
www.regwilkinson.ca

My Size

After years of trading fashion tips and shopping for clothes together, Shirley Kuni and her daughter, Kim Russell, are now teaming up to help other ladies have fun with clothes. Open since 2003, My Size carries up-to-date styles for women sizes six to 28. The selection includes funky jeans and perky tops, as well formal dresses and sporty swimsuits. Both owners do the buying, supporting Canadian designers as much as possible. "Minden really needed a store with this concept," say Kim and Shirley, who measure success not by how many things they sell, but by how many women they help look good and feel good about themselves. The owners take the time to help customers put an outfit together. They have moccasins to go with that smart hemp tops, and purses to complement an elegant evening dress. In fact, My Size is a one-stop clothing store for everything from scarves, hats and jewellery to robes and pajamas. Active in their community, the owners hold a fashion show twice a year with women from the local hospital as models. All proceeds go to the hospital. Find clothing that flatters and celebrates you at My Size.

112 Main Street, Minden ON (705) 286-4260

Tiggs for Him & Her

Winters can be cold in the rugged terrain of Bracebridge's cottage country, but Tiggs for Him & Her meets the challenge. Tiggs supplies a great variety of hardy, quality clothing. Greg and Julia Watson are a husband and wife team who had the foresight to open a store for men's fashion and work clothing. The store was so well received that the Watsons recently added women's clothing and a new shop a few doors down: Tiggs for Kids. Large glass windows display the attractive fashion layouts, designed for the season, in the downtown shopping district the couple have worked so diligently to promote. The selection is impressive. Formal wear includes internationally known, impeccable Cohen suits. Classic and hardy Haggar fashions support rugged work as well as a casual after-work and recreational wardrobe. Leo Chevalier dress shirts, sport shirts and pajamas contribute contemporary chic, and Cotton Reel provides weekend wear, from shirts to fine sweaters. Customer service in Tiggs is exemplary, far above expectations. Considering the selection and the service, Tiggs for Him & Her promises to be there to fill your fashion needs for many years to come. Stop in and try them on for size.

48 Manitoba Street, Bracebridge ON (705) 645-4743

Petticoats

At Petticoats, owners Michelle O'Reilly and Angela Barager know how to cater to the needs of their clients with a beautiful selection of lingerie and sleepwear, bras and shapewear. Proper fitting undergarments can make a woman feel good and improve her figure. Petticoats offers professional bra fittings to help each woman achieve comfort, fit and shape. For expert help with intimate apparel in a relaxed setting, visit Petticoats.

8-A Main Street, Huntsville ON (705) 788-5191

Penny Varney
Jewellery Gallery and Gifts

Goldsmith and jewellery maker Penny Varney began her career in nursing and pharmacy but discovered her passion for creating art when she took classes at a design school. She was later accepted into a prestigious jewellery and metals program, in which inspiration for Penny Varney Jewellery Gallery and Gifts was born. Penny's enthusiasm for her work and for supporting the local art scene is evident before even entering her shop. Creative displays and distinctive pieces glitter in the front window, and just outside the doorway a funky metal sculpture of a kangaroo on roller skates welcomes visitors. Whether you're in the market for an originally designed necklace or just want to browse some of the local artwork on display, the shop offers a friendly, relaxed atmosphere to find pieces from some of the area's finest artisans. In addition to offering Penny's silver, gold and other precious metal work, the gallery displays a number of accessories, boutique-style clothing and gifts, such as candles and oriental tableware. Trendsetters will revel in the eclectic mix of stylish handbags and funky attire. The shop also offers jewellery repair services and custom jewellery. Penny can create a personalized piece or modernize an old favourite. After perusing the shelves, take a walk up the stairs to the outdoor balcony, where patrons are welcome to sit under umbrellas and have a quiet lunch. Stop in for a bite and get a glimpse of the exquisite originals at Penny Varney Jewellery Gallery and Gifts.

Village Potters Arts and Crafts

Every month, Village Potters Arts and Crafts features the work of a different local artist. Whatever kind of art you admire, chances are you will find it represented at Village Potters, where Sheila Holden and Ulpu Heimonen make a home for pottery, stained glass, tole painting, jewellery, wood crafts, quilts and such native art as dream catchers. If the displays inspire your artistic side, you can take one of Sheila's classes on using a pottery wheel or creating hand-built pieces. The shop also offers tole painting classes. Sheila started the business in 1996 to display her functional pottery. She met self-taught painter Ulpu at a crafts show and invited Ulpu to display her watercolour and acrylic paintings at the shop. The pairing proved so successful that Ulpu joined the business as a partner in 1999. Ulpu's still lifes, landscapes, flowers, wildlife and portraits continue to be popular. The gallery is in the centre of downtown Sault Ste. Marie, just two blocks from the waterfront in the historic Cornwell Building. This 1898 structure once housed Cornish miners working in the Bruce Mines, later become a theatre and, finally, a shopping centre. Sample artistic variety at Village Potters Arts and Crafts.

503 Queen Street E, Sault Ste. Marie ON
(705) 256-5800

Auburn Gallery of Fine Art

This award-winning gallery nestled in a historic cottage displays esteemed local artists and represents a number of artists from Vancouver to Newfoundland. Owner and curator Teresa McLaughlin fills Auburn Gallery of Fine Art with a diverse mix of artistic styles and themes, and the gallery is known for its ever-changing displays and constant flow of fresh and inventive artwork. Varieties range from colourful modern and vibrant contemporary paintings to one-of-a-kind handmade jewellery and ornate line-engraved pictures. Art lovers can find a wide range of artistic mediums in the gallery, such as pottery, paintings, jewellery and even fashion and décor. In addition, Auburn Gallery is one of the only galleries that exhibits sculptures in a beautiful garden courtyard. Services the gallery provides include a wedding registry, art consultations and placement advice, as well as art courses and seminars. The gallery also offers expert restoration to touch up artwork that is aged or damaged. If you're an art admirer, be sure to stop by for one of the gallery's five annual art shows. Teresa welcomes you to Auburn Gallery of Fine Art to experience some of Canada's most inspiring artwork.

597 Muskoka Road N, Gravenhurst ON
(705) 687-1490
www.auburnartgallery.com

The Ethel Curry Gallery

To find some of Canada's most talented artists, look no further than the Ethel Curry Gallery. Dedicated to showcasing Canadian artists inspired by the natural beauty of the regional surroundings of the rugged Haliburton Highlands. Along with co-owner Wayne Hooks, Jody Curry and her husband Pete head up the delightful team that keeps the gallery a place of solace and inspiration. Opened in 1996 and named in honor of Pete's aunt, the gallery now houses works by over 100 artists. Upon entering, you might notice stunning woodwork, sculptures, vibrant handmade vases or a painting bearing the muted seasonal colours. Enjoy abstract pottery or ornate handcrafted jewellery as you browse the gallery's various genres. You can even find beautiful fabric art and sculptures in glass, metal, wood and soapstone. No matter what your eyes are drawn to, each piece is a reflection of the artist's vision of nature from an admiring perspective. Feel free to browse for your own enjoyment or find a one-of-a-kind gift for someone special. All art featured at the gallery is for sale. Don't miss spectacular paintings by artists such as Brian Atyeo, John Lennard, Charles Spratt and many others. Whether you're an avid art lover or just a casual admirer, visit the Ethel Curry Gallery to see original, inspired work of Canada's finest artists.

94 Maple Avenue, Haliburton ON (705) 457-9687
www.theethelcurrygallery.com

The Christine Marshall Gallery

Christine Marshall, one of Canada's foremost wildlife artists, typically works in acrylics on canvas. Born in London, England, in 1946, Christine displayed an interest in art from an early age. Like many realist painters, she initially worked in an abstract style, but soon returned to representation, her true interest and skill. Few painters of wildlife have a fresher approach than Christine. Her style of painting, called Romantic Realism, presents the warmer side of nature. "I try to show the animals I paint at their best, in their most impressive or characteristic poses, and in idealized, almost magical settings that convey my romantic view of nature," she says. "I strive to make the animal appear so real that the viewer can almost sense its thoughts." Christine's work has appeared in hundreds of publications and numerous TV documentaries. She has held more than 350 exhibitions across Canada, the United States and overseas and has acquired a long, prestigious list of corporate collectors. Christine Marshall invites you to visit her studio and gallery and perhaps catch a glimpse of a new painting or project underway. It is open regular hours in the summer months and by appointment in the winter.

1009 Strachan Point Road, Bala ON (705) 762-6622
www.wildlifegallery.ca

Bent Offerings Studio

After a long career of painting and drawing and an art degree from Haliburton School of the Arts, Charles O'Neil turned to sculpture about a decade ago, naming his Haliburton studio Bent Offerings Studio in honour of the wire sculptures that dominate his new work. Charles works with coloured wire, copper wire and screening material to create everything from large public sculptures to corporate commissions, small animals and human figures. You'll find his work installed at the Toronto International Airport and Mount Sinai Hospital. Large human figures grace a woodland setting at Haliburton Sculpture Forest. His red shoes set a classy tone for New York City designer Stuart Weitzman Shoes. Since turning his cottage studio into a home in 1996, he's added wire figures to his gardens. His work appears in prestigious galleries and in private collections around the world. Charles' work has earned the respect of such publications as the *Toronto Sun*, the *Toronto Globe & Mail* and *Canadian House & Home* magazine. In 1997, Charles began teaching wire sculpture and drawing at Haliburton College of the Arts. For a revealing look at sophisticated wire sculpture, make an appointment to visit Bent Offerings Studio.

1054 Elk Drive, Haliburton ON (705) 754-1090
www.charlesoneil.com

Jane Selbie Art Studio & Gallery

Colour, texture and creativity come together in this stunning medium mastered by artist Jane Selbie. At Jane Selbie Art Studio & Gallery, you can find these truly original works of art and the artistic soul that is inspired by the natural world. By layering fabrics, Jane creates stunning nature scenes that are visually rich in colour and detail. Formed entirely by fabrics, the art has a mosaic nature, with many layers of varying patterns and textures. Like the natural world, it is often the simplicity that make these pieces stand out. What may seem a simple blue strip of cloth becomes a piece of sky or bend in the river with the precise snip of Jane's scissors. Upon entering the studio, your eyes might be drawn to the seasonally themed works, where the pastels of spring or muted colours of winter can evoke a warm breeze or chilly frost. Whether you're an art aficionado or just interested in exploring a new medium, the Jane Selbie Art Studio is the place for you. Take time to browse the original works hung about the shop or sign-up for a workshop. Jane offers lessons from beginner to advanced so you can put your muse to the test. The Jane Selbie Art Studio & Gallery is a destination not to be missed.

87 Bayshore Acres Road, Haliburton ON (705) 457-3412
http://home.interhop.net/jselbie

Anne McCallum Gallery

Gazing at the variety of paintings on display at Anne McCallum Gallery, visitors might assume that they are admiring the work of several different artists. They see acrylics, watercolours and oils depicting subjects as diverse as the canals of Venice and the sunset on Georgian Bay. They observe styles showing the influences of realists and impressionists, and they even sense something of Georgia O'Keeffe's fascination with color and form in the close-ups of flowers. A few compositions are totally abstract. Surprisingly, just one person has created this richness of artistic expression. Anne McCallum began devoting her time to creating art in 2003, following a career as an elementary school art teacher and principal. "I spent a good part of my working life teaching visual arts and now it is my turn to paint," she declares. Living on the shores of Georgian Bay provides her with the inspiration for her scenes of the harbour, rugged cliffs and boats on the water, but she loves to experiment with her art and refuses to stick to any one theme. "I go wherever the day takes me," she says. Anne, who gladly accepts commissions, has worked with designers and architects to fit paintings into the spaces that they will occupy in their clients' homes. Call Anne to arrange a visit to her home-based gallery where you will find variety worthy of a dozen artists.

16 Ryder Drive, Parry Sound ON
(705) 342-7725
http://mccallumgallery.googlepages.com

Earth & Fire Pottery

From the humble beginnings of starting a hobby in pottery, Grahame and Debbie Wales were transformed into artisan potters over the past 30-plus years. They opened Earth & Fire Pottery Studio in 1990, just west of Carnarvon, Ontario. The work is done in porcelain and stoneware, hand-built or thrown on the wheel and then glazed in rich, luscious colours. Grahame (a.k.a. The Hairy Pottery) handles most of the wheel-thrown production work while Debbie concentrates on one-of-a-kind hand-built or thrown and altered pieces. From functional tableware to distinctive wall murals depicting the Haliburton Highlands, their personalized styles and artistic voices build an incomparable body of work that can be enjoyed in your own home. Each year, they participate in the Haliburton County Studio Tour on Thanksgiving weekend and the weekend before. Earth & Fire Pottery has developed a Clay Camp for Kids in the summer and for adults, it offers a Play with Clay Day where a small group can create functional or whimsical works of art. The new gallery is located in Grahame and Debbie's inviting log studio. Make a work of art or purchase one from the artisans in the picturesque setting that is Earth & Fire Pottery.

1234 Crooked House Road, Minden ON (705) 489-3177
www.earthandfirepottery.ca

Rickie Woods, Potter

"Making pottery is a constant learning process," says Rickie Woods, pinching a bit of clay between her fingers. "I am always experimenting with the clay and colours." The results of her latest experiments are everywhere you look in her studio and showroom—beautiful mugs, bowls and dishes that show her preference for no particular color. Instead, they demonstrate a subtle understanding of a range of reds and browns as well as blues and greens. Stark contrast is key to many of these pieces. For example, a single cloudy band of color bisects an otherwise all-black plate, bringing to mind the Milky Way spreading across the night sky. A few pieces integrate silhouettes of evergreens and other figurative elements into the design. Preferring functional over decorative pottery, Rickie says that her maple syrup jugs are hot sellers these days. Her relationship with clay began in the 1970s, when she was working as a secretary and felt she needed a hobby. As soon as she put her hands on the clay in that first class, she knew she had found her passion. To reach her gallery, located in the basement of her home, visitors follow a winding road that offers pretty views of the hills and lakes. Drop by to see how her latest experiments are going.

2023 Blairhampton Road, Minden ON (705) 286-1556
www.rickiewoodspotter.ca

Whispers North Gallery and Gifts

Whispers North is an art gallery that truly showcases the talents and skills of creative community artists. Susan Kellar opened the gallery to exhibit original works of art and crafts and personally selects everything she displays. Kellar is an artist with a master's degree in Canadian art who has worked for previous art galleries before opening her own. She also served as the Head of Visual Arts for the province of Nova Scotia. She admits there is little time to create her own work since opening her space, and Whispers North has become her main creative focus. Susan's husband, Robert, is a cabinet maker who built all of the displays and cabinet work in the gallery. Whispers North holds a dynamic blend of fabric work by local weavers, handmade jewellery, paintings and photography. More than 100 artists are represented. Some visitor favourites include the pottery, painted and kiln art glass. Susan chose the gallery name for the soft windy sounds the words evoke and for the northern images it conjures upon seeing or hearing it. She welcomes all visitors and enjoys the creative interactions between visitors and artists. Come to Minden in the Haliburton Highlands and find an exceptional representation of contemporary art at Whispers North Gallery and Gifts.

101 Main Street, Minden ON (705) 286-2042

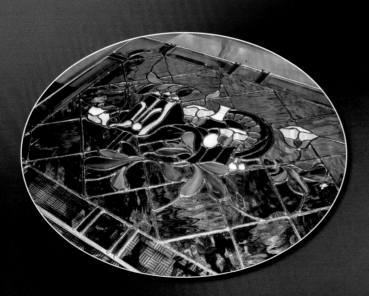

Round House Stained Glass

Round House Stained Glass is Gail Wilson's gallery. Her work shows not only command of her craft but an artist's willingness to surprise and intrigue the viewer. You'll recognize the shapes of two polar bears and an iceberg in the piece called *Iceberg*, but most striking are the geometric patterns themselves, which move the composition towards abstraction rather than realism. Gail's subjects, such as flowers, may be common, but her vision is entirely her own. For example, her signature piece, *Spring*, shows a flower not quite fully bloomed, thus avoiding the cliché of heralding the season with depictions of bright and lush flowers. What's more, Gail pays equal attention to the bulb beneath the ground, from which the slender stem with its flower has emerged. In this way, she celebrates new life completely, by showing the process behind the miracle. Gail loves the medium of stained glass "because it is ever changing in the light of day as the sun moves and the seasons change in the background." She was making her living by running a construction company when she took her first class in stained glass in 1999. Once she discovered her passion and gift for creating stained glass, she went all out, even making her studio herself out of logs. From semi-abstract nudes to elegant still lifes, Gail's pieces are as beautiful as they are original. View these works at Round House Stained Glass, which is open by appointment or chance.

3855 Highway 118, Port Carling ON (705) 765-6532 *www.roundhouseglassart.com*

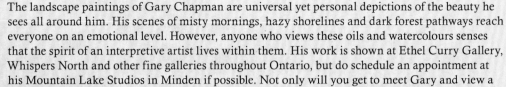

The Chapman Studios

The landscape paintings of Gary Chapman are universal yet personal depictions of the beauty he sees all around him. His scenes of misty mornings, hazy shorelines and dark forest pathways reach everyone on an emotional level. However, anyone who views these oils and watercolours senses that the spirit of an interpretive artist lives within them. His work is shown at Ethel Curry Gallery, Whispers North and other fine galleries throughout Ontario, but do schedule an appointment at his Mountain Lake Studios in Minden if possible. Not only will you get to meet Gary and view a wide sampling of his work, but you will also meet his wife, Judy Chapman, an extraordinarily gifted handweaver. She blends both contemporary and traditional weave structures into her pieces with seersucker being her specialty. This technique, which creates a puckered texture in the cloth, requires extra time to set-up and weave, but the results are spectacular. She creates beautiful blankets, shawls and jackets, as well as gorgeous skirts, vests and tops. Judy calls every hand-woven textile a small miracle and hopes that her work will prompt reflection upon the mystery of weaving. Discover the works of Judy and Gary Chapman as you explore the Haliburton area.

1084 Parallel Falls Lane, Minden ON (705) 489-2675
www3.sympatico.ca/judith.anne

Studio Rose

Raku pottery is created by a process of trial by fire, and is a specialty of Studio Rose, owned by pottery artists Wayne and Sylvia Rose. Wayne is a potter, printmaker and sculptor who specializes in raku and stoneware pottery, and is a former teacher with a master's degree in art education. Sylvia is a graduate of York University with 30 years experience in education, and has written articles about creative art approaches and curriculum documents to support teachers. Her work focuses on large carved raku vases and delicately decorated majolica pieces. Their work is in private and corporate collections. Raku is an exciting process that creates lustrous textures, patterns and colours in the finished piece. It is never totally predictable and some pieces do not survive the intense process. Viewers often wait to see the kiln opened, to catch sight of the glowing red art. These pieces can often be purchased right out of the pit as a special treat for visitors. The functional pieces at Studio Rose, fashioned from porcelain and stoneware, are equally unusual, featuring cut-outs and distinct glazing. Studio Rose is on the annual Haliburton County Studio Tour and open to the public by chance or appointment.

1895 Duck Lake Road, Minden ON (705) 286-3383
www.geocities.com/studiorose

Artistic Endeavours

"Every framing is a challenge," says Jennie Pillgrem, owner of Artistic Endeavours, who has framed everything from gorgeous Georgian Bay paintings to hockey jerseys signed by local hero Bobby Orr. She started framing as a part-time business housed in her father's basement, and her desire to do a perfect job every time continues to drive her. Customers visiting Artistic Endeavours find thousands of different frames from which to choose, along with the enthusiastic owner who is always eager to help with selection. Laminating, plaque mounting and shadow box framing are a few of Jennie's specialties. Known for her personal service, she will even pick up your item from your home, frame it and deliver it back to you. Jennie's father, Bill, was a photographer who did all his own framing, a skill requiring patience, precision and artistry that he passed on to his daughter. When she isn't framing, Jennie likes to collect Georgian Bay paintings and photographs. Be sure to view the selection on display, along with other works by local artists, when you drop by the shop. Put Jennie's skill to the test by bringing your challenging framing job to Artistic Endeavours.

42 James Street, Parry Sound ON (705) 746-5753

Magda Szabo, Miniature Painting

While some painters strive to make grandiose statements with their work, this miniaturist invites the viewer to see the beauty in small things. One of Magda Szabo's larger paintings might measure four by six inches. According to Magda, a miniature painting should not be underestimated. In that small scale, it contains all of the details of a large painting. Look closely at one of her Hawaiian scenes, such as a brightly colored parrot on a branch, and you will observe an astonishing attention to detail in the feathers and the beak. Magda, who works strictly with watercolors, has painted all her adult life, but fell in love with miniature painting in the late 1980s. Since beginning to specialize in this medium, she has won 23 awards from major miniature art societies. She spends half the year in Hawaii, paintings its palm trees, sandy beaches and wildlife, and is represented by Village Galleries on the island of Maui. Although it takes much longer to paint a miniature than a small canvas, the format comes naturally to her. "I must have a small mind," she jokes. Visit the showroom that she keeps in Parry Sound to see the works of this gifted artist.

20 Kristen Heights, Parry Sound ON (705) 746-9465
www.villagegalleriesmaui.com/profiles/szaboprofile.htm

Trilogy of Art

Like many legendary artists, Mary Jane Zissoff was inspired early in life and soon developed a passion and skill for her form of expression: stained glass. As a child, Mary Jane was fascinated by the colours of stained glass when intensified by light. Mary Jane's gift with glassware soon developed into Trilogy of Art, a custom window design project for the Toronto Housing Industry. After years of study and a grant to work with artists at the Banff School of Fine Arts, Mary's stunning creations grace the windows and doors of a number of buildings and are displayed in art shows, exhibits and museums throughout the area. In addition to designing custom windows for homes and businesses, Mary Jane has been commissioned to do private and commercial projects. As part of a six member team of artists, Mary painted two murals depicting vintage trains, the Canadian National and the Canadian Pacific Railway, which will be prominently displayed in Parry Sound. Whether you want a colourful lampshade, a floral window or a contemporary tabletop, Mary Jane can use a variety of techniques and styles to complement your décor and enhance your home or business. Give her a call today to find the perfect piece to make your space a distinctive and artful place.

Parry Sound ON (705) 746-4147

Oxtongue Craft Cabin & Gallery

A log cabin nestled in a woodland setting holds one of Ontario's finest selections of crafts for sale. Oxtongue Craft Cabin & Gallery represents more than 100 Canadian artists working in everything from leather and glass to clay and forged iron and original paintings. Collectors take note that this gallery is the place to find exquisite hand-carved decoys. Other wooden objects include bowls, cutting boards and utensils—perfect as functional mementos of your time spent in Muskoka or as gifts for that friend who loves to entertain. Pottery in stoneware, porcelain and raku abounds at the gallery. Many varieties of jewellery are on display featuring the Muskoka Collection, an exclusive design in rings, pendants, earrings and more depicting the dynamic Muskoka landscape. The shopping experience is made special by the distinctness of the gallery itself. Back in 1977, a husband and wife teamed up to build the log cabin. While constructing the cabin they hung their artwork on a fence—it sold and the idea for the gallery was born. Enjoy delightful shopping for Canadian crafts at Oxtongue Craft Cabin & Gallery.

1073 Fox Point Road, Dwight ON (705) 635-1602
www.oxtonguecraftcabin.on.ca

Photo by Helen Millard

The Organic Salon

If you care about the environment or suffer from sensitivities to chemicals, toxins or pollutants, you will appreciate the organic products used by the Organic Salon, a therapeutic hair salon. Hairdresser, healer and educator Anna Le-Grie wants her clients to experience balance and wellness as well as beauty from a visit to her salon, a part of the Sudbury scene since 1999. She searches the globe for products that meet her high standards, and has selected hair, skin and body care products, and organic supplements from Australia, Britain, the Amazon Rainforest, Canada and the U.S. Her caring attitude and professionalism comes from her extensive experience while teaching within the industry for many years. The salon is open daily and welcomes appointments from those seeking healthiness and organic alternatives. Beyond organic colouring and perms, Anna promotes whole wellness with her Lightbody Energy Point Healing treatments, and workshops for this gentle method of reconnecting, replenishing, aligning and balancing a clients energy fields. Anna contends that nature's alchemy offers everything we need to thrive. By decreasing exposure to harsh toxins clients can avoid detrimental reactions, responses and debilitating symptoms.

Sudbury ON (705) 673-1043
www.lightworlds.net

the Yoga Door

Sault Ste. Marie's first yoga studio, the Yoga Door offers a place for students of all levels to learn and explore the transformative gifts of this system of exercise. Open since 2003, the studio was founded by Dar Charlebois as a natural extension of her deep interest in the healing arts. She teaches weekly classes and workshops in addition to directing a faculty of highly motivated instructors. Dar's students cherish her gentleness and her way of infusing her teaching with joy and accessible spiritual wisdom. A former performance artist who combined creative movement and text to create three original works, Dar came to yoga with a background in educational drama and expressive art therapies. She also co-wrote several plays that toured extensively in Ontario. Imminent yoga teachers, with whom she trained in Canada and the United States, have influenced her intuitive and integrative approach to yoga. She also cites the street-level spirituality of Sean Corn and the therapeutic approach of Molly Kenny, founder of the Samaryia Centre for Integrated Movement Therapy and Ashtanga Yoga, as major sources of inspiration. Celebrate vitality and open yourself to spiritual discovery by taking a yoga class at the Yoga Door.

740 Queen Street E, Unit 2, Sault Ste. Marie ON (705) 257-7707
www.theyogadoor.com

Soapstones
Soap & Skincare Products

The key to a tranquil experience is just a stones throw away at Soapstones. Since 2003, owners Darla and Tom Stipanovich have been handcrafting spa-quality soaps and skincare products. Each product is eco-friendly and made with natural ingredients such as lemon, moisturizing oatmeal honey and sensuous vanilla buttercream. Complete your experience with an exfoliating body scrub, smoothing body butter or rejuvenating body lotion, each with a variety of enticing natural scents. Bath salts made with Dead Sea salts and oils, including eucalyptus and patchouli, melt the cares away while detoxifying the skin. Soapstone's gentle baby products, such as Nighty-Nite Oil, Chamomile Baby Soap and Sweet Cheeks Powder, are natural, come in fun, gender specific or neutral colours and make the perfect baby gift. Take home a bit of luxury when you visit Soapstones Soap & Skincare Products.

6B Brunel Road, Huntsville ON (705) 789-4405
www.soapstones.ca

OM Yoga Space & Manipura Boutique

The first yoga studio in Sudbury was OM Yoga Space & Manipura Boutique. OM Yoga Space provides a safe environment within the community for self-exploration and personal growth in a variety of classes and services, guided by qualified and dedicated instructors. Group classes take place regularly in the studio, but it also offers private, corporate, partner, prenatal and men's yoga classes. One of OM Yoga Space's very effective services is the Shamballa Reiki treatment. In this procedure, hot stones placed on the body connect energy paths and reunite body, mind and spirit. The stones are then replaced by gemstones chosen for their properties and connection to the energy centers of the body. Essential oils are selected for their therapeutic value and administered to each of the seven main energy centres. The instructor then uses her own energies to detect and dissolve energy blockages in the client. After experiencing this treatment, visitors have reported a deep relaxing sense of inner calm and wellbeing. Locals have also embraced the holistic lifestyle coaching, ecstatic dance and chakra exploration services. OM Yoga Space practices Karma yoga, donating all proceeds from the Friday all-level classes to local causes. A small on-site boutique offers yoga accessories and specialty gifts. Lana Boyuk took over the studio from the original owner, Jen Wilson, in 2002. Boyuk and her experienced staff welcome you to a journey of life-enhancement, growth and inner peace at OM Yoga Space & Manipura Boutique.

61 Elm Street, Sudbury ON
(705) 662-1359
www.yogasudbury.com

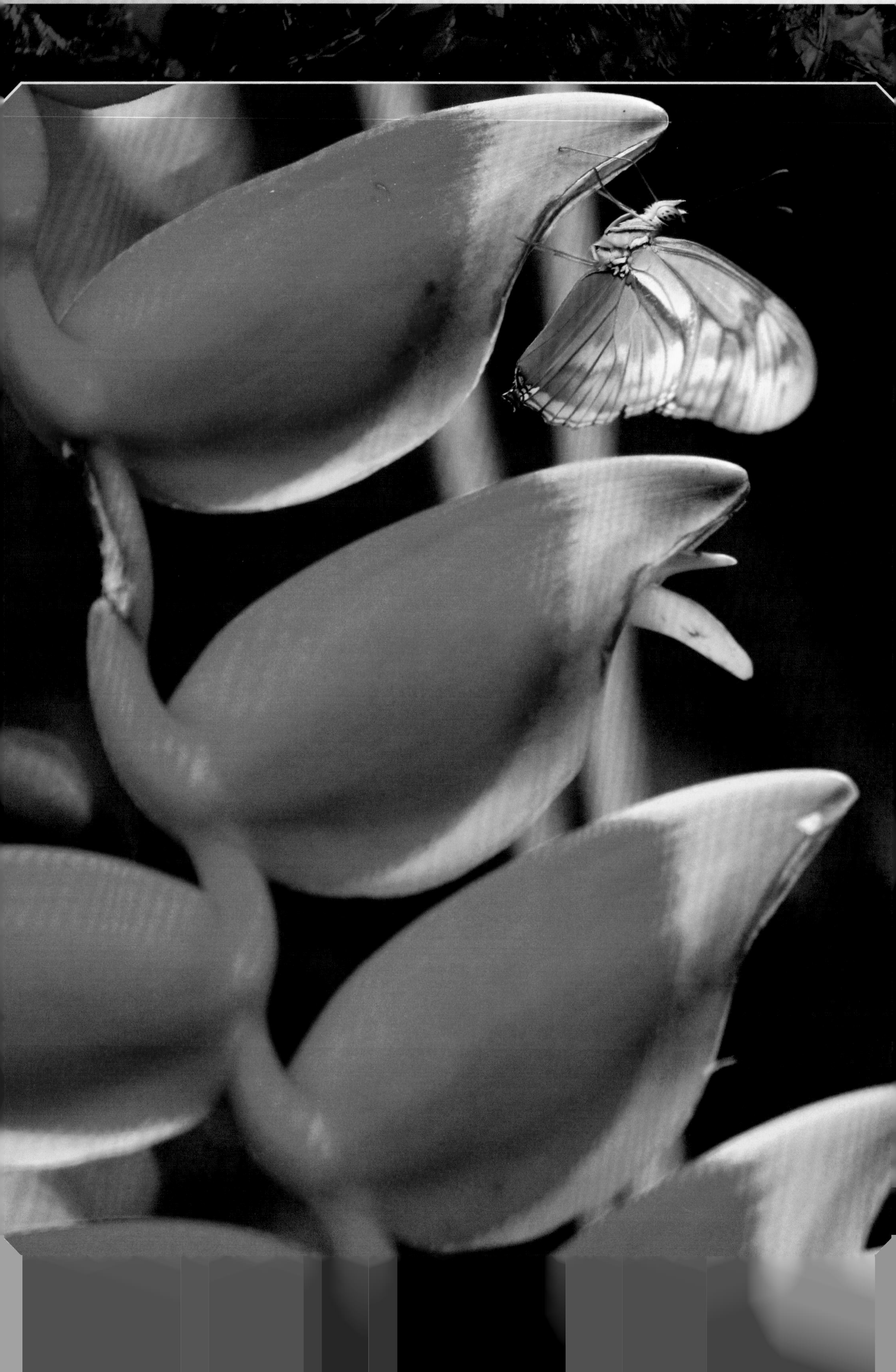

The Corner Cabinet

What initially started as a retirement project for Maureen Wylie quickly developed into this ever-successful home décor and cabinet shop. The Corner Cabinet is a favourite for crafty designers and those wishing to find distinctive gifts such as wooden carvings, rustic decorative signs, artistic framed prints and other home and garden items. Maureen is proud to offer the community a retail option that allows for creativity to blossom. The store is located in a late 1800s building, once home to a local blacksmith's shop. The original brick wall, complete with original wood trim, makes the perfect backdrop to the shop's products. You might walk in and see a dried wreath or small pine end-table that inspires the theme of an entire room. If you're looking for larger pieces, The Corner Cabinet has a selection of pine furniture as well as a variety of classy rustic pieces painted in muted tones. Linens, candles and hand-painted boxes make perfect gifts and you'll delight in the funky purses and shoulder bags adorning the walls. If you're looking for a special touch for your kitchen, take a look at the original pottery items, perfect as decorative canisters or flower vases. You can even decorate yourself with the funky and classic handmade jewellery throughout the store. In addition to being an everything-you-can-imagine store, The Corner Cabinet offers custom cabinetry to really give your home a personal touch. Whether you've got an idea in mind or would like to discuss design options, the shop is always ready to start a new project. Make The Corner Cabinet your destination for all your gift, décor and custom design needs, and see your house become a home.

3–3 Manitoba Street, Bracebridge ON
(705) 645-2810

Muskoka Amore

Persistence pays off for Judy and Dominic Cistrone, who obtain most of the stock for their antiques business, Muskoka Amore, at estate sales and auctions. Amassing a collection large enough to fill two buildings at their retail site in Port Sandfield is an ongoing feat, but one that they deeply enjoy. The compliments that their inventory constantly inspires make the hunt worthwhile. Strengths of the collection include fixtures, mirrors and interesting wooden pieces. Also expect to find an abundance of tables, lamps and rugs as well as pottery and china. Although some pieces are local, many come from as far away as France, Italy and Belgium. Both Judy and Dominic held careers in advertising before deciding to pursue their love of antiques and décor through Muskoka Amore. Judy expresses her creativity in wicker basket flower arrangements as well as in her inventory. Established in 2004, Muskoka Amore is well-situated just north of the Sandfield Arena with lots of parking. Drop by and reap the benefits of the owners' hard work and taste.

134 Thomas Street, Oakville ON
(705) 765-7758

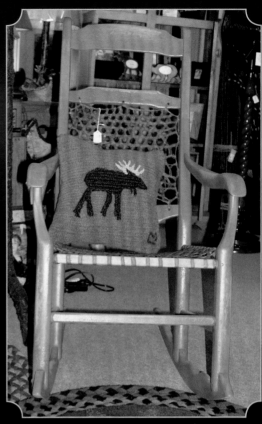

The Old Palmer House

To master the art of casual living, you must first learn to relax, preferably in a deck chair or hammock. The Old Palmer House, a home store housed inside an 1870s log building, offers a selection of both for sale. An appreciation for handmade things is also essential to the casual lifestyle. Again, the Old Palmer House leads the way, promising to deepen your admiration for fine carpentry with its selection of handcrafted harvest tables and chairs. The complete list of handmade merchandise is lengthy and includes everything from Canadian-made pottery to lodge-style quilts. The hooked and braided wool rugs are also popular sellers. Of course, casual and natural go hand-in-hand, as the nature-inspired bedroom suites at the Old Palmer House make perfectly clear. Throughout the store, wildlife images adorn décor items and lamp shades, and many of the lamps themselves seem scarcely removed from the trees by which they were made. A local poll named the Old Palmer House the Best Gift Shop in Muskoka, no doubt because it promotes a rustic lifestyle that is so popular to the area. Janine Scott, who purchased the business in 2007, keeps the store loaded with inspiring ideas to add personality to your home or cottage. You will feel a little bit of the North in anything you take home from her place, whether it is an oil painting or a garden accent. Drop by the Old Palmer House, open May until October, for a primer on casual living, Muskoka style.

2827 Highway 60, Dwight ON (705) 635-9376 *www.theoldpalmerhouse.com*

Antiques & Neat Stuff

Owner Joan Ward applies her eye for good form when she selects merchandise for Antiques & Neat Stuff. Shoppers are guaranteed to find a funky yet tasteful selection of home décor items, including throws, lamps and mirrors. Other popular items include metal sculptures handcrafted by Canadian artists, as well as McBlooms Skin Therapy body products. Joan graduated from Ryerson University with a degree in design about 30 years ago. After helping her husband run a resort for the last three decades, she needed a retirement project that would put her back in touch with her creative side. Since opening Antiques & Neat Stuff in 2001, she has enjoyed creating a fun shopping environment for her customers. The merchandise itself sets the tone. Joan describes it as "a little different," and you can tell that she puts much energy and imagination into arranging it in a way that honors her design background. Joan is almost always present at Antiques & Neat Stuff, located in Haliburton Village. Drop by with your gift list and enjoy the store that she has designed.

**5167 County Road 21, Haliburton ON
(705) 457-1160**

Kitchens etcetera

In 2000, Mary and Andy Chvedukas combined their talents for interior design to form a successful cabinetry and décor business. Kitchens etcetera provides the area with a reliable and cost effective way to get quality creations and custom designs. If you're ready to make a change, but unsure of where to begin, Mary and Andy are happy to provide personalized consultations to conceive an idea that works with your budget and preferences. Kitchens etcetera has constantly changing stock and continually evolving designs so you'll have a multitude of choices. Whether you want to turn your kitchen into a modern chef's paradise, or you're just looking to spruce up a vintage look, you'll find everything you need at Kitchens etcetera. Some of the best-selling items include wall prints with elegant patterns and a selection of colours that can complement any décor. Be sure to check out the classy imported products, which come from stylish countries such as Italy, Spain and Portugal. The French linens are also among some of the most popular products. Stop in for your consultation today and let Mary and Andy make your dream home a reality.

**183 Highland Street, Haliburton ON
(705) 457-3535**

Harris Furniture & Antiques

Since 1923, the Harris family has done a little bit of everything from its property in Parry Sound, including farming, selling ice and boarding horses. The current venture, Harris Furniture & Antiques, has been going strong since 1982. Dean and Colleen Harris sell comfortable furnishing for home and cottage life, including leather and fabric sofas, beds and solid-wood tables and chairs. Canadian-made furniture is the specialty. A dealer of Marshall, Bayrest and Simmons Beauty Rest mattresses, the store is also a place to find blankets, quilts and linens. A tasteful complement of antiques and collectibles blends with the area rugs, cupboards and bedroom suites on display in the showrooms. Worthy of special note is the memorabilia pertaining to hockey legend Bobby Orr, whose hometown is Parry Sound. With cabinet and finishing shops on the premises, this business welcomes custom orders. Not surprisingly for people whose family has been doing business with its neighbors for many decades, Dean and Colleen say, "We place a strong emphasis on customer service and satisfaction." Check out Harris Furniture & Antiques for furniture and accessories to make your house a home.

17 Parry Sound Drive, Parry Sound ON (705) 746-5100 or (800) 633-9066
www.harrisfurniture.ca

Cottage Country Interiors

It was always Suzanne Morrow's dream to open a store that reflected her passion and natural gift for interior design. Cottage Country Interiors is the realization of that dream, and a testament to Suzanne's success with interior décor. Suzanne can help you turn your home into a work of art with her country classic flair and distinctive items. Antique reproductions complete the project with a touch of class and offer an original look to suite your personality and needs. With Suzanne's individual design consulting, it's hard to walk out without inspiration. Her knack for creating an inviting space is obvious from the moment you step onto the porch of the shop. Adorned with bright flowers, rustic décor and aged furniture, the entryway to the store is a taste of some of the delightful items within. Find sophisticated giftware for friends and family, or discover a treasure for yourself. No matter what you find, Suzanne has the expertise and creative eye to make it into a central theme for an entire room or use it as a creative accent in an already decorated home. Look no further than Cottage Country Interiors for interior decorations that will bring elegance and a personal touch to your home.

13513 Highway 118, Haliburton ON (705) 457-2250

Generations Antiques

Dave and Francie Smith always enjoyed collecting and restoring antiques. The day came when their garage was too full of treasures to hold them all. Opening Generations Antiques in 1999 allowed them to expand their hobby. The store not only shows off their interesting finds and careful restorations but gives them an excuse to find more. Generations Antiques specializes in mid-19th century furniture, especially regional furniture made of country pine. Muskoka folks enjoy items with local history, and Dave and Francie find a lot of pieces when retirees clean out or downsize their homes. Dave also makes popular reproduction antique cupboards and harvest tables. Francie specializes in chair seat weaving—bring your bedraggled family treasure to her and she'll make it good as new. You'll find a wide variety of early electrical lighting and oil lamps at the shop, including Aladdin's world-famous kerosene mantle lamps. Antique signs, toys and gadgets complement the furniture. Generations Antiques has won the *Muskokan*'s Muskoka Best Award three years running. Come by and see why. Interesting pieces will draw you in, and the cozy atmosphere will make you want to spend the day.

2368 Highway 11 N, Gravenhurst ON (705) 684-9113
www.generationsantiques.ca

Muskoski Urban Rustic Living

Tary and Ed Roosien, owners of Muskoski Urban Rustic Living, enjoy helping folks bring country comfort to their home or cottage. From iron lighting to harvest tables, the merchandise embodies sturdiness and unpretentious charm. The business offers two floors of displays inside a century-old brick church building. Among the fabulous décor items are many pieces worthy of being called art. Ample consultation space gives Tary room to confer with customers. Not only does she do all the buying for the store, but, as an interior designer, she works with homeowners to develop a decorating plan. She and Ed, who handles the administrative side of things, opened the business in 2006 and soon found that they had outgrown their original location, because of the demand for their products. The former Baptist Church building is very spacious. Also, having a town landmark associated with their store helps give the business a stronger identity. The Roosiens have kept the original stained glass windows and hardwood floors. The chamber of commerce nominated them for Business of the Year in 2006. If you seek a country look for your home drop by Muskoski Urban Rustic Living.

15 Main Street W, Huntsville ON (705) 788-2612

Muskoka Living Interiors and Seasons Retreat

Impeccable taste, classic styling and exceptionally high standards—these are the things that drive the people at Muskoka Living Interiors and Seasons Retreat. Whether it's the award-winning design services or the timeless collection of quality products, the full-service design facilities and retail locations have long been regarded as a virtual must-see. Muskoka Living Interiors and Seasons Retreat has garnered praise and accolades from both design professionals and homeowners alike, further solidifying its reputation as one of Canada's premiere full scope design operations.

3655 Highway 118 W, Port Carling ON (705) 765-6840
499 First Street, Collingwood ON (705) 444-1093
www.muskokaliving.com

Kirkony Custom Iron Work

To the clang of metal striking metal, blacksmith David Hollows works at making a railing in his shop. Once he has finished this project, he has orders to fill for chairs, iron candle holders and outdoor garden accessories. Indeed, if you thought that the days of blacksmithing were over, a visit to Kirkony Custom Iron Work reveals a thriving professional who clearly loves what he is doing. The grandson of a blacksmith, David spent many years learning the art of forging iron before opening his own place in 1992. Kathy McKelvey-Brown does most of the designing at the shop, while David handles the heating and hammering of the metal. The process is fascinating to watch. Most of their work is custom orders, often for repeat customers, such as the man who commissioned David to make a glass door for his fireplace with a wrought iron screen behind it. Satisfied with David's fine craftsmanship, he ordered a set of fireplace tools next. David has made things as small as racks to hold keys and excels at making large pieces such as table frames and gates. He even does the installing. If you have a project for this talented blacksmith, call David or Kathy at Kirkony Custom Iron Work for an appointment.

4025 Gelert Road, Minden ON (705) 286-6837

Brown's Appliances

The selection at Brown's Appliances far exceeds what you would expect to find in a small town store, and the view is superb as well. Since 1957, Brown's has stood atop a hill overlooking the town. The store has made itself indispensable to the community with a hand-picked inventory of cutting-edge appliances. Out-of-towners with summer cottages in Port Carling often shop for appliances at Brown's, satisfied that the selection rivals that of any store back home in the city. The professional series of ranges and cooktops will excite anyone who takes cooking seriously. High-end, commercial-quality refrigerators, dishwashers and washers/dryers are always in stock, too. Built-in models for upscale homes are among the best-selling items. The Grigg family proudly stands behind every appliance it sells. Peggy and her husband, Bill, have run the business for many years. Peggy's father, Clive Brown, founded it in the 1950s. Her children, Jennifer and David, are now key players as the store continues smoothly along in its sixth decade. Find reliable modern appliances to accommodate your lifestyle at Brown's Appliances, a Port Carling standby.

108–6 Maple Street, Port Carling ON (705) 765-5700
http://brownsappliances.com

Prosperi Plastering Co.

The story of the rise of Prosperi Plastering Co. is indelibly linked to the history of one family, beginning when Guglielmo Prosperi immigrated to Sudbury from Italy with his wife and children in 1905. Sudbury was booming when he opened Prosperi Plastering. When Guglielmo passed away, he left the company to his son, Joseph. The trade was seasonal because of the Sudbury climate. Under Joseph's guidance, residential work was phased out in favour of industrial, commercial and institutional construction. Many area businesses, including universities and retail complexes, benefited over the years from the expertise of Prosperi. Joseph's sons, Bill and Bob, joined the company and the third generation led the company forward. The new team expanded the frontiers of Prosperi Plastering and built their name in the community. Today the company sponsors local sports teams and donates to community causes. Bill served on the Board of Directors for Legal Aid in Ontario. Bob's sons, John and Anthony, have come on board to continue the legacy. The fourth generation stands ready for a future of innovation in the construction industry, strengthened by the skills of each generation. Call Prosperi Plastering Co. and link your project to a legend.

154 Regent Street, Sudbury ON (705) 673-1376
www.prosperi.ca

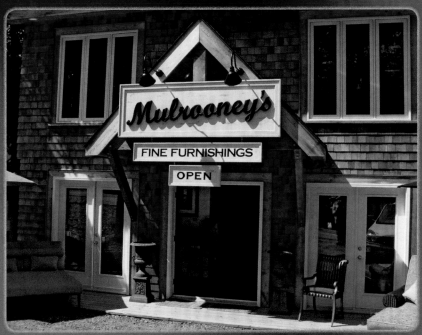

Mulrooney's Fine Furniture

Only five minutes from the locks in Port Carling, Mulrooney's Fine Furniture occupies a 100-year-old, post and beam, natural cedar building on Medora Street. Owners Tom and Rob Sullivan named the business with their mother's maiden name. The store is on the hill that heralds Port Carling, with a large deck in the back for displaying its fine patio furniture in a scenic outdoor setting. In addition to casual living collections, Mulrooney's specializes in furnishings for the hospitality and healthcare industries. Much of Mulrooney's product can be seen in restaurants throughout the region. The name has become synonymous with superb craftsmanship, style, comfort and durability, and its reputation continues to grow. The store was recently featured in *Muskoka Magazine.* Mulrooney's uses crypton fabrics, the only textile that is stain, water and bacteria resistant. An extensive combination of fabrics and finishes allows clients to customize the furniture to accentuate the style of their home or business. Take a look at the smart, practical designs at Mulrooney's Fine Furniture, made with your home and business needs in mind.

124 Medora Street, Port Carling ON
(705) 765-1387
www.mulrooneysfurniture.com

Photo by Ray Thoms

Ristorante Verdicchio

Treasured family recipes and wine pairings have been drawing international customers to Ristorante Verdicchio since 1994. Owners Willie Gregorini and her son Mark create seasonal menus that reflect the foods of the central Italian regions of Umbria, Marche and Tuscany. The restaurant has received many awards, including the Silver Spoon Award for its rice cookery, the Golden Fork Award 2004 to 2007 for food and service, and the Golden Plate Award 2007 from the Independent Restaurant Association. It earned the Best of Award of Excellence from *Wine Spectator* from 2004 to 2007 for its distinct collection and wine program. Ristorante Verdicchio's wine library exceeds 600 labels and represent all regions of Italy. Quality is of utmost importance here. Antipasti include innovative and traditional starters. Entrées offer specialty local meats all completed with homegrown fresh herbs and vegetables. Consider fresh Manitoulin trout rolled with marinated tiger shrimp and crab, wrapped with locally made prosciutto and pan-seared with a chardonnay white wine sauce. Nipissing quail, Quebec cornish hen and locally grown ostrich are also delicious. The restaurant's freshly made pastas include gnocchi and ravioli. Desserts include *Dolce della Nonna*, which was created by Willie's mother, Lina, and is still a family secret. Ristorante Verdicchio has two dining rooms, Il Girasole and La Mensa, displaying the colours of the vineyards, olive groves and fields of Central Italy. Il Casale del Verdicchio banquet facility is a classic room for up to 120 people. Prepare for enchantment at Ristorante Verdicchio. You can depend on the staff to bring you innovative, traditional quality food, attentive service and something exciting for every palate.

1351–D Kelly Lake Road, Sudbury ON (705) 523-2794
www.ristoranteverdicchio.com

Tapps Cottage Eatery

What Adam Szelei and Lexx Varghese wanted for their restaurant seemed impossible. They envisioned a place where the whole family could eat, but they had in mind a pub with nightlife as well. Now that Tapps Cottage Eatery has been going strong since 2004, their idea seems perfectly logical. Each day the restaurant feeds scores of hungry diners in its dining room and on its two large patios, while the pub becomes the site for good times when night falls. Live entertainment is featured on Thursday, Friday and Saturday nights during the summer. Almost all the food at Tapps Cottage Eatery is homemade. Chef Eric Mulder's schnitzel, chili and fish dishes are especially popular. Try a juicy burger or a plate of zesty wings with one of the 12 draughts on tap. The view of the hillside is gorgeous from the veranda out back. Adam and Lexx wisely hire only those individuals who are committed to providing great service. They put their heads together and built Tapps Cottage Eatery from the ground up. Bring the whole family, or drop by with a few friends, and experience for yourself how well they have succeeded in doing the impossible.

125 Medora Street, Port Carling ON
(705) 765-6983

McKeck's Place

Which Canadian hockey player opened a top pick sports bar and restaurant after retiring from a stellar career in hockey at the age of 37? The answer to that question would be Walt McKechnie, and the restaurant and bar is McKeck's Place. The interior is warm and welcoming, with light cedar walls and a log cabin style. Of the four floors, three are non-smoking. The jerseys of Wayne Gretzky and Walt McKechnie are displayed on the wall, along with hockey memorabilia from McKechnie's illustrious game days. The outdoor patio overlooks the lake, and downstairs, a cozy pub opens to the outdoors. The food is every bit as good as the game, starting with the Pre-game Warm Ups and ending with a satisfying main course, such as a steak sandwich from the Coach's Corner Specials or a 2nd Period hamburger. The Lord Stanley Escargot and the awesome chicken wings are local favourites. Walt McKechnie entertained the public for many years on the ice, so offering his fans a comfortable sports bar and restaurant where they can sit back with a brew or eat a mouth-watering meal is a natural extension of his skills. If you're not already a fan, you'll soon become one after a visit to McKeck's Place.

207 Highland Street, Haliburton ON (705) 457-3443

3 Guys and a Stove

"Put simply, I like to have fun and cook good food," says 3 Guys and a Stove owner and cooking show host Jeff Suddaby. Jeff started 3 Guys and a Stove 10 years ago with, as the name would suggest, two other guys. Those two guys have left—but two more have replaced them. The aim at 3 Guys and a Stove is to make dining a treat for all five senses. Your sense of taste is definitely in for a treat here. Jeff's cooking incorporates several levels of flavours and seasonings. Dishes such as the curried pumpkin and sweet potato soup mix flavours and textures in ways that will thrill those with a sense of culinary adventure. Jeff's hearty casseroles are a favourite during the fall and winter months. The signature dessert here is a white chocolate cheesecake warmed in a phyllo pastry and topped with Scottish honey and fresh strawberries. Your other senses will delight log cabin feel of the surroundings, with comfy fireplaces on both floors of the 92-seat restaurant. Those looking to bring home the flavours of 3 Guys and a Stove can purchase Jeff's cookbook, Who's Coming to Dinner —named for his television show—as well as a variety of Jeff's private label food products. Treat yourself at 3 Guys and a Stove.

143 Highway 60 E, Huntsville ON (705) 789-1815
www.3guysandastove.com

Arturo Ristorante

The personal touch is alive and well at Arturo Ristorante. Owner Arturo Comegna not only welcomes you as if you were visiting his home but will make a dish to your specifications, should you find yourself longing for an Italian specialty not shown on the menu. Arturo was born in Italy and started his restaurant career at the age of 17 by working at an Italian ski resort. After training as a chef and working throughout Europe, Arturo came to Canada in 1978, serving as a waiter in Sault Ste. Marie for two years before opening Arturo Ristorante. Lamb, veal chops and fresh fish are some of the specialties at Arturo. The menu features Italian cuisine with accents from other parts of the world. The extensive wine list includes such classic Italian red wines as Brunello di Montalcino, Barbera and Barolo. Arturo's skills extend beyond cooking to knowing how to create a comfortable dining environment that makes good food created from scratch all the more endearing. He loves to paint, and while he never had the funds to pursue his art full-time, he finds a venue for his oils and acrylics on the walls of his restaurant. Experience the best in personalized service and Italian style hospitality at Arturo Ristorante.

515 Queen Street E, Sault Ste. Marie ON (705) 253-0002

Just Crepes

After enjoying an Eggs Benedict crepe for breakfast, don't be surprised if you feel an urge to return to Just Crepes in the afternoon to check out the lunch and dinner menu. The seafood crepe is hard to resist. Indeed, since Just Crepes opened in May of 2007, scores of locals and out-of-towners on holiday have found this charming creperie habit-forming. Owner Janine Heaslip always believed that Port Carling needed something like her restaurant. Janine envisioned "a place to eat just before golfing or snowmobiling or to get a really nice lunch while shopping that also offered the ambience of finer dining." As her model, she considered the excellent creperies that she had experienced on her frequent skiing holidays. The food was always simple yet delicious, the atmosphere comfortable and inviting. How have folks reacted so far to Just Crepes? "I would venture to say that they love it," says Janine, citing feedback that she gets by talking with customers and reading their comments in the guestbook. With its creamy yellow clapboard exterior, blue doors and inviting patio, the building boasts plenty of character. Start a good habit by eating at Just Crepes next time you're coming through Port Carling.

118 Medora Street, Port Carling ON
(705) 765-5878
http://justcrepes.ca

La Dog House

Parisian music floats upon the air at La Dog House, a boutique for dogs with exquisite taste. From beaded leads to chic clothing, the store carries everything your dog needs to make a fashion statement. Owner Debbie Pilon has been breeding dogs for years, particularly poodles, pugs, Yorkies and Maltese. Bothered by the lack of a pet boutique in the region, she decided to open La Dog House and fill it with high-end pampering accessories for pooches of all types and sizes. Items exclusive to her store include her own line of designer leads. For the dog fancier who also loves coffee, she offers something truly special: coffee roasted just for La Dog House, packaged in bags with labels of different breeds. You can even pick up a mug to match. Stock up on natural dog food and treats at Debbie's store, and count on it for grooming and boarding. If you are thinking of bringing a puppy into your home, you are bound to find one for sale at La Dog House that will melt your heart. Check out the Eiffel Tower of stuffed animals when you drop by, just one of the things that lends Parisian flair to La Dog House.

26 Manitoba Street, Bracebridge ON (705) 645-9959

The Gingerbread House

Christmas is not a day in the year but a state of mind at the Gingerbread House. Featuring a permanent Christmas section, this cheerful store would make even Scrooge break out into a smile. Owner Jennifer Specht carries a fabulous array of gift items to keep her customers in the spirit of giving throughout the year. Whether you are shopping for a birthday, wedding or anniversary, you are bound to find that special something at the Gingerbread House. A café serving homemade soups, quiche and such specialties as poached pear salad awaits you after your first round of shopping. Sate your appetite, and then begin your second round by browsing the tables of gourmet items. Syrups, jams and teas are just a few of the featured items. Established in 1981, the Gingerbread House is a familiar part of life in Bracebridge. Thanks to its beautiful exterior of cream-colored stucco with brown trim, it stands out among the row of stores on Main Street. Originally the Grand Theatre, the building has served many purposes before housing the store that makes everyone see snowflakes and hear sleigh bells, even in the middle of July. Add some Christmas cheer to your day by dropping into the Gingerbread House.

75 Manitoba Street, Bracebridge ON (705) 645-4246

JACE

This gift shop is the creation of a third generation family made up of Grandmother Grace, mother Jacqui, and son Jacob Van Dyk. They call their store the Something for Everyone Place, where anyone of any income can find unique and fun items. The five rooms hold an eclectic mix of handcrafted items and specially selected giftware. Looking for a one-of-a-kind gift? Want to treat yourself to something special? Shoppers will love the homey atmosphere of the store and Grace, Jacqui and Jacob welcome visitors. If you're looking for a truly original shopping experience, JACE is the place.

**355 Muskoka Road S, Gravenhurst ON
(705) 687-9254**
www.welcometojace.piczo.com

SAS Home & Gifts

Sue Wilson and Sue Rueger are cousins and best friends, so when they opened a lifestyle store together in 2006, they named it SAS Home & Gifts—for Sue And Sue. SAS also stands for Substance And Style, and of course, for Sassy, which sums up the kind of inventory these fashion-conscious ladies offer. Their pretty storefront on the main shopping street of Bracebridge brings a touch of urban chic to the Muskoka cottage country, hence their motto: Just North of Urban. You'll find home and garden accents, fun giftware and gourmet treats to help spice up your home life. SAS carries contemporary goods, such as mirrors, lamps, jewellery, photo frames, bath and spa products, books, cards, baby gifts and delectables, like chocolates by The Cocoa Room, and the elegant Tea Forte and Lampe Berger lines. The owners are always looking for that gift to make you smile. They get such a kick out of hearing people laugh at their fun finds. SAS has been written up in *Chocolat Magazine*. For sassy gift ideas and home décor, check out SAS Home & Gifts.

**3 Manitoba Street, Bracebridge ON
(705) 645-7727 or (877) 645-4727**

JanKnit's Studio

JanKnit's Studio created a buzz when it opened in 2007 for bringing fashion with celebrity appeal to Haliburton. Specifically, this yarn shop carries garments by Paula Lishman International—coats, jackets and vests knitted from fur yarn. Shown on the runways of Toronto, New York and Milan, the Paula Lishman line is favored by such Hollywood stars as Barbra Streisand and Sissy Spacek. Janet Sheehey, owner of JanKnit's Studio, served as a manager for Paula Lishman, who makes her home in Port Perry. While in charge of selling fur yarn to home knitters, Janet also helped develop fur knit kits, which she now features at her shop. "I know that fur is controversial, but it's a part of our heritage," says Janet, who devotes an entire wall at her store to fur yarns. Keeping to the theme of natural products, she also offers angora, mohair, cotton and many other kinds of yarns. What is the most exotic material that she sells? That would have to be the antibacterial yarn with fibre made from shrimp and crab shells. Another contains aloe vera. For the place where yarn shop meets high fashion, go to JanKnit's Studio, located in Haliburton Village.

214 Highland Street, Haliburton ON
(705) 457-4000 or (888) JAN-KNIT (526-5648)
www.janknitsstudio.com

Lou's Barn & Norm's Smoke House

The secret to Lou and Norm Weber's marital bliss is to work next to each other, pursuing different interests. She runs her own business, Lou's Barn, while he runs his, Norm's Smoke House, on the same property out in the country. Lou started her enterprise, an antiques and collectibles store, first. An artist, she was always looking for old items that she could embellish with her paintings. Soon, she had amassed a collection of furniture, tubs and headboards that was interesting in its own right. She opened her store in 1987 and continues to buy small cottage estates, cleaning and refinishing the items to give them a new life before offering them for sale. Poking through the merchandise is part of the fun, as you never know what you might discover. It's all housed inside a 1940s barn that was once the center of a dairy farm. Norm, meanwhile, spends his time in the smoke house, using Old World recipes to make his own sausage, salami and loads of other mouth-watering treats. His pepperoni and jerky are especially popular. For a fun and uncommon shopping experience, try the combination of Lou's Barn & Norm's Smoke House.

3055 Gelert Road, Minden ON (705) 286-1862

Tis the Season

Tis the Season is the invention of three admitted Christmas fanatics. Snowy white lettering emblazons the shop's cheerful red canopy. Nutcrackers and wreaths serve as charming reminders that it's never too early to shop for your Christmas decorations. Tis the Season is known for its famous Lucky Duck fudge and its distinctive decorations. Along with a plentiful array of ornaments, trees and garlands, you'll find woodsy cottage gift items, china and lanterns. The shop features work by Canadian artists Brook Knight and Jacqueline Kent. Brook crafts winsome Santas and gnomes by hand. An assortment of linens, candles and decorating accessories fill out the shop's stock of cheer. Tis the Season offers its decorating services for homes, cottages, businesses and resorts. When you're ready to take the decorations down, Tis the Season returns for end-of-the-season clean up. The seasonal store is a favourite place to get in the holiday mood. Come see for yourself.

101 Maple Street, Port Carling ON (705) 765-7731

Dwight Trading Post

With a teepee and two mounted black bears in front of the store, Dwight Trading Post allows you to imagine that you have stumbled upon a place on the edge of the frontier. Once inside, you glimpse the many wildlife mounts on display and half-expect to be greeted by a gruff and grizzled trader wearing a huge bearskin coat. Alas, owners Warren and Julie Shewfelt are not only well mannered but also up-to-date in their attire. Nevertheless, their inventory is faithful to that of an old trading post, with jewellery, clothing and native crafts topping the list. None of it is pawned. It is all brand new, representing the work of many talented artists and craftspeople from throughout Canada. Many customers tell Warren and Julie that they have trekked to Dwight just to visit their place. They have heard that it's worth the trip for the selection of Inuit art alone, especially sculpture. These serpentine pieces, depicting whales, bears and traditional hunters, express the deep relationship of native peoples to the land, waters and animals. Pick out one that strikes your fancy, or leave with a new pair of moccasins or a knife with an exquisitely carved handle. As you bid farewell to the moose, deer and bear heads on the walls of Dwight Trading Post, you sense that you will always remember your visit to this special place. Stop by again the next time you are near Dwight.

2825 Highway 60, Dwight ON
(705) 635-1055

Stage & Street Dance & Theatrical Supplies

If ever a business was fated to be born, Stage & Street Dance & Theatrical Supplies is it. Evelyn Davie was approached by a local dance school to make some of its dance recital costumes. Through this experience, Evelyn became keenly aware of the shortage facing the dancers. She opened Stage & Street to fill the need for costumes and dance supplies. This is the only costume shop in Sudbury, and the largest of its kind north of Toronto. Evelyn is famous for her custom theatrical and custom body-builder's costumes. The dance costumes have gone international since their inception. The clothes come in a conveniently large selection of sizes. The retail store is divided into three sections, including dance, shoes and all-body wear. Stage & Street is trained to fit dancer's shoes to the performer, an important detail when purchasing pointe shoes. More than 1,000 costumes are available for rental, from historical designs to celebrity recreations. Evelyn's designs extend to Victorian wedding gowns, theme weddings and skating costumes. She has won various awards in recognition of her excellent craftsmanship and creativitiy, including the New York Dance Alliance award for Ballet Costumes. If there is a dancer in your household, fear not. Stage & Street Dance & Theatrical Supplies has them covered.

24 Elgin Street, Sudbury ON (705) 673-7973
www.stageandstreet.com

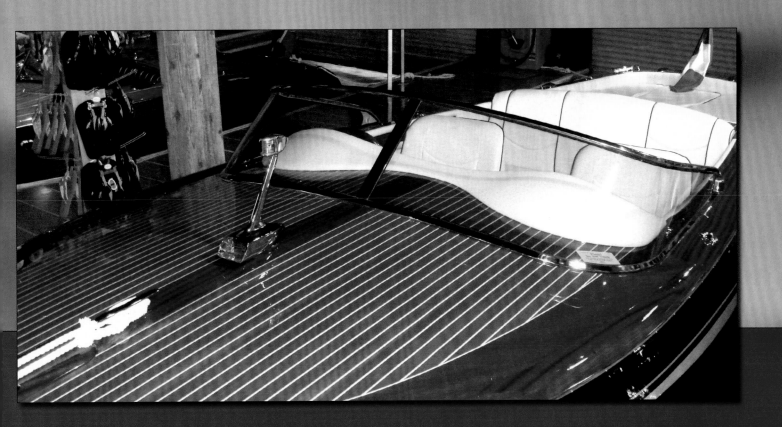

Port Sandfield Marina

One of the largest marinas on Lake Joseph, Port Sandfield Marina has been tending to the needs of boats owners since 1952. If you are looking to purchase a boat, the marina is the oldest Sea Ray dealer in Canada, and has achieved the prestigious Ambassador status for premium sales, service and customer satisfaction. Folks who like to do a little shopping while having fun at the lake will enjoy browsing the two stores located at the marina. The Boathouse is one of the most unique shopping destinations in Ontario, offering a cappuccino bar, premium cigars, footwear, unique gifts, watersport equipment, premium stainless steel barbecues and much more. The Boathouse also offers an exclusive collection of casual clothing by Paul & Shark, Lacoste and Burberry Golf. Specifically for the boater, the store carries a large selection of marine accessories, including safety equipment, dock hardware and boat care products. The second store, The Upper Loft, features fine indoor wicker and willow twig furniture, art, home décor, outdoor wicker and patio furniture and clothing by Blue Willis, Burberry, Terre Mer, Saint James and C.C. Filson. The Muskoka Launch and Motor Company, also located at the marina, specializes in the sale and service of antique wooden boats, and always have some on display. Jonathan and Nada Blair own and operate Port Sandfield Marina. Beautifully situated where Lake Joseph and Lake Rosseau meet, it was founded by Jonathan's grandparents. Make the Port Sandfield Marina part of your lake holiday.

1327 Peninsula Road #7, Port Sandfield ON (705) 765-3147
www.portsandfield.com

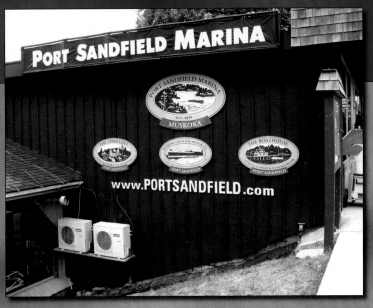

The Wolf Den

The spirits seem to speak through the beautiful handmade objects featured at the Wolf Den. A fixture in downtown Parry Sound since 1967, this shop showcases the work of native Canadian artisans and craftspeople. Present-day Ojibway, Mohawk and Inuit follow the ways of making drums, masks and shields that have been passed down through centuries. You will find masterful examples of all these things at the Wolf Den, plus jewelry, moccasins and soapstone carvings from many cultures. The selection of porcupine quill baskets is particularly remarkable. Doris Muckenheim, who owns the business with her husband, Oliver, runs the shop. She is always eager to share her knowledge of native cultures with customers, pointing out that the pieces often depict mythological characters as Raven, Beaver and Sun. Masks and other objects are similar to those that were once used in important ceremonies. Doris ships items to collectors all over the world. Her small shop is overflowing with everything from dreamcatchers, pottery and leather goods to cedar boxes and personal-size totem poles. Stare into the eyes of a Mohawk medicine mask at the Wolf Den, and be moved by its beauty and power.

35 James Street, Parry Sound ON
(705) 746-8477 or (866) 746-8477
www.wolfden.ca

Sunset in Parry Sound
Photo by Richard Peat

Moon Shadows Estate Winery

The whole time Eric and Carol Thompson were making maple syrup as a hobby, they were thinking of what else they could do with the sweet liquid besides pouring it over pancakes. The ingenious results of their research and experimentation can be sampled in the maple-based wines from their Moon Shadows Estate Winery. Established in July of 2005, it is not only Haliburton's first winery but also Ontario's first maple winery. Using dark maple syrup in the fermentation process, the Thompsons, assisted by expert wine maker Brian Morneau, produce around 20 varieties of fruit wines, ranging from pear and cranberry to rhubarb. Try the Strawberry Shortcake, the winner of a Crystal Cork award from the *Ontario Wine Review*. The few wines that actually feature a maple taste, such as the Golden Maple and the Maple Sugar Dessert Wine, are among the bestsellers. The syrup originates from the 43-acre bush that Carol and Eric purchased and began tapping in the 1990s. Bottling the wines is a family affair. With sons Matt and Luke helping, the Thompson team can manage about 300 bottles an hour. The couple sells its Moon Shadows Estate wines at its Maple Moon gift shop. Take your first taste out of curiosity, and be won over.

12953 Highway 118, Haliburton ON **(705) 455-9999** *www.moonshadowswinery.com*

THE ADVENTURE DOESN'T END HERE...

Learn more about our Treasures of America series by visiting
treasuresof.com

▼ Search for a Treasure
▼ Read our testimonials
▼ Purchase a Treasure book
▼ Recommend a Treasure